The Cleansing of the Heavens

The Accuser Cast Down

The Cleansing of the Heavens

The Accuser Cast Down

Dr. Mark C. Roser

Treasure House

An Imprint of

Destiny Image® Publishers, Inc.
P.O. Box 310
Shippensburg, PA 17257-0310

"For where your treasure is,
there will your heart be also." Matthew 6:21

ISBN 1-56043-311-6

For Worldwide Distribution
Printed in the U.S.A.

First Printing: 1998   Second Printing: 1999

This book and all other Destiny Image, Revival Press,
and Treasure House books are available
at Christian bookstores and distributors worldwide.

For a U.S. bookstore nearest you, call **1-800-722-6774**.
For more information on foreign distributors, call **717-532-3040**.
Or reach us on the Internet: **http://www.reapernet.com**

Behold, He putteth no trust in His saints;
yea, the heavens are not clean in His sight
(Job 15:15).
It was therefore necessary that the patterns of things
in the heavens should be purified with these;
but the heavenly things themselves
with better sacrifices than these
(Hebrews 9:23).

Dedication

This book is dedicated to my father, Clarence E. Roser, who served the Lord with me for 12 years in Uttermost Missions and now resides in a Heaven cleansed of the accuser. He died one week after the book's completion.

This book is dedicated also to all those who love the Word of God and who seek to know the truth regarding the cleansing of the heavens.

Acknowledgments

With deep appreciation to my wife, Patricia, who allowed me many hours of writing and has always encouraged me to give God my best.

To Rusti Henderson, who tirelessly typed the text, enabling me to write and rewrite regardless of how many changes she had to make.

To Jim Conners, who graciously used his time and talent to coordinate the footnotes, headings, and editing details.

A very special thanks to Dr. C. Peter Wagner and Sarah Craig, who were both a great source of encouragement by taking an interest in the message of this unknown author and his controversial book.

Contents

Foreword

As the months go by, I am increasingly amazed at the rapidity with which God seems to be providing to the Body of Christ new (to many of us) weapons of spiritual warfare, while sharpening the ones we already have. Why would He be doing such a thing? My judgment is that God is mobilizing His people as a massive spiritual army commissioned to move the Kingdom of God into the remaining territories of the earth where satan and his forces have been the most deeply entrenched and where they still enjoy almost free reign. God is still in the business of bringing people out of darkness into light and from satan's power into His saving power.

I have had the privilege of rubbing shoulders with some of the most anointed leaders of this extraordinary move of God on all six continents. My role as Coordinator of the International Spiritual Warfare network allows me to interact constantly with top-level intercessors, prophets, prayer leaders, teachers, apostles, prophetic intercessors, pastors, and other anointed leaders of the formidable army that God is assembling in our days. As such, I have at times been among the first to know what the Holy Spirit has been saying about such things as strategic-level spiritual warfare, spiritual mapping, identificational repentance, prayer walking, commitment to the land, prayer expeditions, and the like.

I mention this as background for relating my initial reaction on reading Dr. Mark Roser's *The Cleansing of the Heavens*. I was barely into the earliest chapters when I began saying to myself, *Wait a minute! I am reading things that I have never heard before!* If you are like me, your first reaction to such a thing is suspicion—where is this man coming from? As I continued to read, I began running down in my mind the roster of the outstanding leaders I had helped bring together in the Spiritual Warfare Network, quickly reviewing the discussions in the several meetings we had convened. Then, after looking over at the five shelves of current literature on spiritual warfare that I had collected in my library, I concluded that the issues that Mark was dealing with were issues that have largely been bypassed.

All this would have little significance if those issues were unimportant, but questions such as what immediate influence the cross of Christ might have had on the *modus operandi* of satan in the invisible world can hardly be considered insignificant. Reading further and paying special attention to the Scripture references and their application, I became more and more convinced that Roser's thesis was correct. At that point, I approached Dr. Colin Brown, who is considered by many to be Fuller Seminary's top theologian, and checked out Roser's ideas with him. When I asked him what he thought about the suggestion that satan was cast out of Heaven by Jesus' death, Dr. Brown replied that he believed the same thing and taught it in his classes. He admitted, however, that it was a subject that he usually passed over quite rapidly.

What all this means is that although not many people know about or have thought through the implications of the accuser being cast down from Heaven, Mark Roser has, and he has done the Body of Christ a tremendous service by collating the results of his research into the pages of this book. All of us who have been dealing with spiritual warfare in recent years are well aware that Paul says, "Lest Satan should take advantage of us; for we are not ignorant of his devices" (2 Cor. 2:11 NKJ). Speaking for myself, I must confess that I have previously been ignorant of some of the devices of satan that Mark Roser exposes so convincingly in this book.

Understanding *The Cleansing of the Heavens* will put all of us as believers in a place where satan will have less and less possibility of taking advantage of us, and therefore, we will be better equipped to serve in the great spiritual army to which God is calling us in these exciting days.

C. Peter Wagner
Fuller Theological Seminary

Introduction

Although *The Cleansing of the Heavens* may seem like an unusual title, it is a fully biblical designation for a completely scriptural subject. According to Job 15:15, "...the heavens are not clean in His [God's] sight." In the New Testament the writer of Hebrews says, "It was therefore necessary that the patterns of things in the heavens should be purified with these; but the heavenly things themselves with better sacrifices than these" (Heb. 9:23). But why would the heavens not be clean in God's sight and how could they be purified? The answer involves a thorough examination and exposé of satan's career from start to finish, Genesis to Revelation.

The Cleansing of the Heavens does not magnify the devil, but instead exposes his background, explains his defeat, and clarifies the position that he has occupied ever since. This is a vast subject, and the available books are incomplete. Even textbooks on systematic theology fail to provide a convincing biographical sketch of satan's origin, the timing of his fall, and his present position. Many claim that the biblical data itself is inconclusive. Percy Shelley goes so far as to say:

> "Who or what he is, his origin, his habitation, his destiny, and his power are subjects which puzzle the most acute theologians and on which no orthodox person can be induced to give a decisive opinion. He is the weak place of the popular religion, the vulnerable belly of the Crocodile."[1]

Others deny the devil's very existence, considering him a scapegoat and the creation of man. Professor Leslek Kolakowski, author of *Conversations With the Devil*, said in an interview, "The devil serves to identify what evil is and became an entity who was responsible for evil that let God and ourselves off the hook. That has been the function of the devil in history."[2]

There are 243 direct references to satan in Scripture without counting the verses that refer to his legions.[3] I believe that the devil not only exists but, considering the many names that depict his nature and activity, his place in creation and history is foundational to our knowledge of God and man. I am utterly convinced that without this knowledge we are ill equipped to deal with the difficult questions of life. However, understanding the theology and chronology of satan's cleansing from Heaven gives new appreciation for the warfare dimension of the gospel and its absolute necessity in man's redemption. Moreover, I believe that satan's place and movements are revealed consistently throughout the Old and New Testaments and that this information is essential to understanding the nature of spiritual conflict.

Herbert Lockyer has written that "it is necessary for every believer who would wage a successful spiritual warfare against his avowed and diabolic enemy, to ascertain a knowledge of his history and might so as to victoriously withstand him."[4] Although the earliest known book on the topic of the devil, written by Bishop Melito of Sardis in Asia, appeared as early as A.D. 150, J.B. Russell has pointed out that "serious historical studies of the devil have been very few, considering the importance of the topic."[5]

The Cleansing of the Heavens uniquely addresses central issues related to intelligent spiritual warfare. For example, can satan still bring an accusation against us in Heaven as he did against Job? I don't know of a more important spiritual warfare question. If he can, the implications are far-reaching. If not, why not? Where is satan now? Is he in hell, or is he confined to the earth somewhere?

In most circles, the popular view is that lucifer was cast out of Heaven before man's creation. The great difficulty with this view is that if satan was then violently cast out of Heaven, why would he still have access to Heaven in the days of Job? Some claim that even today satan can accuse us before God in Heaven. One author writes, "Strange as it may sound, satan still has access to God's throne. Although cast out of heaven, he is still permitted by God to appear back in heaven." This author quotes another author who envisions satan presently "sauntering about among the angels, hands in pockets, picking his teeth, disdain for all the angels, looking for the opportunity to accuse."[6] This view has been around for a long time. An eighteenth-century author wrote that "the greatest event in Heaven before the creation of the visible universe...is the fall of satan and his host from heaven." Like many others, this writer believed that "satan is allowed to come before the throne of God... For example, he tells Jehovah that tomorrow at 10 o'clock a.m., John Smith Christian will meet a certain temptation and fall. If the prediction comes true, the evil stands and grins in the face of the Almighty."[7]

Satan's access to Heaven after his forced removal would be strange indeed. What landlord would forcibly evict someone from his house and still permit that person to come and go as he pleased? Could the evicted one enter in the morning for breakfast, at midday for lunch, and again in the evening for dinner? Such theology is foreign to Scripture. Nowhere does the Bible teach a pre-Adamic eviction of lucifer, and allowing him access after violently evicting him is unthinkable.

The Cleansing of the Heavens provides convincing proof from an abundance of Scripture, explaining when, how, and why satan was removed from Heaven. This is a crucial point for Christians overcoming the devil, and a main aspect of Christ's redemptive work. Instead of a pre-Adamic eviction, satan, the accuser before God's throne, was cast out at the ascension of Christ. As a result, he can no longer bring a charge against us in Heaven. Christ's substitutionary death and triumphant resurrection broke satan's Old Testament position of authority in Heaven, causing his dethronement and downfall. The ramifications are earth-shaking and revolutionary for our faith.

Recognizing the devil's former habitation and authority in Heaven will enhance understanding of Scripture. For example, since satan's abode was Heaven, the Book of Job becomes clearer, as well as such difficult Old Testament passages as "an evil spirit from God troubled Saul," and "God sent an evil spirit between Abimelech and the men of Shechem," or how a lying spirit could come from Heaven.[8] Such verses often are avoided and left unexplained because of a lack of biblical insight on lucifer's rise and fall. Most important are the understanding that the cross of Christ is the place to rightly divide the Word of Truth and that the timing of satan's removal from Heaven is critical to understanding the Bible as a whole. The proper approach to Bible study can be compared to a systematic method of assembling jigsaw puzzles. As a boy, my brother loved working huge 5,000-piece puzzles. He would first gather all the border pieces, then separate the other pieces by color. When he put the puzzles together, he was very careful not to lose any pieces or force any to fit in the wrong place. It is important to approach Bible study in a similar manner. We should never disregard passages just because they do not fit our doctrinal tradition, nor should we try to force verses to fit a pre-conceived doctrinal or theological framework.

In keeping with the approach that biblical doctrine must be supported by the full counsel of God's Word, I will, in the chapters that follow, present line upon line everything that the Scriptures teach on the subject of lucifer's fall. My desire is to let the Word of God speak for itself on this vital subject, so the discussion will be carefully referenced throughout. At the conclusion, since Scripture cannot be broken,[9] everything should fit into place, and it should become clear how Heaven was forever cleansed of satan.

The book is built around the organizing theme of satan as the accuser, because that describes his work in Heaven. The combined meaning of the names *satan* and *devil* is "to accuse as an adversary." It will be clearly shown that accusation was the basis for satan's heavenly authority.

Satan's accusatory work was unique when compared to his other works since it was performed in Heaven, not on earth. His authorization to do other works came as a result of the accusations he brought before God. Christ terminated this business of satan in Heaven and delivered us from bondage to demonic powers on earth: "…For this purpose the Son of God was manifested, that He might destroy the works of the devil" (1 Jn. 3:8). Many Christians are at a loss, however, to explain how the cross disarmed the accuser because they do not understand his past activity in Heaven or his place in the Old Testament. Another problem relates to the question of how satan could be judged and defeated yet still be active today.

Part One of this book, "The Cleansing of the Heavens Explained," discusses how Scripture exposes satan's activity in the Old Testament, reveals his origin, foretells his judgment, explains his defeat through the death, resurrection, and ascension of Christ, and describes his current position under our feet. Part Two, "The Cleansing of the Heavens Applied," reveals the cleansing of the heavenlies and satan's ultimate end, explains how we overcome satan by the blood of Jesus and the word of our testimony, and describes how man's original relationship with God is restored and how we can live without guilt and fear. (See the chart following.)

Since most Christians are more familiar with the "overcoming" topics of Part Two, the primary focus of this book is on the theological and biblical framework of the casting down of the accuser as it is established in Part One. The application in Part Two is more on an individual rather than corporate level because that is where spiritual warfare must begin. Although this is not primarily a "how to" book on spiritual warfare, there are extensive applications to "war a good warfare" and to "fight the good fight of faith."[10]

The Scriptures presented, connected, and explained in *The Cleansing of the Heavens* have answered for me the most important questions related to engaging the enemy as we advance the Kingdom of Christ into the entire world. As a missionary in Africa for the past 12 years, I have worked out the truths I share in this book in the crucible of the mission field. Although theological in nature, this book is more than mere theory, for it addresses the vital issues of our position and authority in Christ in relation to satan.

Understanding the casting out of satan from Heaven is instrumental to aggressively advancing the Kingdom of God. Unfortunately, many Christians lack this comprehensive understanding of the devil's defeat, and so fail to take possession of their inheritance. As with David and Goliath, God's people have heard the sound of satan's fall and even participated in moves against the enemy host. Many, however, have not seen their giant enemy beheaded and stripped of his armor. We need to see how the strongman has been bound and his evil principalities disarmed.[11] May the Holy Spirit enlighten our eyes to the full understanding of how "the prince of this world" has already been judged![12]

Endnotes

1. Cited in Peter Stanford, *The Devil, A Biography* (New York: Henry Holt and Co., 1996), 93.

2. *Ibid.*, 14.

3. Morton Kelsy, *Encounter With God* (Minneapolis: Bethany, 1972), 242-245, note 568. References to demons and the devil in the New Testament compared to 340 references to the Holy Spirit. Although others identify beelzebub, abaddon, wormwood, etc. as proper names of ruling spirits under satan, our use is in the generic sense: satan, 153 times; devil, 116 times; serpent, 27 times; belial, 17 times; dragon, 16 times; beelzebub, 7 times; adversary, 3 times, leviathan, 5 times.

4. Herbert Lockyer, *Satan: His Person and Power* (Waco, TX: Word Books), 1946, 7.

5. *Select Library of Nicene and Post Nicene Fathers of the Christian Church,* Philip Schaff, ed., Volume 3 (Oxford: The Christian Literature Co., 1891). See also Jeffrey Burton Russell, *The Devil: Perceptions of Evil from Antiquity to Primitive Christianity,* (Ithaca, NY: Cornell University, 1977), 36.

6. S.J. Lawson, *When All Hell Breaks Loose, You May Be Doing Something Right* (Colorado Springs: NavPress, 1993).

7. B.W. McClung, *The History of the Devil* (printed T. Warner at the Black Bay in Patemoster, 1726), 8,11.

8. See 1 Samuel 16:14-16,23; Judges 9:23; 1 Kings 22:19-23.

9. See John 10:35.

10. 1 Timothy 1:18; 6:12.

11. See Mark 3:27; Colossians 2:15.

12. See John 16:11.

A Chronology of Satan's Career

His Habitation in the Heavenly Places Since Creation

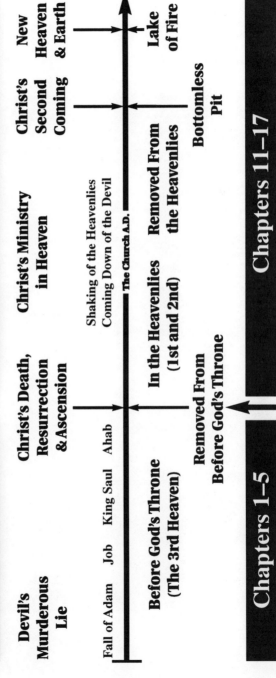

Old Testament

New Testament

Devil's Murderous Lie

Christ's Death, Resurrection & Ascension

Christ's Ministry in Heaven

Christ's Second Coming

New Heaven & Earth

Fall of Adam   Job   King Saul   Ahab

Shaking of the Heavenlies Coming Down of the Devil

The Church A.D.

Before God's Throne (The 3rd Heaven)

In the Heavenlies (1st and 2nd)

Removed From the Heavenlies

Removed From Before God's Throne

Bottomless Pit

Lake of Fire

Chapters 1–5

Chapters 6–10

Chapters 11–17

Part One

The Cleansing of the Heavens Explained

Chapter One

The Accuser in Heaven Exposed

One night while in deep prayer, my wife Pat encountered what she described as a spirit of death in the room. Frightened, she awakened me from a dream in which I was in the intensive care unit of the hospital standing watch over my son's incubator. There was an eerie quality to my dream, with dim lights and alarms all around. It was as though I expected an intruder at any moment.

Johnathan, our eldest child, had been born a full two months premature and was barely clinging to life. Due to the immature development of his lungs at birth, he had been unable to breathe on his own. I had watched with sinking heart as he gasped for air with his first cry and the medical staff forced a breathing tube down his throat. He had been placed on a lung machine and rushed off to intensive care. It was so touch-and-go that I was given papers to sign relieving the hospital of any liability in the event of blindness or mental retardation due to the oxygen treatment.

Pat and I thought, *What have we done wrong?* This trial of faith seemed completely foreign to what we knew of our position in Christ and the promises of God's Word. Before Pat went into labor, we had often prayed for our baby. The Scripture, "Every good *gift* and every perfect *gift* is from above,"[1] had ministered deeply to me since the only name we had chosen was Johnathan, which means "beloved gift." When

Pat went into early labor we prayed, "Let him come now only if he will be all right!" Christian friends encouraged us with scriptural promises, and I was convinced the baby would be fine.[2]

Now all we could do was pray and sing to him as we stroked his little head. Weighing only three pounds, three ounces, he had needles for an IV stuck into his tiny body and experienced other regular needle pricks for blood samples. He was hooked up to an alarm that went off frequently. Whenever he stopped breathing, a nurse would come and shake him to restart his breathing.

Outside the intensive care unit were hundreds of ceramic tiles painted with words from parents either grieving over defeat in death or rejoicing in victory over the grave. One of these contained a Scripture that greatly encouraged us:

> *For our light affliction, which is but for a moment, worketh for us a far more exceeding and eternal weight of glory; while we look not at the things which are seen, but at the things which are not seen: for the things which are seen are temporal; but the things which are not seen are eternal* (2 Corinthians 4:17-18).

After Pat sensed the spirit of death and woke me from my strange dream, we spent much of the rest of that night in prayer before we fell asleep again. The next morning we learned that two other infants in the unit, one of which was a larger baby that had been lying alongside our Johnathan, had died that very night! God showed us then that we were engaged in a great life and death struggle with the devil. A hurtful spirit had come to snuff out the life of our child, but, warned by God in a dream, we escaped this messenger of death.[3]

After seven weeks, with Johnathan weighing five pounds and breathing on his own, we took our son home, rejoicing in the victory. Many battles still lay ahead: three and a half years of horrendous febrile seizures, as well as almost losing him again on the mission field in an incident when he required mouth to mouth resuscitation. He has since matured, outgrown these seizures, and today is a robust, healthy teenager who is already taller than his dad!

There are probably many answers to the question "Why do people suffer?" but they are seldom simple. It is not enough to say "The Lord gave, and the Lord hath taketh away,"[4] regardless of the context, nor to ask as Jesus' disciples did, "Master, who did sin, this man, or his parents?"[5] We may not discern why people go through what they do, and unless God clearly shows us, we must be careful not to judge them. Rather, we must pray for them. Because suffering is deeply personal, God normally reveals the reason only to those who seek Him with a vested interest.

At any rate, any explanation of suffering that fails to include satan's malice is as incomplete as if God's sovereignty or man's responsibility were left out. Nowhere is satan's malicious role in human affairs revealed with greater clarity than in the Old Testament Book of Job.

The Accuser and Job

Again there was a day when the sons of God came to present themselves before the Lord, and Satan came also to present himself before the Lord (Job 2:1).

Satan's activity in the Old Testament is hidden for the most part. He can be seen operating behind the scenes, however. Yet in the Book of Job (and occasionally elsewhere in the Old Testament), God draws back the curtain from the hidden counsel of Heaven to reveal satan standing before God's throne as the accuser of men. This influential, heavenly position was of great consequence, causing significant results on earth. Recognizing satan's place in Heaven in Old Testament times is crucial to a proper understanding of the Bible. Lucifer was a lofty figure in the courts of Heaven and possessed an exalted place of influence. Without this understanding, certain portions of the Old Testament are almost incomprehensible.

The first two chapters of Job, totaling only 35 verses, picture satan in Heaven twice. The angels appear before the throne of God to report on their administrative duties on earth, and satan is among them. When God singles out Job as an example of righteousness, satan accuses Job of serving God for his own ends and challenges God to test Job's righteousness. The devil claims that, if tested, Job will curse God to His face. God allows satan to try and prove his accusation against Job.[6] The accuser is unable to induce Job to curse God, even after Job has lost his children and his wealth. In chapter 2 satan seeks further grounds to prove his charge, claiming that when Job is touched in his own body, his true colors will show and he will curse God. Though afflicted severely in his body, Job still refused to speak evil of God.[7]

*And the **Lord said unto Satan**, Hast thou **considered** My servant Job, that there is none like him in the earth, a perfect and an* *upright man, one that feareth God, and escheweth evil? and still he holdeth fast his integrity, although* **thou movedst Me against him,** *to destroy him* **without cause** (Job 2:3).

This verse makes it clear that Job was blameless.[8] His suffering was not due to any sin or unbelief in his life. Instead, satan was directly responsible for afflicting Job, permitted on the basis of his accusation, yet limited by God's sovereignty.[9] Satan's activity, though evident in Heaven, was hidden from men on earth. Job did not understand why he was suffering. It is no surprise then that Job cried out in his affliction for an advocate with God, and challenged his adversary to fully state his case against him.[10] No other book in the Bible reveals as clearly as Job the activity of satan as the *accuser of the brethren in Heaven* and the trials he creates on earth as he seeks man's condemnation.

The Accuser in Heaven Day and Night

The Bible teaches that in Old Testament times satan dwelled day and night in Heaven. Revelation 12:10 says that "the accuser of our brethren...accused them before our God *day and night.*" The phrase *day and night* appears three other times in the Book of Revelation, and always refers to a *continual* action:[11]

- The damned have no rest *day nor night* (see Rev. 14:11).
- The devil "shall be tormented *day and night* for ever and ever" (Rev. 20:10).
- The redeemed are "before the throne of God, and serve Him *day and night* in His temple: and He that sitteth on the throne shall *dwell* among them" (Rev. 7:15).[12]

It seems clear from these examples in Job and Revelation that at least in Old Testament times satan had continual access to Heaven and the throne of God and acted as the accuser of men. This raises two immediate questions. First, how can satan remain in the presence of a holy and righteous God? And second, can he still accuse us before God?

Many have argued that satan could not have remained in Heaven for a single moment after he sinned because God cannot tolerate evil in His presence. One of the verses used to support this idea is Habakkuk 1:13, which says, in part, "Thou art of purer eyes than to behold evil, and canst not look on iniquity...." This is a misconception concerning the holiness of God.[13] Even though it is certainly true that God cannot be enticed by looking at evil and His purity is beyond acts of iniquity, at the same time Proverbs 15:3 says, "The eyes of the Lord *are* in every place, beholding the evil and the good." Also, the writer of Hebrews says, "Neither is there any creature that is not manifest in His sight: but all things *are* naked and opened unto the eyes of Him with whom we have to do" (Heb. 4:13). God's presence is everywhere, and He sees everything.

If God could neither look on evil in Heaven nor tolerate lucifer for a moment in His presence after he sinned, how then could He allow the devil to stand before His throne and accuse the brethren "day and night"?[14] If God cannot endure evil, why didn't He destroy the devil altogether as soon as he sinned? God is sovereign and long-suffering, and He does everything in His own timing and order. In due course, He removed satan from Heaven. First, though, it was necessary for God's Son, the perfect representative of the Father, to come and endure much evil to deliver mankind from satan's domain. In like manner, the Holy Spirit deals with us and dwells in us as believers in spite of our sin and iniquity. God's long-suffering nature is our salvation (see 2 Pet. 3:15); otherwise, both the devil and mankind would have been destroyed long ago. The nature of both Jesus and the Spirit reveals that the Father was well able to endure the accuser before His throne day and night before casting him down. The apostle Paul knew this to be true:

*What if God, willing to show His wrath, and to make His power known, **endured with much longsuffering** the vessels of wrath fitted to destruction* (Romans 9:22).

God justly managed the evil in His presence, enduring satan for a season until Christ came, making known in the process His sovereign power and His anger against sin.[15] This is proof of His incorruptible holiness and justice. Unlimited in wisdom, greatness, and power, the God of the Bible is able to work all things together for good, even acts of rebellion. The Bible declares that in this way He alone is holy.

Can satan still accuse us before God? The answer is no. Further evidence will bear this out. Satan can no longer appear before God to accuse us because he was defeated when Jesus died on Calvary. With the victory of Christ our Advocate, the accuser has been cast down, and the scene in Heaven has dramatically changed.[16] Our open access to God is secure, and we have a tremendous position of strength, a far better covenant than Job had for dealing with the devil.[17] Satan's accusatory authority against us has been overthrown, and we have been raised up in Christ to a privileged position. We must differentiate, therefore, between the extent of satan's authority in the Old Testament as compared to the New.[18]

When we read the Old Testament, let's be aware of satan's place as the accuser in Heaven. We can be discerning like David was when a woman of Tekoah came to him in mourning. She claimed to be a widow who sought to protect her son from the death sentence. Touched by her sad story, David graciously promised her son a pardon. But the real agenda emerged when she applied her fabricated case to David's son Absalom. "Why should the king not bring back to Jerusalem his son Absalom?"

David responded immediately, "Is not the hand of Joab with thee in all this?"[19] He quickly discerned that Joab was the one *behind the scene* seeking permission for Absalom's return to Jerusalem. Like Joab in David's kingdom, we discover that satan was a lofty figure in the courts of Heaven and possessed an exalted place of influence. Without understanding this, portions of the Old Testament are incomprehensible. On the other hand, realizing his Old Testament role exposes satan's hand in many places.[20] For example, when the Old Testament speaks of God bringing evil upon people, we realize that they reaped evil at the hand of satan because of their sin.[21]

Several additional examples will clarify further satan's position and influence in Heaven during Old Testament times.

An Evil Spirit From the Lord

*But the spirit of the Lord departed from Saul, and **an evil spirit from the Lord** troubled him* (1 Samuel 16:14).[22]

*Then God sent an **evil spirit** between Abimelech and the men of Shechem; and the men of Shechem **dealt treacherously** with Abimelech: that the cruelty done to the threescore and ten sons of Jerubbaal might come, and **their blood** be laid upon Abimelech their brother, which slew them; and upon the men of Shechem, which aided him in the killing of his brethren* (Judges 9:23-24).

These are troubling verses. How could there be an *evil spirit* from a good, righteous, and holy God? The New Testament never mentions an evil spirit coming from God. Some scholars explain this as primitive Hebrew thought that attributed all things to God, even evil spirits. Other scholars reason that the spirit was not evil in its nature, but only hurtful in its effect. These interpretations are neither necessary nor consistent with a proper view of Scripture. The biblical record is inspired in its very words, so the adjective "evil" describes the nature of the spirit, not merely its effect, and the word "from" denotes its prior location. God *sent* an evil spirit *from* His presence.

These verses reveal satan exercising his authority from Heaven. Saul was the God-chosen and anointed king of Israel, but he had backslidden into disobedience and rebellion. His sin enabled satan to accuse him before God and to obtain the right to oppress him. Abimelech had murdered his 70 brothers with the help of the men of Shechem in order to secure his position on the throne. Their sin and treachery opened them up for satan's accusations before God, resulting in their judgment and death. Job 1:12b says, "So Satan went forth *from the presence of the Lord.*" Likewise, in the cases of Saul and Abimelech and the men of Shechem, an evil spirit went forth *"from the presence of the Lord."* The phrase *the presence of* is the key to understanding these passages. Unlike Job, to whom God restored double, Saul, Abimelech, and the men of Shechem lost everything because they brought suffering upon themselves and opened themselves to deadly attack from the heavenly adversary.

If there is demonic oppression in our lives, we need to ask ourselves, "Where am I giving place to the devil? Am I practicing a particular sin? Am I unforgiving toward anyone?"[23] Satan goes about like a roaring lion seeking to afflict us in our minds, wills, and emotions so that he can devour our souls.[24] He overcame Saul because he could accuse him in Heaven and gain quick, strong access to Saul's soul. We too may be tormented and devoured if we do not avail ourselves of our God-given rights and responsibilities.[25] Unlike Saul, however, we have a sure, steadfast anchor for our souls: Christ our High Priest who intercedes for us within the veil of God's Most Holy Place.[26] The advocacy of Christ in Heaven and the Holy Spirit on earth can now support us even when we fail because our accuser is now barred from Heaven.[27]

Satan was a strongman unbound in the Old Testament because he exercised an authority from Heaven that he does not possess today. In Luke 11:21-22, where Jesus speaks of an armed strongman, protecting his goods, being overcome by a stronger man who binds him and spoils his goods, He is referring to the devil as the strongman and Himself as the stronger one! The devil's guarded treasures are the souls of men.

Satan has been bound by Christ so that the souls of men can be released. (This binding of the devil by Christ is discussed in detail in Chapters Five and Six.)[28]

Before I gave my life to Christ, evil spirits tormented me and sought to destroy me. I would come home from a night on the town, full of alcohol and high on marijuana, and my mind would race as I lay in my bed hearing voices. One night, while drinking in the park with a friend, a police officer confronted us. Being under the legal drinking age, I ran into the woods and hid in the darkness among the trees. Later, walking out into a housing subdivision, I was greeted by a large, growling dog who followed me step for step, eyeball to eyeball. As I made my way up the dead-end street, a second dog joined the first, and then a third, all growling, snarling, and threatening every moment to tear me apart. "Get your dogs," I cried out, but no one answered. What moments of torment! I dared not make a wrong move. Although satan had access to my soul, he was unable to devour me. I thank God that I was born on the New Testament side of the cross where satan has no audience with God; otherwise, today I might be in the belly of some dog! My mother, however, through her intercessory prayers to Jesus, our great High Priest, found mercy for me before God's throne of grace.

A Lying Spirit in Heaven

First Kings 22:19-23 reveals satan's strong heavenly position in the Old Testament through a "lying spirit" in the presence of God. An evil spirit from God is commissioned to administer sin's deception to a wicked king. If this were not in the Bible, it would be hard to believe:

> And [Micaiah] *said, Hear thou therefore the word of the Lord: I saw the Lord* **sitting on His throne**, *and all the* **host of heaven** *standing by Him on* **His right and on His left**. *And the Lord said, Who shall persuade Ahab, that he may go up and fall at Ramothgilead? And one said on this manner, and another said on that manner. And there came forth a* **spirit**, *and stood before the Lord, and said, I will persuade him. And the Lord said unto him, Wherewith? And he said, I will go forth, and I will be a* **lying spirit** *in the mouth of all his prophets. And He said, Thou shalt persuade him, and prevail also: go forth, and do so. Now therefore, behold, the Lord hath put a* **lying spirit** *in the mouth of all*

these thy prophets, and the Lord has spoken evil concerning thee (1 Kings 22:19-23).[29]

Micaiah pulls the curtain back to reveal the realm of the spirit: "I saw the Lord sitting on His throne." The prophet takes us behind the veil of the flesh into the hidden chambers of Heaven where a lying spirit is authorized to go and fill the mouths of all the prophets. Heaven thus divulges the hidden motives of men and the unseen influences that shape their words and actions, disclosing a struggle that does not originate with flesh and blood.[30] By rejecting the truth, Ahab opened himself to the deadly influence of a lying spirit. Just like the prince of demons himself, this spirit was by nature a liar, and not merely a liar in his effect upon the prophets.

Micaiah's vision of God on his throne with "*all the host of heaven standing by Him on His right and on His left*" is noteworthy. Here the angels in Heaven, separated on God's right and left hands, portray a future judgment of all creation. "And He shall set the sheep on His right hand, but the goats on the left. ... Then shall He say also unto them on the left hand, Depart from Me, ye cursed, into everlasting fire, prepared for the devil and his angels" (Mt. 25:33,41).[31] These verses and other related Old Testament Scriptures suggest that satan and his fallen angels were on God's left hand, and Michael and the other elect angels were on God's right hand. (Further evidence for this will be presented shortly.) Therefore, the *lying spirit that stood before the Lord* came from the *left* side of God's throne. Ephraim Syrus in the ancient *Nisibene Hymns* may have had this in mind when he wrote:

> "The Voice made proclamation...for they saw that Jesus had triumphed to the grief of all them on the *left* hand. Woe He has doubled to them that are of the *left* hand; to evil spirits and demons...Joy to them that are of the *right* hand has come to-day."[32]

The angels in the prophet's vision of Heaven present themselves before God as in the Book of Job. Each of them had their own measure of rule as they administered the affairs of men.[33] In Job's case, the heavenly assembly considered his righteousness; in wicked Ahab's case they discussed his impending judgment.[34] Since Ahab gave place for a spirit of deception to dominate his life and kingdom, a lying spirit had the right to speak about his fall and was afforded the dubious honor of leading Ahab into his final battle at Ramothgilead. When Ahab appealed to Micaiah in the name of Jehovah to speak the truth, however, Jehovah gave him the truth. Nonetheless, Ahab still went out to battle and died.

Ahab demonstrated how totally deceived one can be. His death also fulfilled a prophecy pronounced by Elijah.

It is sad to see someone who is deceived; sadder still when the truth is so evident. Today, the gospel of Christ is proclaimed worldwide on television and radio. Often, family members and friends give personal witness to the truth of God. Like wicked Ahab, though, men still reject the truth of God in exchange for a lie that leads to death. "But if our gospel be hid, it is hid to them that are lost, in whom the god of this world hath blinded the minds of them which believe not...," because they refuse to receive a love for the truth.[35] Is there nothing we can do?

Thanks to Jesus, lying spirits no longer have access to the throne of God. We can now not only try the spirits to see whether they are from God, but also intercede for those whom satan has blinded.[36] Through the Word of God and the Spirit of Truth, we can walk free of deception and set others free. Prayer is our chief weapon. It quickens the *logos* of God into the sword of the Spirit and cuts through the rulers of the darkness of this world.[37] If Micaiah could expose the deception of the prophets of Baal and Elijah could move a deceived nation back to God, should we expect and attempt less now that the true Light has come and the end of the age approaches? God forbid.[38] The Church is the light of the world, but she has yet to fully harness the power that flows from Heaven.

The Egyptians and the Angel of Death

Did you ever wonder why Moses' rod turned into a serpent? This symbolized the fact that God had given Moses power over the plagues in which satan and his angels would be the active agents. Moses had power to cast the rod of the serpent down upon the land and to take it up. When *the serpent* came down upon Egypt, it resulted in the death of their firstborn. The Book of Psalms could not be clearer in this respect:

> *He gave up their cattle also to **hail**, and their flocks to **hot thunderbolts**. He cast upon them the fierceness of His anger, wrath, and indignation, and trouble, by sending **evil angels** among them. ... And **smote** all the firstborn in Egypt* (Psalm 78:48-49,51a).

Satan is a messenger of destruction. In Job's case, when the fire fell and burned up the sheep, satan did the destroying.[39] It was his hand also that brought a great wind from the wilderness, destroying the house with Job's children in it.[40] Although Job's servants called it *"the fire of God"* and perhaps "*the wind of God*," it was a demonic fire and wind that came from Heaven. Remember that all Job's possessions were in satan's power.[41] Likewise in Egypt, satan demonstrated his destructive powers: polluted water, frogs, lice, flies, boils, hail, locusts, disease, and death. By casting the serpent upon the Egyptians, God expressed His fierce wrath against them in ten plagues and gave the world a sample of the seven last plagues, which fully express His anger upon a Christ-rejecting world. In the Book of Revelation, satan's name is apollyon and abaddon; both names, the Greek and the Hebrew, mean "destroyer."[42] The world experiences final devastation with the pouring out of these bowls of wrath, which coincide with the coming down of an angry devil as he realizes that he has but a short time remaining.[43]

When the children of Israel in the wilderness rebelled and complained, fiery serpents bit them, and many died. Others were saved when they looked upon a brazen serpent that Moses raised up on a pole. Jesus likened Himself to that brazen serpent because when He died on the cross He bore the curse of man's rebellion against God.[44] Jesus entered satan's realm of sin and death to save us from the wrath to come.

Although it should be clear by now that in Old Testament days satan had access to the throne of God as the accuser of men, further evidence is found in the Law and religious practice of the nation of Israel. The tabernacle and other physical elements, as well as the worship rituals themselves, were designed to be earthly representations of heavenly realities. It should come as no surprise, therefore, to find satan's role and activity in Heaven represented in them also, as we shall see in the next chapter.

Endnotes

1. James 1:17a.

2. God does not promise us an easy, trouble-free life. There are tests, trials, and even martyrdom for some, but this is inherently different in nature from God's chastisement and judgment. Although we are not free from demonic attacks, when we walk uprightly in Christ "we keep ourselves and the evil one cannot touch us" (see 1 Jn. 5:18). We can resist the devil by standing steadfast in faith, and he must flee, leaving his evil schemes unfulfilled.

3. During this ordeal, God spoke strength and encouragement to us through the Scriptures, particularly Matthew 2:13,16; First Peter 5:7-10; and Philippians 1:19.

4. Job 1:21.

5. John 9:2.

6. See Job 1:9-12.

7. See Job 2:4-10.

8. There is no need for us to seek in Job himself a cause for his suffering. Some think that if they do not teach that Job opened the door to the devil through fear and unbelief, Job-like suffering could happen to them also. Job says, "Ye see my casting down, and are afraid. ...cause me to understand wherein I have erred" (Job 6:21b,24b). A study of Job reveals that his "fear" was the wholesome reverence of God that is *the beginning of wisdom*, not fear that is related to unbelief. Job suffered not because he erred or gave place to the devil, but because satan was able to accuse him before God in Heaven.

9. If not limited, satan would have gone too far and killed Job. God said, "Spare his life." Although satan tried to contradict God with his own imprudent assessment of Job, he was yet responsible to and under God's direct authority.

10. Job cried out for a mediator and for his adversary to write out the charges against him (see Job 9:33; 31:35). Answering him out of the whirlwind with a series of questions that Job is unable to answer, God reveals to Job his lack of knowledge and power in dealing with his adversary (see Job 38:1ff). Job could not explain even one thing out of a thousand that God does in nature, let alone in a world of free moral agents influenced by a malicious devil.

11. It is always *day or night* (see Deut. 28:66; Josh. 1:8; 1 Kings 8:59; 1 Chron. 9:33). Therefore, this phrase allows for no artificial distinction, as some claim, between satan's access and residence. How can Old Testament references to satan in Heaven be reconciled to the doctrine of a pre-historic eviction of satan?

12. In the New Testament, the phrase *day and night* is transposed as *night and day,* but it still refers to a continual order (see Ps. 32:4; 55:10; Is. 60:11; 62:6; Jer. 9:1; Lam. 2:18; Mk. 5:5; Acts 9:24; 1 Thess. 2:9; 3:10; 2 Thess. 3:8; 1 Tim. 5:5; 2 Tim. 1:3).

13. Habakkuk is appealing to God because the wicked Babylonians are to take Israel captive, which seems contrary to divine justice.

14. If a *day and night*, why not 1,000 years since 1,000 years are as a day in God's sight (see 2 Pet. 3:8)?

15. See Habakkuk 1:1-5,9,12. This Old Testament pattern, often found in the prophets, reveals how God used one nation to judge another, then judged the nation He used.

16. See Ephesians 6:10ff; James 5:11; 1 John 5:18.

17. See Job 9:33.

18. We live in Christ on the New Covenant side of the cross, which is the place to rightly divide the Word of Truth (see 2 Tim. 2:15). Our understanding and application of the Old Testament are crucial at this point. When Christ came, He brought God's Kingdom, delivering men from satan's domain. The united testimony of the apostles and prophets is that Jesus the Messiah disarmed, bound, defeated, judged, and cast down the evil one. At the very least, this translates to a restriction on satan's authority and power in the gospel era and our own empowerment.

19. See 2 Samuel 14:1-20.

20. See Job 1:12; 2:6: "thine hand" and "behold, he is in thine hand."

21. There are less obvious examples of satan's Old Testament position, such as the puzzling attempt to destroy Moses immediately after his call, the death of men at Bethshemesh who looked into the Ark of the Covenant, and Uzzah who illegally touched it (see Ex. 4:24-26; 1 Sam. 6:19; 2 Sam. 6:7; 2 Kings 1:1-3,6; Jer. 19:3,15; 21:10; 23:2,12; 25:29; Ezek. 5:16; 6:10; 14:22-23).

22. The inspired writer of First Samuel states several times that the evil spirit was from God (see 1 Sam. 16:14-23; 18:10; 19:9).

23. Oppression from within due to sin is different than appointed difficulties that press upon us from the outside. We cannot abide in Christ if we continue in sin or act as accusers in Heaven against our brothers. Forgiveness is connected to forgiving others, or else we will be tormented (see Mt. 5:23-26; 18:21-35).

24. See 1 Peter 5:8.

25. See 1 John 5:18.

26. See Hebrews 6:19-20.

27. The application of this truth, discussed in Part Two, relates to living a victorious Christian life (see 1 Jn. 2:1ff).

28. Dr. C. Peter Wagner, writing in *Warfare Prayer*, says, "Jesus' coming was such a radical event…if we think satan has formidable power these days, we must realize that he had even more power before Jesus came" (*Warfare Prayer*, [Ventura, CA: Regal Books, 1992], 52).

29. See the full account in First Kings 22:1-40. Ahab, king of Israel, a hater of truth, and Jehoshaphat, king of Judah, a seeker of truth, were in a strange alliance against Syria. The 400 prophets of Baal on Ahab's royal payroll had prophesied success in the upcoming battle. Jehoshaphat, however, desired to hear from a "prophet of the Lord." Micaiah, whom Ahab had imprisoned, was brought before them. Encouraged to conform his message to that of the others, Micaiah replied that he would speak only what Jehovah bid him to say. Then, when he prophesied success like the others, Ahab adjured him in the name of Jehovah to speak only the truth. At that point, Micaiah's prophecy suddenly changed; he exhorted everyone to return home and prophesied Ahab's death.

30. Books such as Frank Peretti's *This Present Darkness* (Westchester, IL: Crossway Books, 1986) and C.S. Lewis's *The Screwtape Letters* (New York: New American Library, 1988) are appealing because they dramatize this unseen realm.

31. See also Ecclesiastes 10:2.

32. *Select Library of Nicene and Post Nicene Fathers of the Christian Church*, Philip Schaff, ed., Volume 13, Part 5, "Concerning Satan" (Oxford: The Christian Literature Co., 1891).

33. See Deuteronomy 32:8; 2 Corinthians 10:13; Ephesians 6:12; Hebrews 2:5.

34. In the several Old Testament passages that record the celestial council, satan is there and appears to exercise a greater voice and independence of movement than the others. The angels of God enter the world only as God bids them to; satan, however, intently roams the earth with the purpose of uncovering the sins and iniquities of men. Although God initiates the conversations regarding Job and Ahab, satan has much to say, as well as a malicious desire to see men harmed. Psalm 82 is another example of God presiding over the divine assembly. In this case, He accuses the gods (i.e., angels) of failing to exercise their duties with regard to the protection of the poor and powerless. H.T. Page points out that "The text is silent about the circumstances of their fall from innocence, but obviously these

are fallen beings whose sin had a devastating impact on human society. The angels stand accused of aiding and abetting the wicked in their exploitation of the poor and powerless. So great was their influence that verse 5 says, '[A]ll the foundations of the earth are shaken....' So great is the evil of social injustice that it can only be accounted for by the activity of cosmic forces opposed to God." Page also cites Psalm 29:1; 89:6; and Isaiah 24:21-22 as examples of these "powers in the heavens above." It is likely that they are among angels who were given administrative duties over the nations (see Deut. 32:8; Dan. 10:13,20-21; 12:1). (Sydney H.T. Page, *Powers of Evil* [Grand Rapid: Baker Books, 1995], 27, 54–61.). In the fragment of Papias, we read, "He assigned some of them [angels] to preside over the regulation of the earth but...their administration came to no good end." Papias and Polycarp were regarded as companions of one another and hearers of John the Apostle, A.D. 100.

35. 2 Corinthians 4:3-4; see also 2 Thessalonians 2:9ff.

36. See 1 Timothy 2:1-8; Jude 22; 1 John 4:1; 5:16-17.

37. See Isaiah 60:1ff; 2 Timothy 3:13; Ephesians 6:12,17-20.

38. Chapters Ten through Fourteen will discuss at length the Church's position and authority in this world. The main objective at this point is to prove that satan had a place in Heaven prior to the ascension of Christ, for that is the starting place for understanding the nature of our conflict with the devil. Thank God for the current prayer movement, which is embracing spiritual warfare and strategic level intercession.

39. See Job 1:15-17.

40. The wildernesses and desolate places from where the wind came are associated with the devil and his demons. (See Leviticus 16:10,21-22; Isaiah 13:21; 34:14; Matthew 4:1; Luke 8:29.) The angels, whether of God or of satan, are likened unto fire and wind. Under certain conditions they can influence the weather and the elements of creation (See Rev. 7:1-3; 9:14-15). Dr. C. Peter Wagner points out that in May, 1991, a cyclone again struck Bangladesh, leaving 200,000 dead, and that although meteorologists cannot explain why seven of the ten deadliest storms of the twentieth century struck Bangladesh, a Bengali poet attributes it to the Rudra, the storm god, who is fearfully worshiped.

41. See Job 1:12.

42. See Revelation 9:11. See also Exodus 12:23; 1 Corinthians 10:10.

43. Like the Assyrians through whom Jehovah chastened Israel, satan was the rod of God's wrath. Calvin, in his commentary on Genesis, speaks of satan as "God's executioner," "a minister of God's wrath," and that "God executes his judgments by reprobate angels." It is a historical fact that Luther, Zwingli, and all the other leading Protestant theologians stood with Calvin on the sovereignty of God. We can learn from their perspective of God's sovereign relationship to satan: "Whatever, then, Satan and the wicked attempt to do...though they rage against God, He yet holds them in by His bridle...and their purposes to answer His own ends." (John Calvin, *Commentary on the Minor Prophets*, [Banner of Truth, 1991]).

44. See John 3:14; Galatians 3:13; Hebrews 12:2-3.

Chapter Two

The Accuser and the Law

We have seen how the Book of Job and other Scriptures reveal satan's position and influence in Heaven "day and night" prior to the coming of Christ and how this reality makes understandable the puzzling references to "evil" and "lying" spirits coming from God. Satan was the accuser of men and also the agent of death and destruction issued in judgment from the presence of God. Positionally, satan and the other fallen angels were at God's left hand, while Michael and the other elect angels were at His right. Evidence for this is also found in the Law, religious practice, and the national experience of Israel.

Satan at the High Priest's Right Hand

As in Job, the Book of Zechariah exposes satan as the accuser of the brethren in Heaven. In this scene Joshua the high priest (not the Joshua of the Book of Joshua) has approached God in the Holy of holies:

*And he showed me Joshua **the high priest** standing before the angel of the Lord, and **Satan** standing at his **right** hand to **resist** him* (Zechariah 3:1).

Micaiah's vision of the heavenly host in First Kings chapter 22 positioned satan and his lying spirits at God's left hand. Zechariah's vision shows satan at Joshua's right hand as the high priest faces the ark of the covenant in the Holy of holies. Positionally, then, satan standing at

Joshua's right hand means that he is standing at Jehovah's left hand. The Bible is a wonderful, supernaturally consistent book, often confirming this right-hand/left-hand arrangement of the angelic host in Heaven. For example, when the angel Gabriel appears to Zacharias regarding the birth of John the Baptist, he is standing on the *right side* of the altar of incense. Facing the altar and burning incense in the temple, Zacharias suddenly looks up and sees Gabriel.[1] This same arrangement is found in Psalm 109 as part of one of David's imprecatory prayers of judgment against his enemies: "Let Satan stand at his *right hand.* When he shall be judged, let him be condemned: and let his prayer become sin" (Ps. 109:6b-7).[2]

If the high priest entered the Holy of holies contrary to the Law, his sacrifice would be rejected, the accuser would prevail, and the high priest would die before the Lord. It was even customary for the high priest to have a rope tied around his waist so he could be dragged out in case he died before the Lord. No one would go in after him because satan, the angel of death, stood there to execute the judgments of the Law.

> *And the Lord said unto Satan, The Lord* **rebuke** *thee. O Satan; even the Lord that hath chosen Jerusalem rebuke thee: is not this a brand* **plucked** *out of the fire? Now Joshua was clothed with filthy garments, and stood before the angel. And he answered and spake unto those that stood before him, saying,* **Take away the filthy garments** *from him. And unto him He said, Behold, I have caused thine iniquity to pass from thee, and I will clothe thee with change of raiment* (Zechariah 3:2-4).

God alone can silence the accuser and shut the mouth of the lion. He judges among the mighty angels, literally, *the gods.*[3] The divine rebuke has been spoken. We have been plucked from the fire. Our sins are removed, and we may now appropriate what Christ has provided. No more does a dark cloud hide God's face from us. No longer does the cord of sin bind us or the enemy point his accusing finger. No dirty garments defile us, no thieves rob us, no beasts wait to spring on us. There is now no devil in God's presence to condemn us.

The taking away of Joshua's filthy garments in exchange for clean garments is based on the coming Branch who will remove the sin of the land in one day.[4] Zechariah prophesied about the coming of Jesus and the work of the cross, which ensured satan's defeat. Jesus' holy life and sacrificial death as our High Priest cleansed the greater and more perfect tabernacle of Heaven.[5] Jesus disarmed the accuser so that we might enter God's presence unhindered.

The Holy of holies represented God's dwelling place. Satan's presence there resisting the high priest is further evidence of his Old Testament place in Heaven. Since he occupied this position as the accuser before God day and night, it is not surprising to find him depicted in the Holy of holies by the cherubim.

The Cherubim in the Holy of Holies

Moses was commanded to make the tabernacle according to an exact pattern, because the tabernacle and the articles in it were to serve as a visible "example and shadow of heavenly things."[6]

> *And thou shalt make **two cherubims** of gold, of beaten work shalt thou make them, in the **two ends** of the mercy seat. And make **one cherub** on the one end, and the **other cherub** on the other end: even of the mercy seat shall ye make the cherubims on the **two ends** thereof. And the cherubims shall **stretch forth their wings on high**, covering the mercy seat with their wings, and their **faces shall look one another;** toward the mercy seat shall the faces of the cherubim be* (Exodus 25:18-20).

The cherubim on either side of the mercy seat in the tabernacle were earthly representations of the angelic host in the presence of God in Heaven. More precisely, I believe these golden cherubim represented the two chief angels, Michael and lucifer, who exemplified, respectively, the elect and evil angels in God's presence. As surprising as the concept may be, consider for a moment the possibility that satan was visually represented in the tabernacle. He is identified clearly in Ezekiel 28:14 as "the *anointed cherub that covereth.*" The word *anointed* literally means "outspread," and refers to the wings of the cherub that covered the mercy seat. Because satan was "day and night before God's throne" accusing the brethren, it is not mysterious to find him represented in the tabernacle as the cherub on the left hand of the mercy seat.

Every detail of the cherubim was designed to picture a heavenly reality. The pure gold signified the Word of God by which the angelic hosts were originally created, bright and beautiful, full of glory and without blemish. The cherubim overshadowing the mercy seat spoke of their direct administration of both the mercies and the judgments of Almighty God. The mercy seat represented God's heavenly throne, and the stretching out of the cherubim's wings graphically illustrated the awesome influence and power they exerted from on high.[7]

Angelic Face-Off

Picture Michael and his angels on the right, lucifer and his angels on the left, each group facing the other from across the mercy seat and waiting for a word from God's throne. Such nose-to-nose confrontations constitute a pattern in the Bible. Time and again we see the elect and the evil angels squared off. For example, in Daniel's day, when he fasted and prayed, the angels wrestled.[8] When satan and his angels stood up in Heaven to speak against Israel, Michael and his angels stood for the nation.[9] When it came time to cast satan and his angels out of Heaven, Michael and his angels were given the honor.

Jude and Peter also refer to this battle between the angels:

Likewise also these filthy dreamers defile the flesh, despise **dominion***, and speak evil of* **dignities***. Yet* **Michael** *the archangel, when contending with the* **devil** *he disputed about the body of Moses, durst not bring against him a railing* **accusation***, but said, The Lord rebuke thee* (Jude 8-9).

Presumptuous are they, selfwilled, they are not afraid to speak evil of **dignities***. Whereas* **angels***, which are greater in power and might, bring not railing accusation against them before the Lord* (2 Peter 2:10b-11).

The title *dignity,* used by both Jude and Peter in reference to satan, is literally *doxa* in Greek.[10] It is the same word used to describe the cherubim of glory in Hebrews 9:5, "And over it the cherubims of glory [*doxa*] shadowing the mercyseat; of which we cannot now speak particularly." Classified as a heavenly dignity, satan was *one of the glorious ones,* or one of the cherubim of glory [*doxa*].[11]

An angelic conflict occurred *before the Lord* with Michael and satan, the chief contestants in a dispute involving legalities over the dead body of Moses. According to Hebrews 2:14, satan "had the power of death." Perhaps he would not allow Moses future rights of release from the grave without a fight![12]

Michael, unlike satan, did not behave in an accusing manner even toward the devil. Instead he acknowledged satan's position and appealed to Jehovah.[13] Although we have authority in Christ to bind and loose, and to cast out evil spirits, we do not indulge in unscriptural name calling or vain mockery against the devil. Defiled men, however, "speak evil of the things that they understand not."[14] We depend on God's power and authority to stand against the evil principalities and ruling spirits in the heavenlies.[15]

Most Christians are unaware of satan's Old Testament position in Heaven, and yet it is an essential theological basis for spiritual warfare and understanding everything else that followed his rebellion. Before he was defeated and cast out by the work of Christ, satan was a cherub on the left hand of God's throne, with administrative functions related to accusation and judgment.

The Blessings and Curses of the Law

And all Israel, and their elders, and officers, and their judges, ***stood on this side of the ark*** *and on that side before the priests the Levites, which bare the ark of the covenant of the Lord, as well as the stranger, as he that was born among them;* ***half*** *of them over against* ***mount Gerizim****, and* ***half*** *of them over against* ***mount Ebal****; as Moses the servant of the Lord had commanded before...* (Joshua 8:33).

Joshua provided perhaps the most explicit earthly illustration of this heavenly reality. In obedience to Moses' instructions in Deuteronomy 27:1-13ff, Joshua divided the 12 tribes of Israel on two mountains, Gerizim and Ebal, with the ark of the covenant between, along with the tables of the Law and the cherubim overshadowing the mercy seat. As Joshua read the Law of God to the people, the tribes on Gerizim spoke the blessings that would come from obedience while the tribes on Ebal spoke the curses that would come from disobedience.[16] This was a symbolic and highly significant action. The tribes on either side of the ark corresponded to the heavenly host on God's right and left, and to the cherubim on either side of the mercy seat. By this display, Israel testified to the ruling spirits over the nations that he who obeys is blessed, while he who rebels is cursed.

The timing and place of this event were full of meaning. Poised on the edge of Canaan preparing to make war and take the land, the entire nation participated in this somber ceremony on the mountains. Continued obedience to the Law was their only assurance that Jehovah would conquer all their foes and establish them in the land of their inheritance. Obedience demanded that they destroy the idols of the land, for disobedience would lead to their going after other gods.[17] The message of choices between good and evil (blessings and curses, life and death, Jehovah and baal) was driven home that day. Not only would the Israelites dispossess the physical inhabitants of the land, but they would also disenfranchise the gods (evil angels) that the inhabitants worshiped. If Israel would obey Jehovah, every place the soles of their feet walked would be theirs, regardless of the local principalities or powers.

This earthly multitude, patterned after the heavenly host, demonstrated the reality that our moral choices determine whether we are blessed or cursed. Blessings crown the head of the obedient, but curses fall on the disobedient. Indeed, blessings and curses are revealed as originating from two different mountains, or two different kingdoms. The ark of the Lord in the midst illustrates that God is the judge over all powers, whether in Heaven or on earth. The curses of the broken Law, as well as the blessings of obedience, were administered by angelic powers (the cherubim) with God as arbitrator. From God's right hand blessings flowed by way of His ministering spirits, whereas curses fell from the left hand of God by satan's angels.[18]

Curses are never without a cause, however, and it is here that satan found his place to operate.[19] The New Testament teaches that the Law was given by angelic mediation and was subject to their oversight.[20] This message of the Law, which was spoken by angels, was binding, with every violation receiving its just punishment.[21] Although the Law was righteous and confirmed what was already in operation (the principle that rebellion brings cursing, but obedience to God brings blessings), it could not produce spiritual life or empower one to make the right moral choices.

From the day Moses threw down the tablets of the Law in anger at the people's idolatry, the history of Israel is replete with examples of curses coming out of the broken Law. Worshiping other gods resulted in wrath from above and separation in the camp below—those who would choose the Lord's side were *blessed*, while the rest were *plagued* until there was repentance and an atonement for their sin.[22]

The Law afforded satan countless opportunities. Sin is a transgression of the Law, and satan built his kingdom on the "strength of sin…the law."[23] Satan used the Law to tempt man to sin, and once he succeeded, he used it to accuse man to God. Law thereby became a means of death.[24] We can imagine the accuser tempting men, then writing down their transgressions in order to accuse and afflict them in their lives and after death.[25] The apostle Paul says that the Law became an occasion for sin by stirring up our fallen sinful nature.[26] Because of sin, the Law worked wrath, imputing every transgression and calling for an appropriate judgment.[27]

Everyone acknowledges that laws are there for our good, like the laws of the road. Born however with a disobedient and rebellious nature, people continue to do what they know to be wrong.[28] I did. Once while intoxicated, I drove my black station wagon down the wrong way of a one-way street with my lights out. I just missed a head-on collision. In spite of the law, I found myself traveling down the broad way that led to destruction. I was in a terrible predicament, and the law only the more exposed and condemned me.

If we were still under the Law, satan would yet dominate us. By the Law, sin would be strengthened in our weak sinful nature. It is no wonder that satan preaches a different gospel, one that would make the keeping of the Law the basis of our salvation. He wishes to frustrate God's grace by moving us into his sphere of jurisprudence.[29]

Christ did for us what the Law could not do, joining us by grace to Himself and imparting to us His Spirit and nature. Christ empowered me to stop my sinful habits. The vicious and iniquitous cycle of sin in my life was broken when I believed in Jesus' death for my sins. He freed me from the law of sin and death, and a new principle began to operate in my heart, the law of the Spirit of Life in Christ. Christ's Spirit now enables me to fulfill the righteous requirements of the spirit of the Law.[30] Thank God that we are no longer under the Law. This is a vital truth because satan's influential place in Heaven was partially based on man's subjection to the Law.

Satan Provokes David to Number Israel

*Now **Satan** stood up against Israel, and **moved** David to number Israel* (1 Chronicles 21:1 NKJ).

*Again the **anger of the Lord** was aroused against Israel, and **He moved** David against them to say, "Go, number Israel and Judah"* (2 Samuel 24:1 NKJ).

There is an apparent contradiction in these verses. One verse says satan moved David, the other that God moved him to number Israel. In both verses the same Hebrew word is used. Often translated as "provoked," it carries the idea of instigating; "to bring about by inciting, especially to do evil." Understanding satan's activity before God's throne makes it easier to reconcile these verses.[31]

The context of both passages makes it clear that David's numbering of Israel was an act of pride.[32] David and Israel had repeatedly defeated the Philistines,[33] but by numbering the men of war, they were counting on themselves and turning away from an earlier trust in God.[34] Even Joab realized that this was a serious insult against God. Satan then obtained grounds to accuse David and the nation. David's sinful pride and presumption provoked God's holy anger and reflected the moral climate of the whole nation at that time.

God included David in the heavenly debate by allowing him to choose the punishment the devil would be permitted to exact in the land: famine for seven years, flight from enemies for three months, or pestilence for three days. A type of the New Testament saint, David here foreshadows a place in God where we are raised up to sit with Christ in heavenly places. There was a brief but deadly plague. David saw the spirit of the destroying angel over Jerusalem and cried out to God for mercy.

*And David said unto Gad, I am in a great strait: let us fall now into the hand of the Lord; for His mercies are great: and let me not fall into the hand of man. So the Lord sent a pestilence upon Israel from the morning even to the time appointed: and there died of the people from Dan even to Beersheba seventy thousand men of the people died. And when **the angel stretched out his hand** upon Jerusalem **to destroy it**, the Lord repented Him of the **evil**, and said to the **angel** that **destroyed** the people, It is enough: stay now **thine hand**. And the angel of [from] the Lord was by the threshingplace of Araunah the Jebusite. And David spake unto the Lord when he saw the **angel** that smote the people, and said, Lo, I have sinned, and I have done wickedly: but these sheep, what have they done? let thine hand, I pray Thee, be against me, and against my father's house* (2 Samuel 24:14-17).

When David offered a blood sacrifice, the angel's hand was stopped because God accepted an atonement.

Matthew 5:25 says, "Agree with thine adversary quickly, whiles thou art in the way with him; lest at any time the adversary deliver thee to the judge, and the judge deliver thee to the officer, and thou be cast into prison." This is a good picture of our adversary's activity in the Old Testament, and Jesus' counsel is still very applicable. When satan accuses us of a transgression that we've committed, it is best to quickly confess (agree=acknowledge) and seek God's mercy as David did. There is no use defending our sin.

The Limitations of Satan and His Demons

Satan and his demons are fallen angels. In the space of three verses they are called demons, serpents, scorpions, and spirits.[35] Concerning the angels of God we read: "Are they not all ministering *spirits*, sent forth...."[36] In angelology there are different classes, ranks, and types of angels, both among the holy and the unclean. These ranks enable us to understand their diverse operations, manifestations, and habitations. Nevertheless, demons are fallen *angels*. Many Old and New Testament passages prove this point: "They sacrificed *unto devils*, not to God; *to gods* [i.e., *fallen angels*] whom they knew not."[37]

What should be absolutely clear at this point is that no matter how powerful satan and his legions appear to be, and no matter how much strife, anguish, and trouble they cause mankind, they are limited in their power and authority by the sovereignty of God. In every instance that we have examined it has been apparent that God has power over satan and his angels!

Satan possessed delegated authority and moved on legitimate grounds, but always under God's sovereign control. In the example of righteous Job, God permitted and yet limited satan's attack. In the case of wicked Ahab, God commissioned and concluded satan's employment. At all times God displayed His sovereignty in wisely governing His creation. We must therefore continually assert God's power to rule lest we espouse a grievous error in which satan appears to be forcing God's hand contrary to His will. Instead, we must see that God justly handled the devil, and so revealed His unparalleled majesty.

Satan's influential position in Heaven prior to Christ's coming and his power there must be held in balance by God's absolute authority to judge. Judgment belongs to God alone. He knows all the details, even the thoughts and the intents of the heart, and therefore He alone is qualified to judge. Psalm 82:1 says, "God standeth in the congregation of the mighty; He judgeth among *the gods* [angels]."

Satan's position has changed dramatically since the Old Testament days. The atoning work of Christ has defeated and demoted satan. The chapters that follow will describe and explain when and how this happened and clarify satan's position today with regard to Christians. This knowledge is important in the realm of spiritual warfare and in claiming our true inheritance as children of God.

Endnotes

1. See Luke 1:11,19,26; 2:15.

2. See also Psalm 109:3-17; 1 Samuel 28:15ff; Matthew 27:3-5; Acts 1:18-20. In principle Saul reaped this judgment because he treated David with such contempt. He hated David and fought against him without a just cause, rewarding him evil for good, hatred for love. When his case came before Jehovah, satan brought condemnation on Saul even though the king prayed. Psalm 109 ultimately was fulfilled by Judas Iscariot when he betrayed Christ before hanging himself.

3. See Psalm 82:1.

4. See Zechariah 3:8.

5. See Hebrews 9:11ff.

6. Hebrews 8:5. The word *example* means to exhibit the representation of a thing. *Shadow* is defined as the image or outline cast by an object.

7. See Acts 7:53; Galatians 3:19; Hebrews 2:2,5.

8. See Daniel 10:1ff.

9. See 1 Chronicles 21:1; Daniel 12:1.

10. In both places, the New American Standard version translates *doxa* as *angelic majesties*.

11. Because of the death, resurrection, and ascension of Christ, satan's position has changed; he no longer resides in glory. No wonder the writer of Hebrews says of the cherubim, "...we cannot now speak particularly." See also Exodus 36:8,35. Chapter Six, "The Accuser and the Cross," addresses the significance of the cherubim represented on the veil of the temple and the veil being torn.

12. Chapter Seven, "The Accuser and Christ's Descent Into Hell," addresses this in context with the Mount of Transfiguration and the appearance of the dead saints in Jerusalem.

13. It is noteworthy that the Mosaic cherubim were used in the idolatry of ancient, heathen religions. In Egyptian, Canaanite, and Hittite ruins there are many representations of demons as winged lions with human countenances. Colossal winged bulls and lions with human features were also found at the gates of Assyrian temples and palaces. Most archaeologists connect these hybrid cherub forms with the Israelite cherubim, but why did Israel have this in common with the cultic worship of the surrounding nations? I believe satan was the connecting link. Because he was a defiled cherub who desired worship as a god, it makes sense to find cherubim involved in the idolatry of the nations. The winged bull and lion cherubim of the heathen were thus perversions of lucifer, the anointed cherub, who along with his angels corrupted their beauty, and became the strong bulls of Bashan and ravenous lions. Ever since Eden, satan has had a large following. Today, multitudes still bear his mark and worship his image by their mind-set and lifestyle. Some unwittingly promote the satanic through the media, while others openly serve satan in the occult.

14. 2 Peter 2:12.

15. "When an ungodly man curses satan, he curses his own soul" (Apoc. Surach 21:27). Though perhaps overstated, that statement drives home the point that outside of Christ it is vain for men to rebuke satan. In Christ, however, we can engage even the highest ranking principalities and powers. Chapters Ten and Eleven explore our present position in relation to satan and his forces. Dr. C. Peter Wagner also discusses this issue at length in *Confronting the Powers* (Ventura, CA: Regal Books, 1996).

16. Mount Gerizim matches Mount Moriah where Abraham by faith offered up Isaac. There the temple was built, and there the penalty of the curse was borne by the sacrificial victim. Gerizim was thus the mountain from where the blessings of the Law were pronounced, whereas Ebal, on the opposite side, was where the curses for disobedience were read. See Deuteronomy 27:12-13ff.

17. See Deuteronomy 7:25; 11:16.

18. Cursing is attributed to certain angels, enabling demonic powers to act (see Judg. 5:23; Job 3:8-9a).

19. See Proverbs 26:2.

20. See Acts 7:53; Galatians 3:19.

21. See Hebrews 2:2. Note in the text of Joshua 8:33, "their elders, and officers, and their judges" were responsible for implementing and enforcing the requirements of the Law on a national level. If they failed to judge themselves, God would judge them via angelic powers.

22. Exodus 32 is a great illustration of these truths. Each individual required an atonement for sin, and the sins of the community affected each individual. Choices had to be made by the nation and by each person, with corresponding consequences. See also Numbers 14:24; Joshua 24:15; Jeremiah 24:1ff; Ezekiel 18:1ff.

23. 1 Corinthians 15:56.

24. See Romans 5:14.

25. Based on God's law, angels were authorized to bless those who continued in well-doing, but to curse those who practiced wickedness. This angelic administration called for records and retribution. Individuals, villages, and entire people groups came under their jurisdiction. Deuteronomy 32:8 in the LXX (the Septuagint, the Greek translation of the Old Testament) reveals that this angelic administration involved the entire angelic host and included all nations. (See also 2 Kings 19:35; Ecclesiastes 5:6; Daniel 10:12-13, 20-21; Luke 1:19-20; Ephesians 6:12; Revelation 20:12.) Apoc. Zeph. 3:8-9 refers to the angels of the accuser who write down all the sins of humankind so that he can accuse them in the afterlife. A physical description of the accuser is given in 6:8. This apocalypse is dated around 100 B.C.–A.D. 175. According to Jean Daniélou, the Jewish tradition and the later Christian writers teach that the whole economy of the Old Testament was not only communicated but administered through the medium of angels (see Acts 7:53; Gal. 3:19; Heb. 2:2-5). The Church fathers went a step further and taught that the entire physical creation was under their power. "St. Thomas Aquinas, moreover, confirms this as a traditional teaching: 'all corporal things are governed by the angels. And this is not only the teaching of the holy doctors, but of all the philosophers' " (Jean Daniélou, *Angels and Their Mission: According to the Fathers of the Church* [Westminster, MD: Newman Press, 1957], 4-5). Although a startling assertion in our rationalistic, scientific age, it does reveal the extent to which many have viewed the ministry of angels, and their views do have biblical support.

26. See Romans 7:5,8,21-23.

27. See Romans 4:15; 5:13; Galatians 3:10-11; James 2:10.

28. See Romans 7:12-21.

29. See Galatians 1:7-9; 2:16–3:1.

30. Romans 8:1-4.

31. The Bible always maintains man's responsibility and never teaches the idea of "the devil made me do it." Without an understanding of lucifer's rebellion, however, one might conclude that God tempts men to sin (because the element of divine anger against Israel precedes the moving of David to sin by numbering Israel), whereas James says "…for God cannot be tempted with evil, neither tempteth He any man" (Jas. 1:13).

32. See 2 Samuel 11:1ff; 1 Chronicles 20:1ff; 21:17.

33. See 1 Chronicles 20:1-8.

34. In both accounts, this transgression is connected topically, though not chronologically, to David's sin with Bathsheba. During David's time of rest and leisure, satan used pride to seduce him into numbering Israel (see 2 Sam. 24:3). God promised to subdue their enemies and make the Israelites innumerable in the land; whereas numbering was normally a vehicle for military subscription, forced labor, or taxation.

35. See Luke 10:17-20 (NKJ). As in the New Testament, the Old Testament uses a diverse vocabulary when it refers to the fallen angels. They are called "gods," "powers in the heavens above," "demons," "spirits," "princes," and "sons of God." Satan may even possibly come under the designation of "an angel of the Lord." In the case of Balaam, "an angel of the Lord" is said to be "a satan," or an adversary. Balaam was hired by Balak to curse God's people, but he could not curse Israel unless he led them into fornication and idolatry. Then the curse of the Law came upon them. How devilish! Balaam, against God's express wishes, went to Moab, and was met by an adversarial angel from the presence of the Lord. Bible scholars do not consider this angel of the Lord described in this setting to be "*the* angel of the Lord." But because satan acted as a destroying angel on Jehovah's behalf (as demonstrated), this could possibly be an angel from Jehovah under satan's designation. If this was satan or one of his angels, imagine the scope of satan's activity in the Old Testament: "And *God's anger was kindled* because he went: and the angel of the Lord stood in the way for an *adversary* [satan]

against him…" (Num. 22:22). To consider the possibility of satan's involvement here is provocative. Yet, the word *adversary* used here in Numbers is literally *satan* (James Strong, *Strong's Dictionary of the Hebrew Bible* [Peabody, MA: Hendrickson, n.d.]). This angel follows the anger of the Lord as in the case of the Egyptians. God's wrath against sin preceded hurtful angels. This angel, who stood before Balaam, also had a drawn sword and would have slain him. We have already seen that when the death sentence is administered in the Old Testament, satan is there because he had "the power of death." When Balaam responded to the reward offered by Balak, satan had grounds to move against him. His influence here could also explain the enigmatic shift by God in permitting Balaam to go the second time. (Numbers 22:20-35 reveals an unseen struggle over whether Balaam should or should not go with the princes of Moab.)

36. See Hebrews 1:13-14.

37. Deuteronomy 32:17a.

Chapter Three

The Accuser's Origin

All orthodox theologians agree that satan was created upright and, in time, corrupted himself. The question is, precisely when did his rebellion occur and what form did it take? Why did it happen, and how could such a thing take place in a realm created and ruled over by a holy, just, and right-eous God? Many believe that the Bible is silent on the subject and therefore conclude that satan's revolt is shrouded in obscurity, occurring long before the creation of man. Does the Word of God say nothing about this?

I believe the Bible describes satan's fall as clearly as it does man's, and rightfully so. If an individual or group unsuccessfully attempts a military or political *coup d'état*, it is important for national confidence and stability for the government remaining in power to inform its citizens of the when, where, and why of the revolt. In the same manner, God has revealed to His people the chronology of satan's high treason with all its relevant details. This knowledge is important for our continued confidence in the stability of the Kingdom of God, for conducting spiritual warfare, and for understanding our current position as believers with regard to satan and his legions.

The First Sin

For centuries philosophers have debated the origin of evil, and without divine revelation, it would remain a mystery. The Bible plainly states where sin comes from: "He that committeth *sin is of the devil*; for the devil sinneth from the *beginning*" (1 Jn. 3:8a). The Greek word translated "of" indicates that sin is *from* or *out of* the devil. It denotes origin, expressing the two related thoughts of source and beginning. Anything that has a beginning has a source from which it springs. The source of sin, its beginning place, was within the heart of lucifer.[1]

According to Jesus, sin began with a murderous lie of the devil: "He was a murderer *from the beginning*, and abode not in the truth, because there is no truth in him. *When he speaketh a lie, he speaketh of his own*: for he is a liar, and *the father* of it" (Jn. 8:44b). With the phrase *from the beginning*, Jesus links satan's lies with murder, referring to Genesis 3:4, "And the serpent said unto the woman, Ye shall not surely die."

This sin of lying by which satan murdered Adam and Eve is the first recorded sin in the Bible and was the first outward act of his rebellion. It was cold, calculated, premeditated murder because the serpent was fully aware of God's command and the consequences of man's disobedience. Prior to satan's lie in the garden and the response of Adam and Eve, creation was untainted by sin. The creation account ends with the words, "And God saw *every thing* that He had made, and, behold, it *was very good*" (Gen. 1:31a). Sin did not enter creation until satan's murderous lie in the third chapter of Genesis.[2] There is no earlier sin that God overlooked or left unrecorded.

Genesis 3:1 refers to a "serpent" (Heb., *nachash*) who was "more subtle" (Heb., *aruwm*) than any beast God had made. From antiquity this serpent has been identified with lucifer, or satan. Lucifer means "brightness" or "shining one" or "morningstar." The Hebrew word *nachash* also carries the basic meaning of "bright" or "shining."[3] Revelation 12:9 clearly links satan with a serpent: "And the great dragon was cast out, that old serpent [Gk., *ophis*], called the Devil, and Satan...." The Greek word *ophis* means "serpent," but also has a figurative sense of a sly, cunning, malicious person. Because the Hebrew word *aruwm* (subtle) means "cunning" and "crafty," many believe this is an indication that satan had already sinned, but the word also has the positive meaning of "prudent" and "wise." The fact that the serpent stood upright until after he was cursed strongly suggests that he had not sinned prior to this time (see Gen. 3:14).

Although lucifer did not sin outwardly until the third chapter of Genesis, there undoubtedly was an incubation period beforehand, during which his desire to be like God developed. The Bible teaches that sin normally follows a logical progression: "But every man is tempted, when he is drawn away of his own lust, and enticed. Then when lust hath conceived, it bringeth forth sin: and sin, when it is finished, bringeth forth death" (Jas. 1:14-15). Satan's lust combined with his pride to conceive an iniquitous condition in his heart from which his rebellious lie sprang.[4]

Free Will and Moral Volition

Lucifer was able to conceive rebellion in his heart and utter outwardly a murderous lie, even in a sinless environment, because he was created with a free will. His heart was not governed by natural laws, but by moral volition. As He did later with man, God created satan with the power of choice. Although God saw *the iniquity* that was in lucifer's heart before it was on his tongue (God sees everything and knows what is good and evil), He did not intervene and violate lucifer's will because without a free will there is no potential for love.[5]

Angels and men likewise were faced with the choice of whether to live in dependence on God or independence from Him. The serpent (lucifer) was a regular presence in the garden of Eden (Paradise) where God and man also dwelled together in fellowship.[6] I believe that the event that triggered the rebellion in lucifer's heart was the creation of man. Lucifer saw mankind as a means of self-fulfillment and self-exaltation, and those who became his angels followed him out of their own lust for power and position. Scripture tells us that one third of the angels followed satan into rebellion, seeing his cause as desirable and advantageous.[7] Likewise, lucifer became a source of temptation for man by manifesting his own lust when he said, "You shall be *as gods*."[8] Certainly it was lucifer's desire before it was Adam's.

God had warned Adam and Eve not to eat from the tree in the center of the garden because its fruit was deadly, possessing the knowledge of good and evil.[9] The Scriptures often compare individuals to trees;[10] indeed, true and false prophets are recognized by the fruit they produce.[11] Jesus said, "Either make the tree good, and his fruit good; or else make the tree corrupt, and his fruit corrupt: for the tree is known by his fruit" (Mt. 12:33). In the garden of Eden, lucifer, due to his own lust, produced poisonous fruit. The serpent and the tree of the knowledge of good and evil are graphic illustrations of how lucifer's evil influence entered Paradise. If Adam and Eve had stood their ground, listened to God, and resisted the serpent's call to sedition, they could have exposed his evil scheme and lucifer would have had no power over them.[12] They would either have driven the devil out of Paradise in God's stead, or God Himself would have cut lucifer down and thrown him into the fire.[13]

Satan's Kingdom

Instead of confronting satan, however, Adam and Eve gave him a hearing. After all, he was beautiful, and the fruit he offered looked good to make one wise like God. Using his great wisdom and cunning, the crafty and subtle serpent persuaded them to join him in his *coup d'état*![14] In what seemed the perfect crime, well-conceived and well-executed, lucifer's rebellion involved the depths of his corrupt wisdom and the mystery of iniquity and was calculated to achieve his aim of securing a kingdom for himself. His goal was no less than to take mankind and the world to himself and, in so doing, establish himself in authority and dominion over both mankind and the entire heavenly host. Lucifer was not satisfied with the lofty position that he already enjoyed; he wanted to be in control and equal to his Creator.[15]

Satan thus established a kingdom completely antithetical to God's Kingdom: death instead of life, sin instead of righteousness; the list of reversals could go on for pages! As Milton's devil in *Paradise Lost* said, "Evil be thou my good." There was no other way for lucifer to possess what he wanted. Just as all the characteristics of God's Kingdom emanate from God's righteous nature and character, satan's kingdom became simply an expression of his corrupt, perverted nature; an evil realm planted in the very heart of the angelic and human races![16]

Satan tempted mankind to rebel against God because, as the author of sin, he knew he would have a legal right over sinners. He understood the laws of creation and operated as a free moral agent. When he joined man to himself, he could actually claim to God, "If You cast me away, You must also cast them away, because they are what I am! We are one, so they must receive the same as I!"[17] Accordingly, the Scriptures clearly teach that when satan is banished to the lake of fire, rebellious men will be also. Lucifer's and mankind's destinies were united. Satan knew that God could not in justice banish him from Heaven to the dark abyss without leaving man forever in sin.[18] For a time it seemed that satan had secured in Heaven and on earth the preeminence that his heart desired.[19]

By his free will, lucifer lifted up in his heart because of his beauty, conceived the iniquities of pride, lust, and deceit, causing him to misuse his wisdom and lead angels and mankind into sin.[20] Desiring equality with his Creator and dominion over His creation, lucifer tempted man with his own desire to be like God. When man rejected God's rule, he gave his allegiance and earthly authority to the devil. Mankind became, by nature, a child of the devil through sin. As a result, lucifer's lie established him as the god of this world[21] and brought man into an unholy relationship.[22]

None of this took God by surprise. He had a plan all along that would redeem mankind from satan and break his authority over them. For this reason, the Lord did not immediately remove satan from Heaven, lest all of humanity be irretrievably lost. God's wisdom and purpose in this is illustrated in Jesus' parable of the wheat and the tares (see Mt. 13:24-30). The householder sowed good seed in his field but an enemy came at night and sowed tares. When asked by his servants if they should uproot the bad seeds, the householder wisely answered, "...Nay; lest while ye gather up the tares, ye root up also the wheat with them. Let both grow together until the harvest" (Mt. 13:29-30a). In God's creation, an enemy sowed a deadly seed, and mankind was killed spiritually by it. A new life-giving seed was required if man was not to remain dead forever. God promised such a divine Seed to mankind and established enmity between satan's seed and the coming Seed of the woman.[23]

The Promised Seed of the Woman

The third chapter of Genesis is a pivotal chapter in the Bible. Not only does it depict the first sin of satan and the first sins of Adam and Eve with their resulting fall, but it also shows the just and righteous way a sovereign God handled the crisis. The Lord pronounced judgment on the situation, issuing a curse and a promise of hope. The serpent was cursed and Eve received the promise of a future deliverer, which raised up a hope for her and all succeeding generations of the human family.

*And the Lord God said unto the woman, What is this that thou hast **done**? And the woman said, The serpent **beguiled** me, and I did eat. And the Lord God said unto the serpent, **Because thou hast done this** [Not some earlier unrecorded sin that God had overlooked], thou art **cursed**...upon thy belly shalt thou go, and dust shalt thou eat all the days of thy life: And I will put enmity between thee and the woman, and between **thy seed and her seed; it shall bruise thy head,** and thou shalt bruise His heel* (Genesis 3:13-15).

Cursed above all creation as the author of sin, the serpent's character became irreversibly corrupt. God judged his sinful nature immediately, confining him to move in his evil desires. God's curse of satan carried no mention of redemption through a substitute, so the devil was locked into an abiding evil state even more drastic than the change that occurred in Adam's nature after he sinned. Outwardly upright before his sin, the serpent now went on his belly to eat the dust of the earth, symbolizing satan's evil desire to possess and consume mankind. Mankind, formed from the dust of the earth, was sentenced to return to the dust. The devil's dust diet figuratively depicts his dominion over death and sinful flesh:[24] "The thief cometh not, but for to steal, and to kill, and to destroy" (Jn. 10:10a). So it would be "all the days of [his] life."[25]

It is noteworthy that God did not drive the serpent out of Paradise along with Adam and Eve. For a time, satan retained a place in Heaven, called by the apostle Paul the "third heaven," where Paradise is located.[26] As with Adam, who died inwardly on the day he ate but not outwardly for some 930 years, so satan, although judged in his nature, was not removed from Heaven until thousands of years later. Although satan's dominion by usurpation grew during this time, God nevertheless had set in motion His coming judgment through the promised Seed of the woman. In Heaven everything is done decently and in order, even the removal of the devil.

Adam and Eve were judged for their sin. But God's grace is revealed in the fact that before He pronounced judgment on them, He promised a deliverer who would thoroughly defeat the serpent. God's vengeance on the serpent would result in mercy for mankind. Israel's exodus from Egypt is an excellent natural parallel, as the breaking of Pharaoh's power meant release from bondage for God's people. The serpent's head, depicting his power and authority, would be broken by the Seed of the woman. As a result, men would be delivered from sin and death.

The promised Seed of the woman is the first striking prophecy of Christ's virgin birth and vicarious death. The last Adam would defeat the serpent, although the serpent would bruise His heel. This very lust of the devil, moving him to destroy the promised Seed, would lead to his own downfall. Satan's ultimate downfall was first proclaimed in Eden, but he continued to exercise his authority on earth and his position in Heaven until Jesus Christ, the promised Seed, came and was bruised at the cross.

The Angels That Sinned

Once God's curse had been pronounced, satan in his corrupt and perverted nature lost no time plotting and scheming to thwart God's promise of a deliverer for mankind. Prompted by the devil and his legions, sin and evil grew in the hearts of men, who were now under the dominion of the author of sin. With each succeeding generation, the wickedness of man increased in conjunction with a progressive angelic rebellion until the evil reached such a level as to precipitate the Flood. Many students of the Bible believe that chapter 6 of Genesis records an attempt by the unholy angels to destroy any possibility of a promised Seed.

> *And it came to pass, when men began to multiply on the face of the earth, and daughters were born unto them, that the **sons of God** saw the daughters of men that they were fair; and they took them wives of all which they chose. ... There were **giants** in the earth in those days; and also after that, when the **sons of God came in unto the daughters of men**, and they bare children to them, the same became mighty men which were of old, **men of renown**. And God saw that the wickedness of man was great in the earth, and that **every imagination** of the thoughts of his heart was only **evil continually*** (Genesis 6:1-2,4-5).

According to the belief of many, satan's campaign against the promised Seed took the form of a two-pronged attack: fallen angels (sons of God) began to cohabit with women,[27] and evil imaginations filled men's hearts. The former produced giants, a corrupted seed of woman; the latter, an unsafe world where violence was the order of the day. Both were part of an attempt to cut the human race off from the promised Seed. Because the wickedness in the earth was so great, God decided to destroy man from the face of the earth (see Gen. 6:7). God chose to preserve Noah because Noah was blameless. A footnote in *The Companion Bible* says, "[Noah] alone had preserved their pedigree and kept it pure, in spite of the prevailing corruption brought about by the fallen angels."[28]

If the "sons of God" in Genesis 6:2 who "saw" the daughters of men and "took" them as wives were fallen angels, then theirs were sins with a definite purpose.[29] Is it correct to identify the "sons of God" in this passage with angels? Did certain angels of satan physically unite as one with the human race in order to eliminate a pure Seed? The evidence is persuasive:

- Elsewhere in the Old Testament the "sons of God" are angels.[30] The Septuagint, the Greek translation of the Old Testament, even renders Genesis 6:2: "...the angels of God saw the daughters of men...."

- The "sons of God" as angels is a view held from ancient times, both by Jews and Christians.[31]

- Apparently, both Jude and Peter refer to this incident in the sixth chapter of Genesis as a sin of angels.[32] Jude likens the sin of these angels who left their first estate to the sin of Sodom where perverse men committed sexual immorality with lower creatures.

Jesus compared this time before the Flood both with Sodom and Gomorrah and with the last days when many are demonized in the area of sexual lust.[33] A supernatural dimension to this area may account for why it so powerfully enslaves. Although it is true that Jesus said that the angels do not marry, He did not say they were sexless or incapable of sexual activity.[34] Abraham entertained angels who were able to eat and drink. They appeared as men to the degree that the wicked people of Sodom, to whom they were sent, wanted to have sexual relations with them.[35]

I personally believe these were angels who took evil beyond measure in their lustful attempt to place mankind beyond redemption.[36] Although they had joined with lucifer earlier, this was a further step in their rebellion. Here the development of sin in the heavenlies and on earth attained its utmost wickedness through intercourse between fallen angels and depraved mankind.[37] Satan could not have envisioned the extent of sin's misery and ruin on earth over the centuries.[38] One sin has a way of leading to an even more serious one. This constitutes the progressive working of the mystery of iniquity and God holds satan responsible for spreading evil: "By the multitude of thy merchandise [iniquities]…they have filled the midst of thee with violence…by the iniquity of thy traffic" (Ezek. 28:16-18). The bad seed grows up and matures to full stature as in the time of harvest.

This decline is reflected in the downward spiral of standards in today's movie industry, which is filled with occult violence, sex, and profanity. We have come far from the days of strict censorship. In the early days of movies, cursing, illicit sex, nudity, and even *excessive and lustful kissing* could not be shown. The code (mutually agreed upon by the production house and the church council) stated that *passion should be treated in such* *a manner as **not** to purposefully stimulate the lower and baser emotions.* Gradually, movie makers inserted minor violations. Becoming bolder with less regard for any form of restriction, filmmakers now treat passion in such a manner as to purposefully stimulate baser emotions. Just as the scarlet woman of Revelation "the inhabitants of the earth have been made drunk with the wine of her fornication." Hollywood's "profaneness [is] gone forth into all the land[s]," and she is "too bold to blush."[39] Harvey Wilcox, a temperance leader who purchased and named Hollywood in 1886, would never have dreamed what his 120-acre ranch near Los Angeles would become. In its early days it was a quiet Christian community of high moral values where alcohol was banned except for medicinal purposes.

When evil runs its course and is full-grown, God's response is swift, severe judgment. With the Flood, He judged the world and bound these angels in everlasting chains under darkness until the judgment of the great day.[40] Indeed, He did not wait to judge this crowd of angels, nor the world that they had so completely corrupted. Instead, satan's angels and mankind were left with a good example of judgment. As with the waters of the ocean, there is a limit to how far God will allow evil to go. The period of the Flood also parallels the judgment of the earth by fire, which is to be foreshadowed by a short time when God temporarily allows restraint to be cast off before He again judges fallen angels and mankind. Thus as time runs out, satan and his angels are desperate and will do whatever they can in their enmity against the promised Seed.[41]

The Condemnation of the Devil

When Paul presents Timothy with the qualifications for a bishop, he warns against appointing a novice because of the danger of pride and self-exaltation.[42] Satan is given as an example because, although he possessed a very high and lofty position before God, he was not content. He coveted God's very throne, a place above everyone else. The picture is clear. Lifted up with pride, lucifer wanted to be like the Most High.

In writing to Gaius, John admonished the church's leadership not to follow such evil pride. One among them, Diotrephes [whose name means *nourished by Zeus*, the supreme god of the Greek pantheon of gods], "loveth to have the preeminence among them."[43] This man ascended to a high, influential position in the church, but not by righteousness. Indeed, John exposes in Diotrephes the same satanic scenario:

*So if I come, I will call attention to what he is doing, **gossiping maliciously about us**. Not satisfied with that, he **refuses** to welcome the brothers. He also **stops** those who want to do so and **puts them out of** the church* (3 John 1:10 NIV)

Gainsaying for position, slander against the brethren, casting them out of the assembly, and using one's position to achieve preeminence is the condemnation of the devil. But where did Paul and John learn that such pride was the condemnation of the devil? Was it not from the Old Testament prophets such as Isaiah and Ezekiel?

These prophets spoke of satan's judgment, not looking back to a prehistoric event, but anticipating one still to come at the first advent of the Messiah. Relegating these prophecies to refer to an unknown time before man's creation fails to explain when and how Heaven was cleansed of the accuser or account for his presence in Heaven as discussed earlier. When satan sinned, God judged his nature immediately, but his full condemnation and removal from Heaven was delayed until the fullness of God's redemptive plan could come to pass. Speaking through godly prophets, however, the Lord clearly foretold the judgment awaiting the accuser.

Endnotes

1. John of Damascus, considered the first to compose a volume of the Church's teachings, wrote, "Concerning the devil and demons...they became wicked, turning away of their own free choice from good to evil. They determined to rise in rebellion against Him: and he [satan] was the first to depart from good and become evil." Irenaeus and Athenagoras both believed that satan caused man's fall at the same time as his own. This is found throughout an entire tradition of Church fathers that can be easily followed in their writings. (*Select Library of Nicene and Post Nicene Fathers of the Christian Church*, Philip Schaff, ed., Volume 9 [Oxford: The Christian Literature Co., 1891], 20).

2. One of the many difficulties with the Gap theory is that it presupposes that everything was not good after Genesis 1:2. The Gap theory suggests that lucifer's revolt occurred in a "gap" between Genesis 1:1 and 1:2 because "the earth was without form, and void" due to satan's judgment along with a pre-Adamic race of bodily beings. This pre-Adamic race also accounts for the demons, hence the call for Adam to "replenish the earth and subdue it" (Gen. 1:28). The creation account,

however, ends with God's declaration that everything was "very good." Evil did not enter creation until later, and it is reasonable to expect the Bible to record such an important event. It does so, in Genesis chapter 3.

3. Ray C. Stedman, *Expository Studies in Genesis 2 and 3: Understanding Man* (Waco, TX: Word Books, 1975), 56-57. In the subsection entitled "The Shining One," Stedman writes: "I am very sorry that this word in the Hebrew was ever translated serpent, because it has given rise to a very false idea about this story....But the interesting thing is that this account does not really say that there was a snake in the garden of Eden. The Hebrew word here is *nachash* which means literally 'to shine,' or in the noun form as here, 'a shining one.' If you read it that way an entirely different being emerges: 'Now the shining one was more subtle....' Undoubtedly, snakes were created to represent this being who appeared in the garden as the shining one...."

4. Lust and pride were the main ingredients of his iniquity. "Fifteen root words are translated iniquity in the English language Bible, which tells us something about the subtle aspects of this sin. It is of great significance that all appearances of iniquity have to do with religion-perversion of the truth...The whole mad scheme of iniquity...stems from the earliest enterprise of satan—that enterprise, in fact, that made him the devil" (Charles W. Conn, *The Anatomy of Evil* [Old Tappan, NJ: Revell, 1981], 27-29).

5. Theologians call this a probationary period—a time of testing for both angels and mankind. I prefer to see it as an opportunity to become conformed to God's image—or to become like God—in the right way. It is one thing to desire what someone else possesses, such as his house or position, but quite another to aspire to be like him in his honest and loving character. The devil wanted God's elevated position over creation but not His holy character.

6. See Genesis 3:1; Ezekiel 28:13.

7. See Revelation 12:4.

8. Genesis 3:5.

9. See Genesis 2:17.

10. See Psalm 1:3; Proverbs 11:30; 15:4; Isaiah 56:3; Jeremiah 17:8; Daniel 4:10ff.

11. See Matthew 7:15-20.

12. How long were Adam and Eve in Eden before they fell? Early rabbis say 150 years; whereas Second Enoch says five and a half hours. Five hours seems too short a time to have named all the animals, whereas 150 years seems too long.

13. See Genesis 2:15; Luke 3:9.

14. Although Eve was deceived, Adam, with full use of his great intellect, chose to side with lucifer against God. Following lucifer's lustful example, Adam's sin was willful and treacherous. See 1 Timothy 2:14; Hosea 6:7 (Lit. *adam* in Hebrew, translated *men* in KJV and *Adam* in NIV).

15. See Isaiah 14:13-14.

16. See Ephesians 2:1-3; Colossians 2:13; 3:5-10.

17. See Hebrews 2:11-17. The principle of identification and oneness mentioned here also formerly applied to man and satan.

18. I believe that this truth alone settles the question of why God allowed satan to remain active after his rebellion. God's primary purpose in doing so was not to develop character but to provide redemption. It was not God's will for man to know evil. See Genesis 2:16-17; 3:5,22; Romans 16:19.

19. See Isaiah 14:13; Ezekiel 28:17.

20. See Ezekiel 28:15,17.

21. The terms and semantics vary, but the concept remains—legal dominion was transferred. Satan could therefore offer the kingdoms of the human world to Jesus as a legitimate temptation.

22. See Genesis 2:17; Isaiah 28:18.

23. See Genesis 3:15.

24. See Hebrews 2:14.

25. Genesis 3:14c.

26. See 2 Corinthians 12:1-4

27. The apocryphal book of First Enoch, chapters 6 through 16, describes how 200 angels under the leadership of Semyaza intermarried with human women. In addition to fathering giants by these women, the angels further corrupted the human race by instructing people in occult arts, by teaching them how to make instruments of war, and by showing them how to beautify themselves with cosmetics and jewelry.

28. Noah was *perfect*. The Hebrew word *tamiym* may be a reference to physical purity. The same word is translated *without blemish* in Exodous 12:5 and Leviticus 1:3; 22:19. Noah's family may have been one of the only ones not to have intermingled with these fallen angels.

29. The Hebrew words *raa* (saw) and *laqah* (took) correspond directly and deliberately as a repeat of the sin in the garden of Eden; they *saw* the fruit of the tree and *took* it. Evil is not just a human affair, but is transcendent in its character.

30. See Job 1:6; 2:1; 38:7; Psalm 29:1; 89:7.

31. Philo, Tertullian, Josephus, Delitzsch, the Talmud and all identified and interpreted them as angels. Justin Martyr, Methoius, and Martin Luther also held this position.

32. See Jude 6-7; 2 Peter 2:4-5

33. See Jude 6-8; Luke 17:26-30; Romans 1:26-27.

34. See Matthew 22:30; Mark 12:25. He even qualified His statement, saying that those who rise from the dead "neither marry, nor are given in marriage; but are as the angels which are *in heaven*" (Mk. 12:25). Possibly, God's angels *in Heaven* are being contrasted with those who left their heavenly estate.

35. See Genesis 19:4-9. These godly angels returned to Heaven, but angels are always in the masculine gender in names and personal pronouns. This would also explain why their offspring are *giants*, supernatural males, *mighty men,* and *men of renown.* Also worth noting is the Hebrew word for "giants", *Nephilim.* It is from a root word that means *fallen ones*, possibly referring to the angels that left their first estate. The truth behind the mythological Greek gods, half man, half god, as well as the advanced achievements of the ancients, may also have their roots here.

36. According to Alexander, the interpretation of the sons of God as angels was dominant for three centuries after the time of First Enoch, being clearly expressed in Jubilees, the Testaments of the Twelve Patriarchs, Second Enoch, and Second Baruch, as well as in the writings of Philo and Josephus. The identification of the sons of God as angels was also made by Clement of Alexandria (c.150–c.215), Tertullian (c.160–c.225), Lactantius (c.240–c.320), and Ambrose (c.339–c.397) (P.S. Alexander, "The Targumim and Early Exegesis of 'Sons of God' in Gen. 6" *Journal of Jewish Studies* 23 [1971], 60-71.) The other position, that the "sons of God" represent the godly line of Seth, or a line of kings,

has several problems. First, the phrase "sons of God" never means the godly line of Seth or dynastic rulers anywhere else since God has not yet begun working through one line. Second, even when He does refer to that line, the term "sons of God" is not used. Third, there is no support for the idea that the phrase "daughters of men" refers to Canaanites. Fourth, this theory does not take into account Adam and Eve's other children. Fifth, nor can the argument stand that human polygamy brought on the Flood since polygamy was practiced after the Flood.

37. There are documented experiences of men and women having orgasms with certain kinds of demons. Research over hundreds of years has produced much evidence. Demons that take on the male role are technically called *incubi* and the female are referred to as *succubi*. As an example of incubi, Lester Sumrall notes a well-popularized case in the Philippines of a demonized prostitute. There is, however a divine post-Flood limitation to angelic intercourse with mankind; they can no longer produce offspring. Although it cannot be proven, I am of the opinion that high-ranking angels who took on bodies were able to manipulate procreative powers. (After all, scientists today can produce *test tube* babies by artificial insemination.) The answer may also be found in the biological conditions of the pre-Flood world that enabled humans to live ten times longer than after the Flood.

38. Perhaps he thought that God would work a deal out with him rather than destroy mankind. Theodicy, the justification of God's ways in the world, seeks to answer the question of why God permits evil to be done. Some have argued that evil is necessary for the greater good as part of the benevolent divine scheme; others, that evil is nonbeing, a privation or absence of good. Christian theologians have also taught that evil is a mystery, or is expedient to test and train us to maturity. Better still is a theodicy that evil is the result of sin, and that sin proceeds from free will. (Since God desired a moral goodness and thus love in His creation, freedom to choose was a prerequisite. God could not give man true freedom and at the same time prevent man from choosing evil with all its effects; otherwise, the creation would have been limited to rocks, trees, animals, and such.) Although each of the above views have elements of great truth, I believe that the picture is incomplete without an understanding of lucifer's rebellion. Evil began with lucifer in Heaven, and when we consider the chronology of his fall, we see that evil's power was dealt with by God Himself suffering on the cross. Without violating human choice God has

passed judgment on evil, excluding it from eternity and limiting the extent of evil in time by means of His redemption in Christ.

39. See Revelation 17:2; Jeremiah 6:15; 23:15.

40. Although their sin is compared to the sin of Sodom and Gomorrah, the timing of their being cast down to hell is the Flood. *"For if God spared not the angels* that sinned, but cast them down to hell, and delivered them into chains of darkness, to be reserved unto judgment; *and spared not the old world..."* (2 Pet. 2:4-5). Because they left their heavenly abode and took on bodily form, God could in all justice chain them in the abyss (see Mt. 8:28-29). Certainly, lucifer and his other angels did not come down in such a fashion, although they probably urged on those who did.

41. The next time water will not be the cleaning agent, but fire. The heavens on fire will remove satan and his angels from the heavenlies.

42. See 1 Timothy 3:6.

43. 3 John 1:9.

Chapter Four

The Accuser's Judgment Foretold

The root of the sin that was conceived in lucifer's heart was pride: in his beauty, in his exalted position in Heaven, and in his estimation of himself, that he was worthy to be considered equal to his Creator. The place was Eden. Genesis provides the account.

Cursed with no hope of redemption, only satan's nature was judged initially. Nevertheless satan lifted himself up in Heaven and established a kingdom of his own that was the very antithesis of God's. Through sin man, by nature, became part of satan's domain. God, however, promised a Seed that would break satan's stranglehold on man and remove the accuser from his high and lofty place.

Just as the Bible relates the origin of satan's evil nature and exposes his malicious work as the accuser in Heaven, it also reveals his dethronement. The prophets greatly anticipated the Deliverer's coming and the accuser's demise. There are several key passages in the Old Testament that describe and outline for us the stages of his judgment and progressive casting down. The prophets Isaiah and Ezekiel, in particular, have much to say about the this and, not surprisingly, the Book of Job has a lengthy section that reveals a great deal about satan's personality. King David, the "sweet psalmist of Israel," had firsthand experience of battle with the evil one and filled his psalms with divine insights and revelations that grew out of those encounters. Together, these passages present a clear picture of judgment on the accuser's position and lay the groundwork for an expectation of his being cast out of Heaven and the cleansing of the heavens.

Isaiah's Proverb to Lucifer

More than one Roman emperor claimed divinity for himself and demanded worship, as did certain pharaohs of Egypt and early kings of Babylon.[1] King Nebuchadnezzar of Babylon was driven out and abased for a season because of his proud delusion of grandeur. After viewing the splendor of Babylon's palace and hanging gardens, he declared, "Is not this great Babylon, that *I* have built for the house of the kingdom by the might of *my* power, and for the honour of *my* majesty?"[2] He became as a beast of the field, losing his mind for a time until he learned that God rules in the armies of Heaven and exalts and abases whomever He wills.

Ancient Babylon was founded on the post-Flood apostasy of Nimrod and derived its name from the confounding of tongues at the tower of Babel.[3] Babylon's rebellion to the true faith became so highly developed that her mystery cults spread throughout the world: "MYSTERY, BABYLON THE GREAT, THE MOTHER OF HARLOTS AND ABOMINATIONS OF THE EARTH."[4] It is no wonder then that Isaiah's prophecy regarding the accuser's judgment begins with judgment against the Babylonian kings who put themselves in the place of God.[5] They were, however, only lucifer's earthly representatives, and although the proverb begins with them, it quickly progresses to satan's ambitious heavenly throne:

> *And it shall come to pass in the day that the Lord shall give thee rest...that thou shalt take up this **proverb** against the **king** of Babylon, and say, How hath the **oppressor ceased!** the golden city ceased! The Lord hath **broken the staff of the wicked....**he that ruled the nations in anger, is persecuted, and none hindereth. The **whole earth is at rest**, and is quiet: they break forth into singing. Yea, the fir trees rejoice at thee, and the cedars of Lebanon, saying, Since thou art laid down, no feller is come up against us. Hell from beneath is moved for thee to meet thee at thy coming: it stirreth up the dead for thee, even all the chief ones of the earth; it hath raised up from their thrones all the kings of the nations. All they shall speak and say unto thee, Art thou also **become weak** as we? art thou become like unto us? **Thy pomp is***

*brought down to the grave, and the noise of thy viols: the worm is spread under thee, and the worms cover thee. **How art thou fallen from heaven, O Lucifer,** son of the morning! how art thou cut down to the ground, which didst weaken the nations! For thou hast said in thine heart, **I will** ascend into heaven, **I will exalt my throne** above the stars of God: **I will** sit also up on the mount of the congregation, in the sides of the north: **I will** ascend above the heights of the clouds; **I will** be like the most High. **Yet thou shalt be brought down to hell**, to the sides of the pit. They that see thee shall narrowly look upon thee, and consider thee, saying, Is this the man that made the earth to tremble, that did shake kingdoms; that made the world as a wilderness, and destroyed the cities thereof; **that opened not the house of his prisoners?** ...But thou art cast out of thy grave like an abominable branch, and as the raiment of those that are slain, thrust through with a sword, that go down to the stones of the pit; as a carcase trodden under feet. Thou shalt not be joined with them in burial, because thou hast destroyed thy land, and slain thy people: the seed of evildoers shall never be renowned.* (Isaiah 14:3-20)

The Hebrew word *mawshawll,* translated "proverb," is both a parable and an axiomatic truth. Lucifer is parabolically the king of Babylon, and the *I will's* of lucifer constitute an enduring principle. As the proverb "Is Saul also among the prophets?" was quoted when someone appeared to be out of place, so also one might reply when someone proudly boasts of what he will do for himself, "Is lucifer still in Heaven?"[6] This prophetic proverb, however, will be taken up against lucifer only when he is taken down; then mankind will fully consider lucifer's fall.[7] It is concerned with the breaking of the staff and scepter of the wicked, which signifies satan's power of sin and authority over death. That breaking of the staff was still a future event in Isaiah's day. The future aspect of this prophecy is demonstrated by the fact that the verbs *shall* or *will* are used seven times in the first two verses.

Essentially, the scope of Isaiah's prophetic proverb can be summarized as follows:

- The proverb begins with the king of Babylon, but it is concerned mainly with the end of oppression, the breaking of satan's evil, angry rule over the nations (Is. 14:4-6).

- The proverb is complete when at last the whole earth is at rest because the oppressor is laid low (Is. 14:7-8).

- The proverb equates *laid low* with being made weak, brought down to hell, and becoming a spectacle to the spirits of former world rulers (Is. 14:9-11).

- The proverb concerns lucifer's fall from Heaven. This is not a declaration of what happened in a time long past. It is a prophecy of what was to come in the future with the advent of the promised Seed many years after Isaiah (Is. 14:12).

- The proverb attributes satan's fall ultimately to his self-will and self-exaltation. With all his might lucifer had tried to seize a position equal to the Most High (Is. 14:13-14).

- The proverb prophesies beyond lucifer's casting out from Heaven to his future confinement to the bottomless pit and hell (Is. 14:15-16).

- The proverb alludes to lucifer's destructive powers on earth through sin and authority to hold prisoners in his house of death, from which he refused to release them (Is. 14:16-18).

- The proverb promises that lucifer will be rejected, pierced by the sword, and trodden underfoot, and his evil seed shall never be propagated again (Is. 14:19-20).

Ezekiel's Lament for the Anointed Cherub

The twenty-eighth chapter of Ezekiel contains a prophecy related to satan that is often used in conjunction with the passage in Isaiah. Together they provide a consistant revelation of the stages in satan's judgment beginning with his nature, followed by his positional authority in Heaven, and ending with his punishment in the fire:

*Moreover the word of the Lord came unto me, saying, Son of man, take up a **lamentation** upon the **king** of Tyrus, and say unto him, Thus saith the Lord God; Thou **sealest up the sum, full of wisdom,** and **perfect in beauty**. Thou hast been in **Eden** the garden of God; every precious stone was thy covering...the workmanship of thy tabrets and of thy pipes was prepared in thee in the day that thou wast created. **Thou art the anointed cherub that covereth;** and I have set thee so: **thou wast upon the holy mountain of God;** thou hast **walked up and down** in the midst of the stones of fire. Thou **wast perfect** in thy ways from the day that* *thou wast created, **till iniquity was found in thee**. By the multitude of thy merchandise they have filled the midst of thee with violence, and **thou hast sinned**: therefore **I will cast thee** as profane out of the mountain of God: and **I will destroy thee**, O covering cherub, from the midst of the stones of fire. **Thine heart was lifted up** because of thy beauty, thou hast **corrupted thy wisdom** by reason of thy brightness: **I will cast thee** to the ground, **I will lay thee** before kings, that they may behold thee. Thou hast **defiled thy sanctuaries** by the multitude of **thine iniquities**, by the iniquity of thy traffic; therefore **will I bring forth a fire** from the midst of thee, it shall devour thee, and **I will bring thee to ashes** upon the earth in the sight of all them that behold thee. All they that know thee among the people shall be astonished at thee: thou shalt be a terror, and never shalt thou be any more* (Ezekiel 28:11-19).

As with Isaiah, Ezekiel's prophecy begins with a man, the prince of Tyrus whose heart is *lifted up*, saying, "I am a God, I sit in the seat of God...." Yet the Lord replied, "...thou art a man, and not God, though thou set thine heart as the heart of God" (Ezek. 28:2). This is a prophecy of judgment, for this prince will be drawn out and put to death: "Because thou hast set thine heart as the heart of God" (Ezek. 28:6b); "Wilt thou yet say before him that slayeth thee, I am God? but thou shalt be a man, and no God, in the hand of him that slayeth thee" (Ezek. 28:9). The prophecy progresses from the human prince who claims to be a god to his lord, lucifer, the anointed cherub, "the king of Tyrus," who is "king over all the children of pride."[8]

Lucifer's history from beginning to end is given in the form of a lamentation. God takes no pleasure in the death of the wicked, and He grieved over lucifer's rebellion. Isaiah spoke of lucifer's "stringed instruments," and Ezekiel speaks of the cherub's tabrets and pipes, which indicated that lucifer was equipped to lead angelic worship.[9] At creation, all the angels sang for joy that God had created them, but when they consider the cherub's defilement, their song turns to a sorrowful cry.[10] The lament explains why:

- The lament concerns one who was created without a blemish, full of wisdom and perfect in beauty, until this iniquity of pride was conceived in his heart. What a waste! No wonder the prophet is told to lament (Ezek. 28:12,15).

- The lament explains that lucifer's pride was the result of his great beauty and wisdom (Ezek. 28:16-17).

- The lament also identifies the lamented as "the anointed cherub that covereth" (Ezek. 28:14) or the angel who was the "guardian cherub" (NIV) to God's throne depicted by the cherubim of glory in the tabernacle.[11] The word *anointed* literally means "outspread," and refers to his outstretched wings. This is the first case of the treasurer seeking to rob the treasury!

- The lament positions lucifer in Eden, the garden of God, and upon the holy mountain of God (Ezek. 28:13-14,16). The garden of God and the holy mountain refer to the third heaven.[12] Ezekiel confirms Eden *after* the creation of man as the *when* and *where* of lucifer's revolt: a perfect parallel to the serpent in the third chapter of Genesis.

- The lament envisions lucifer moving up and down between Heaven and earth among the angels like we see him in Job (Ezek. 28:14; Job 1:7; 2:2).

- The lament reveals lucifer's digression from iniquity, to sin, to defilement, until he is so full of wickedness that he is cast as profane out of the mountain of God (Ezek. 28:15-16,18). Crucifying the Lord of life was the ultimate expression of lucifer's trafficking in and multiplying iniquity. This brought judgment on him and his heavenly position.

- The lament predicts lucifer's casting out of Heaven in the future tense of "I will" (Ezek. 28:16). Although some modern translations render it in the past, the tense of the verb must be rendered future.[13]

- The lament predicts lucifer's judgment and punishment in specific, chronological stages as follows:

  1. "I will cast thee as profane out of the mountain of God" (Ezek. 28:16b).

  2. "I will destroy [Heb., *abad*, separate] thee, O covering cherub, from the midst of the stones of fire [angelic host]" (Ezek. 28:16c).[14]

  3. "I will cast thee to the ground" (Ezek. 28:17b).

4. "I will lay thee before kings, that they may behold thee" (Ezek. 28:17c).

5. "I [will] bring forth a fire from the midst of thee" (Ezek. 28:18b).

6. "I will bring thee to ashes upon the earth in the sight of all them that behold thee" (Ezek. 28:18c).

7. "...and never shalt thou be any more" (Ezek. 28:19).

Lucifer's judgment as prophesied by Ezekiel begins with his being cast out of Heaven; then his wickedness will send him down to the deepest hell. As man gravitates to his own place at death, moving rapidly in the direction prompted by his ruling desires, so satan will hit the lowest hell. His sinful desire to be honored, admired, and universally acclaimed emanates from a perverted, proud, and self-pleasing heart that can only be forever abased. Oh, what torment still awaits him!

The day is coming when satan's murderous lies and evil works will be completely exposed. His past accusatory work in Heaven will be completely unveiled and understood. His evil activity on earth, tempting, deceiving, terrorizing, and afflicting mankind unto death, will be fully disclosed. Even his dark doings in the place of the dead under the earth will be totally brought to light. Jesus said that there is nothing hidden that shall not be exposed. Satan's true nature will be made known to all of creation. Until that day, it is important for us to learn as much as we can about our adversary and his devices, because successful spiritual warfare depends, in part, upon knowing our enemy.

Drawing Out Leviathan

*In that day the Lord with His sore and great and strong sword shall punish **leviathan the piercing serpent**, even **leviathan that crooked serpent**; and he shall slay **the dragon that is in the sea*** (Isaiah 27:1).

*Canst thou draw out **leviathan** with an hook? or his tongue with a cord which thou lettest down?* (Job 41:1)

In these verses, "leviathan" personifies satan, whom John described as "the great dragon...that old serpent, called the Devil."[15] Isaiah prophesied that God would one day punish satan, the "crooked serpent" and "dragon that is in the sea."[16] The sea of glass before God's throne in Heaven is where he emerged to accuse the brethren.[17] Yet, the sword of

God's Word, incarnate in Christ, would draw satan out of this heavenly sea to punish him for his wickedness. Christ is that divine "hook" and supernatural "cord" that drew satan out of the sea of glass and bound his accusatory tongue in Heaven.[18]

The Book of Job says that God charges his angels with folly and judges those that are on high.[19] Elsewhere Job refers to "the crooked serpent," revealing a cosmic conflict with him: "The pillars of heaven tremble and are astonished at [God's] reproof. ...He smiteth through the proud. ...By His spirit He hath garnished the heavens; His hand hath formed the crooked serpent" (Job 26:11-13). The serpent's nature was formed under God's hand of judgment; in Genesis 3:14, lucifer was confined to move in his lustful desires *upon his belly*. The Book of Job reveals some amazing insights into these formative years of satan's diabolical character. It seems particularly fitting that Job, who so contended with the accuser, should expose satan's nature and attributes in the most detailed biblical passage on his personality.

Throughout history God has used men like Job to expose what was in the accuser's heart. Isn't it true that a person's character is especially evident when he contends? When you squeeze a tube of toothpaste, what's on the inside comes out. It is the same with our hearts: What we are on the inside will eventually come out. Over time, satan's character was laid bare. We owe a great debt to people like Job who submitted themselves to the Master's use in contending with this evil creature, leviathan, and revealing him for what he is. When God said to satan, "Hast thou considered my servant Job" (Job 1:8; 2:3), He was using Job to poke at the devil.

I am told that wildlife workers use a long stick in order to draw out and move crocodiles. They provoke the creature to strike, and the crocodile expends all his energy in furious movements against the apparent threat. After a couple of attacks, the crocodile has lost all his strength and is powerless. The workers then simply use masking tape to bind his big, dangerous mouth and lift him onto a truck to transport him. This illustrates how God drew out satan in Old Testament times, before he was bound. By using the integrity of men such as Job, God drew out satan's malice and handled and restrained his movements. Once drawn out, leviathan's nature is exposed. Chapter 41 of Job describes leviathan in detail in the form of questions hurled by God at Job. Implied in the questions is the relationship between leviathan and the Lord. Space

allows only a brief look at several of leviathan's malicious characteristics, which I have keyed to the appropriate verses of Job chapter 41:

- *Leviathan makes many supplications unto God:* "*Will he make
  many* **supplications** *unto thee? will he speak soft words unto thee?*"
  (Job 41:3) We have already seen in Job chapters 1 and 2 numerous
  supplications leviathan made before God's throne. When Jesus said
  to Simon Peter, "Simon, Simon, behold, Satan hath desired to have
  you, that he may sift you as wheat" (Lk. 22:31), He used the same
  terminology in connection with satan's relationship to God. The
  adjective "soft" in verse 3 describes these supplications, expressing satan's subjection to God. It is important to understand that at
  no time was God's hand forced by the devil's power to accuse.

- *Leviathan sought terms of agreement with God and served
  God's purposes, albeit unwittingly:* "*Will he make a* **covenant**
  with thee? wilt thou take him for a **servant** *for ever?*" (Job 41:4)
  The Hebrew word for "covenant" is *beriyth*, which also means
  "confederacy." The confederacy between Ahab and Jehoshaphat
  discussed in Chapter One is especially noteworthy. A righteous
  king and a wicked king were in alliance, each with their own
  agendas! The allowance that Jehovah grants the lying spirit qual-
  ifies as an agreement regarding King Ahab's fall. The decree,
  however, is always finalized in the heavenly court. Leviathan's
  servitude to Jehovah is restated throughout this passage, revealing again God's absolute, unparalleled majesty and sovereignty:
  "Who is like unto thee, O Lord, among the gods?"[20]

- *Leviathan has always been properly handled by God and bound
  by divine limitations:* "*Wilt thou* **play** *with him as with* **a bird**? *or
  wilt thou* **bind** *him for thy maidens?*" (Job 41:5) Satan is no match
  for God, who even laughs at his wicked attempts to break his bonds
  and cast away his cords.[21] Occasionally, birds in the Scriptures
  characterize satan and his activities, partly because of their habitation and travel in the skies, but mostly because, compared to God,
  satan is weak like a bird.[22] He descends to feed on worms, insects,
  and seeds that fall on the wayside.[23]

- *Leviathan, in relation to man, is at enmity in a frightful battle
  in which no man seeks to stir him up nor can any confront him
  apart from God:* "*Canst thou fill his skin with barbed irons? or
  his head with fish spears? Lay thine hand upon him,* **remember**

the battle, do no more. Behold, the hope of him is in vain: shall not one be **cast down** *even* **at the sight of him***? None is so fierce that* **dare stir him up***: who then is able to stand before Me?"* (Job 41:7-10) In the Old Testament, satan is compared to a strongman. His position and power among the angelic host is openly recognized so that even Michael, the mighty warrior archangel, appeals to Jehovah to rebuke him. Repeatedly, however, Jehovah's sovereign power is presented in this passage by means of a comparison. When He answers Job from the whirlwind, He asks: "Who then is able to stand before Me?" In dealing with leviathan, Jehovah's greatness is seen by His glorious ability to work all things together for His purposes: "Even the wicked for the day of evil."[24] The effect upon Job is overwhelming: "I know that Thou canst do all things, and that no purpose of Thine can be thwarted. ...therefore I retract, and I repent...."[25]

- *Leviathan shall be justly recompensed by God, and the evil role he has played in the world shall be fully exposed: "Who hath prevented Me, that I should* **repay him***? whatsoever is under the whole heaven is Mine. I will* **not conceal** *his* **parts***, nor his* **power***, nor his comely* **proportion***. Who can* **discover the face** *of his garment? or who can come to him with his* **double bridle***? Who can open the doors of his face? his* **teeth** *are terrible round about"* (Job 41:11-14). Christ bound the strongman. Although hidden from sinful men, God has already begun repaying satan: His sword of judgment in Christ has severed satan from Heaven and exposed his ungodly kingdom in this world. As the Light of the world, Jesus also brought leviathan to light everywhere He went. Satan's evil spirits fell to the ground, writhing and hissing like snakes. Whether in the synagogue or among the tombs, God in Christ uncovered and overcame satan's evil influence in men.

- *Leviathan's root sin is pride, and it is such great pride that he is beyond the reach of God's grace to redeem him: "His scales are his* **pride***, shut up together as with a* **close seal***. One is* **so near** *to another, that* **no air** *[i.e., grace] can come between them. They are joined one to another, they* **stick together***, that they* **cannot be sundered** (Job 41:15-17). Satan is cursed and damned beyond redemption due to his proud scales. There is no allowance for saving grace because God "resisteth the proud, but giveth grace unto the humble."[26]

- *Leviathan's nose, eyes, and mouth each reveal a consuming, fiery lust:* "*Out of his* **mouth** *go* **burning** *lamps, and sparks of* **fire** *leap out. Out of his* **nostrils** *goeth* **smoke***, as out of a* **seething pot** *or caldron. His breath kindleth* **coals***, and a* **flame** *goeth out of his mouth*" (Job 41:19-21). Like a smith who blows the coals beneath the forge, satan, armed with weapons of destruction, is called a "waster to destroy."[27] The fires that fell upon Job and upon the Egyptians were demonic, destructive fires.[28] They fell because satan had opened his mouth in Heaven to either accuse or to claim what was in his domain.

- *Leviathan's heart is so hard and perverse that he rejoices at another's sorrow and heaviness:* "*In his neck remaineth strength, and* **sorrow is turned into joy before him***. The flakes of his flesh are joined together: they are firm in themselves; they* **cannot be moved***. His heart is as firm as a stone; yea, as hard as a piece of the nether millstone*" (Job 41:22-24). Satan's kingdom is the antithesis of God's and the characteristics of any kingdom are found in the spirit of the king. Sorrow corresponds to joy in satan's spirit and thus in his domain. His heart is harder than Pharaoh's, making him an object of divine wrath.[29] Satan's heart is so hard that he especially rejoices when he causes "one of these little ones" who believe in Jesus to stumble. The millstone is not tied around his neck; it is heavy in his heart.[30]

- *Leviathan's evil nature is so terrifying that in treachery no one is his equal:* "*When he* **raiseth up himself, the mighty are afraid***: by reason of breakings they* **purify** *themselves. ... Sharp stones are under him: he spreadeth sharp pointed things upon the mire. ... He maketh a path to shine after him; one would think the deep to be hoary.* **Upon earth there is not his like,** *who is made without fear. He* **beholdeth all high things***: he is a* **king over all the children of pride**" (Job 41:25,30,32-34).[31] Leviathan beholds "all high things," referring to his presence in Heaven as a covering cherub, where he stood questioning, petitioning, conferring, and accusing. His attacks are like a flash of lightning on a stormy night, striking fear even in the hearts of mighty men. When satan rose up against David and provoked him to number

Israel, David and his mighty men feared in the wake of his rising up against them. They purified themselves, cried out to Jehovah for mercy, and offered a blood sacrifice.[32] In his powerful hymn, "A Mighty Fortress Is Our God," the great reformer Martin Luther, recognizing that this passage referred to the devil, wrote, "On earth is not his equal." A later stanza contains the words, "One little word (of Christ) shall fell him (satan)."

- *Leviathan's nature is such that no natural weapons are of any use against him. Only spiritual weapons mighty through God can subdue him: "The sword of him that layeth at him cannot hold: the spear, the dart, nor the habergeon. He esteemeth iron as straw, and brass as rotten wood. The arrow cannot make him flee: slingstones are turned with him into stubble. Darts are counted as stubble: he laugheth at the shaking of a spear"* (Job 41:26-29). The conflict has never been with flesh and blood! When Israel pursued her enemies or fled before them, it was a reflection of her relationship to Jehovah. Her might in battle was linked to her faith in and obedience to God. The righteousness of God is our breastplate, and the Word of God is our sword when we combat the devil. David is especially an example of this truth!

David and All the Prophets

David belongs near the top of any list of Israel's prophets because the "sweet psalmist of Israel" so typifies the coming Messiah in his conflict with the evil one. Through God's power, David achieved great victories that foreshadowed the devil's downfall. As a result, the Seed of the woman breaking the serpent's head is also the Seed of David, and heir to the everlasting throne.[33]

Show Thy marvellous lovingkindness, O Thou that savest by Thy right hand them which put their trust in Thee from those that rise up against them. ... Like as a lion that is greedy of his prey, and as it were a young lion lurking in secret places. Arise, O Lord, disappoint him, cast him down: deliver my soul from the wicked, which is Thy sword (Psalm 17:7,12-13).

Young David was a brave and righteous warrior. When Goliath, a monster of a man over nine feet tall, called for an Israelite from one of the 12 tribes of Israel to meet him in mortal combat, David alone was prepared to confront the Philistine's champion in the Valley of Blood.

The holy angels in Heaven were like the nation Israel on earth. While Goliath still stood strong, they listened to the taunting of the devil. They waited with expectation for One whom the accuser could find no fault with and who would not fail.

God's people on earth, however, were intimidated and seemingly powerless before their foe, who, like the devil, walked to and fro, cursing the people in the name of Dagon. Although only a shepherd boy, David fearlessly responded in the name of Jehovah, and Goliath became like the lion and the bear that had attacked David's sheep.[34] David cut off Goliath's head with the giant's own sword.

Martin Luther, in his commentary on the Book of Hebrews, explains that Christ nullified the devil's work by using the devil's very own weapon:

"In this way God promotes and perfects his proper work by means of his alien work by a marvelous wisdom He compels the devil to work through death nothing else than life itself, with the consequence that as the devil is working his damnedest against the work of God, he is by dint of his own work but a working against himself and forwarding God's work."[35]

This great truth of how the adversary would be overcome was not only prophesied in the Old Testament, but also illustrated in the lives of the Old Testament saints like David and all the prophets.

David typified Christ's coming in many ways. Along with Joseph, who delivered his jealous brothers after suffering much at their hands, David came to the aid of his brethren, although they despised him. He was consumed with zeal for the Lord. Before David was anointed king over God's people, he demonstrated his zeal as a worshiper. He played his harp and refreshed Saul. His music drove the evil spirit from the tormented king.[36] Saul, however, jealously turned on him, accusing him falsely and pursuing him throughout Israel trying to kill him. Thus, David knew firsthand the accuser of our brethren. Yet, he did not retaliate, but responded in the Spirit of Christ, learning obedience through the things he suffered before he ever sat on the throne. It is little wonder then that David was God's prophetic instrument in writing such psalms as: "My God, my God, why hast thou forsaken me?"[37]

The psalms of David reveal the heart of a man who was well acquainted with hateful enemies. He had adversaries from without, such as the

Philistines; from within his own kingdom, such as Sheba; even within his own household, such as his son Absalom who rose up against him.[38] David also knew the enemy that warred within his own sinful nature: "Let not any iniquity have dominion over me."[39] Continually crying out to the Lord and trusting in His deliverance, David recognized his own wretchedness and impotence to save himself. The Psalms provide literally volumes of material from David's life on this subject, and they contain both the testimony and the principles for obtaining the same sure mercies.[40] David was a man of like passions as our own, yet he overcame the accuser because he had a heart after God.

Like David, all the prophets prophesied of a coming deliverance from the powers of evil. They inquired and searched diligently as to what this great redemption entailed and when it would be accomplished. They prophesied of the coming Messiah who would suffer bruising to bring about the grace and glory of salvation.[41] Such biblical references are as numerous as the promises of God and the hopes of His people.

With the accuser's origin, Old Testament place in Heaven, and impending judgment firmly established, the stage is now set for the entrance of the promised Seed and the climax to this cosmic drama: the casting down of the accuser and the cleansing of the heavens.

Endnotes

1. See Daniel 3:1-12.

2. Daniel 4:30.

3. Due to man's post-Flood apostasy at *Bab-ili* ("gateway of the gods") the place and people were given over to false worship.

4. Revelation 17:5.

5. Here, the law of double reference applies in which a visible human is addressed first and then the invisible personality possessing him.

6. See 1 Samuel 10:12; James 4:13-16.

7. Full appreciation of lucifer's fall awaits the day when the people of God and the entire earth are at rest. Although it seems at times that evil is so entrenched and mighty that nothing will change, the prophets prophesied an end to it. The systematic theologian Chafer recognized the contextual problem of interpreting this as a pre-Adamic fall of lucifer, so he considers it as a description of satan's final judgment. (Lewis Sperry

Chafer, *Satan: His Motives and Methods* [Grand Rapids: Zondervan, 1919, rep. 1977], 18-19).

8. Job 41:34.

9. See Isaiah 14:11; Ezekiel 28:13.

10. See Job 38:7.

11. See Exodus 25:20.

12. See 2 Corinthians 12:2,4; Hebrews 8:5. Moses' tabernacle with the three courts, the third being the Holy of holies, was an earthly pattern of the heavenly places.

13. Using what translators call the prophetic past tense, meaning it is as certain as if it already happened, is confusing, especially considering that it was all future in Ezekiel's day. Besides, part of the prophecy is future even today. The New American Standard translates verse 18 in the past tense: "...I brought fire from your midst; it devoured you, and I turned you to ashes upon the earth...." The New International Version uses the past tense as well. This proves that the Authorized King James Version does the text justice, for satan has not yet been cast into the lake of fire. It should also be noted that the translators must often interpret the tense of the verb in the Hebrew language. For example, here in verse 14, the actual Hebrew reads *thou anointed cherub*. The present tense of the verb *are* has been inserted by the translators. When done properly, the verb insertion helps the reading of Hebrew in the English language.

14. *Abad* is an unusual Hebrew word. It does not mean to annihilate, but simply to cut off (wander away, break), in this case, from among the holy angels (stones of fire). This is one of the stages of satan's judgment. His place is no longer found among the "sons [angels] of God." See Job 1:6; 2:1; Revelation 12:8.

15. Revelation 12:9. "Leviathan," in Merrill Unger's *The New Unger's Bible Dictionary*, is found in the animal kingdom section and is identified as a crocodile, a serpent, a sea monster or possibly a whale (Chicago: Moody Press, 1988). Although William Smith (*Smith's Dictionary of the Bible*, Nashville: Thomas Nelson Publishers, 1979) would choose the crocodile as the animal most clearly denoted by the Hebrew word *liweyatan*, he concludes that the term is not used in a limited sense, and could even be some species of the great rock-snakes which are common in south and west Africa. Another Bible dictionary simply suggests a monstrous

being, like Lotan, identified with the mythological monster of chaos, a seven-headed creature.

16. See also Psalm 104:26.

17. See Revelation 4:6; 12:10.

18. In his commentary on the Apostles Creed (A.D. 344), Rufinus, a friend of Jerome, quotes from this portion of Job. As did others, he saw "the mystery of the Incarnation (the Son of God) was as it were a hook concealed beneath the form and fashion of human flesh that He...might lure on the Prince of this world to a conflict, to whom offering His flesh as a bait, His Divinity underneath might catch him and hold him fast with its hook, through the shedding of His immaculate (no stain of sin) blood...He who had the power of death seized the body of Jesus in death, not being aware of the hook of Divinity enclosed within it" (*Select Library of Nicene and Post Nicene Fathers*, Philip Schaff, ed., Vol. 3 [Oxford: The Christian Literature Co., 1891]). The western tradition after Augustine maintains that the mystery of the Incarnation was known to the angels from the beginning, while according to eastern tradition the mystery was hidden to every creature, including leviathan.

19. See Job 4:18; 21:22b.

20. Exodus 15:11a.

21. See Psalm 2.

22. See Matthew 13:4,19. Jubilees 11:11-13 says that before the time of Abraham, prince mastema (satan) sent birds to eat the seed that was being sown by farmers. Then the land began to be barren. Satan is also associated with birds in the Apocalypse of Abraham 13:3-7; First Enoch 90:8; and Sanhedrin 107a.

23. See Ecclesiastes 10:20; Zephaniah 1:3; Matthew 13:4; Revelation 18:2; 19:17.

24. Proverbs 16:4b.

25. Job 42:2,6 NAS.

26. James 4:6.

27. Isaiah 54:16c.

28. See Job 1:16; Exodus 9:22-26.

29. See Romans 9:17-22.

30. See Matthew 18:6; Mark 9:42; Luke 17:2; Revelation 18:21-22.

31. The NIV translates Job 41:30b as "leaving a trail in the mud like a threshing sledge."

32. See 1 Chronicles 21:1ff; 2 Samuel 24:1ff; Psalm 51:17.

33. See 1 Chronicles 17:11-17; Zechariah 12:8; Luke 1:32; John 7:42; Romans 1:3.

34. See 1 Samuel 17:1ff.

35. "Lectures on Titus, Philemon and Hebrews," *Luther's Works,* Vol. 29, Jaroslav Pelikan, ed. (Am. Ed., Concordia Publishing House, 1968), 135.

36. See 1 Samuel 16.

37. See Psalm 22:1ff.

38. See 2 Samuel 18:33: "...O my son Absalom, my son, my son Absalom! would God I had *died for thee*, O Absalom, my son, my son!" See also Romans 5:8b: "While we were yet sinners [rebellious enemies], Christ [willingly] *died for us.*"

39. Psalm 119:133b.

40. For additional study, the following psalms of David contain both the cry of the conflict and the proven principles for overcoming the accuser: Psalm 7; 9:3,5-7,15-16; 10; 11; 13; 15:1-3; 17; 18; 20; 21:7-12; 22:12-16; 23:5; 24; 25:2,7,19; 26:5-6; 27:2-6; 28:1-3; 31:4,6,11,15,18,20; 33:10,13; 34:16-17; 35:1,11,19-26; 36:1-6,11-12; 37; 38:11-16,19-20; 39:8,11-12; 40:1,12-13; 41; 42:10; 43:1-2; 44:4-7,9-10; 46:1; 50:14; 51:1,14; 54:1-3,7; 55:1-3,16-18; 56:2-3,5,9,13; 57:2; 59:1; 61:1; 62; 64:1-2,5; 66:17; 68:1; 69:1,4,14,16,18; 70:1; 71:2,4,10,12; 74:4; 109:26; 120:1-2,7; 138:7; 140:1-4,6; 141:1-2; 142; 143; 144:1.

41. See Daniel 12:8; 1 Peter 1:11. The Word of God, not just the well-known passages from Isaiah and Ezekiel, is filled with this subject.

Chapter Five

The Accuser and the Advent of Christ

Until the advent of Christ, satan moved with authority up and down from Heaven to earth and back and forth throughout the world, knowing all along that the promised Seed of the woman was coming to break his hold on mankind.[1] The New Testament teaches that the Kingdom of God came in the person of Jesus Christ to release men from the power of satan into the power of God. Thus, the reality of satan's kingdom and power cannot be ignored without changing the nature of the good news of Christ's advent: The Son of God became incarnate in human flesh to demolish the devil's dominion and to establish God's Kingdom in men.

In his book, *The Cross of Christ*, R.W. Stott outlines the progression of the conquest of evil as revealed in Scripture:

- The Conquest Predicted—the Old Testament.
- The Conquest Begun—the Gospels.
- The Conquest Achieved—the crucifixion of Christ.
- The Conquest Confirmed and Announced—the resurrection and ascension of Christ.
- The Conquest Extended—the Book of Acts.
- The Conquest Concluded—the Book of Revelation.[2]

I would add a seventh to Stott's list:

* The Conquest Explained—the New Testament Epistles, particularly those of Paul.

Jesus Christ came to shatter satan's heavenly authority as the prophets had foretold. He is that Seed through whom all families of the earth are blessed; the Messiah or "anointed one" come to free His people from sin; the "last Adam"[3] who would take back from satan's grasp what the first Adam had surrendered through sin. After Jesus was baptized, the heavens opened and the Father spoke, "This is My beloved Son, in whom I am well pleased," and the Holy Spirit descended upon Him, anointing Jesus for His mission and initiating His public ministry.[4]

The Last Adam Anointed and Tested

Once anointed, Jesus was led by the Spirit into the wilderness where He was tempted by the devil, who offered Him the world and everything in it.[5] Referring to earthly kingdoms, satan said:

*...All this power will I give Thee, and the glory of them: for that is delivered unto me; and to whomsoever **I will** I give it. If Thou therefore wilt worship me, **all shall be Thine*** (Luke 4:6-7).

It was absolutely crucial that the last Adam succeed where the first had succumbed.[6] The first man had surrendered his dominion over the world to satan through sin.[7] As a result, death entered the world, spreading to all men so that no one would be able to stop it or escape its power. Man became by nature a child of the devil, establishing satan's power in its manifestations in man, both individually and corporately. Satan became the "god" or "prince" of this world with his overlord position on earth and his seat in Heaven maintained by man's sin.[8] He was, therefore, in a position to offer Jesus the religious, political, and economic control of this world in an attempt to subject Christ's throne to his own. Had Jesus yielded to satan's offer and sinned against His Father, the devil would have secured mankind's bondage to himself for time and eternity. Jesus had to submit to His Father in all things and have no part with the devil; complete obedience to the Father was essential if mankind was to be delivered.[9]

God's holy integrity allowed the accuser to tempt Jesus in every point possible, not only in the desert, but throughout His life. Jesus successfully endured all of satan's temptations, no matter when or where they came: while growing up in submission to His parents; after the

Holy Spirit came upon Him; in hunger or weariness; in pain or sorrow; from hypocritical religious leaders; in the midst of an unbelieving generation; at the hands of tyrannical rulers; from friend or foe; at Gethsemane; and on the cross. As a human controlled by the Holy Spirit, the Son of Man beat temptation and decisively overcame all the seductive power of sin.[10] The Captain of our salvation was thus made perfect, fully equipped to render relief when we are tempted and to deliver us when we sin.[11]

We must recognize that when we become children of God, we too will be tested. Leaders who disciple new believers should be especially aware of this, because it explains why many who receive the Word of God are later offended and fall away from the faith. The tempter comes to take the Word out of their hearts, saying as he did to Jesus: "If you are a child of God, then...." Casting doubt and disbelief, he brings enticements and enchantments in many forms, some quite direct, others very subtle.

Before I became a Christian, I had seven years of my life mapped out, and God was nowhere in my plans. As a political science major on an ROTC scholarship, my tuition, books, and a monthly living allowance were paid for by Uncle Sam. The government agreed also to cover law school if I would serve as an officer in the army for two years on active duty and four years in the reserve. I would then enter politics: Power, influence, and money would be mine! No doubt I would have expressed these aspirations in more noble terms then, but I was impressed with power. The image I had of Christ, however, was one of weakness: an irrelevant Jesus still hanging on the cross, unable to rescue the world or those in it.[12]

When I gave my life to the risen Christ, however, I experienced a powerful transformation with strong conviction. It wasn't long before tests and temptations came. To begin with, was I to continue the career plan that I had mapped out for myself? I decided to return the scholarship. To many people, I must have appeared foolish as I left a prestigious university to wash dishes at a restaurant. In their view, I went from a top university student with tremendous direction and a bright future to a dishwasher in a dingy kitchen working alongside old men who only worked periodically to stay in cigarette and beer money! For a while, it was a wilderness ordeal for me, but such is a necessary part of the Christian journey. There is hope in the wilderness, however. It was in the wilderness that Jesus squared off with the devil toe-to-toe, refusing all that satan had to offer. Because He was victorious, we too can overcome.

The sinlessness of Jesus is consistently affirmed in the New Testament. The apostles understood its necessity and stressed its reality in our deliverance: "[Jesus] was in all points tempted like as we are, yet without sin" (Heb. 4:15b); "who is holy, harmless, undefiled, separate from sinners…" (Heb. 7:26b). He is "a lamb without blemish and without spot" (1 Pet. 1:19b), "who did no sin, neither was guile found in His mouth" (1 Pet. 2:22). Jesus had to be without sin in order to take our sin away. In Scripture, these two factors are related: "And you know that He was manifested to take away our sins, and in Him there is no sin" (1 Jn. 3:5 NKJ), and "For He hath made Him to be sin for us, who knew no sin" (2 Cor. 5:21a). The Old Testament prefigured this requirement in its sacrificial law of spotless offerings and prophesied the same: "And He made His grave with the wicked, and with the rich in His death; because He had done *no* violence, neither was *any* deceit in His mouth. ...My righteous servant shall justify many; for He shall bear their iniquities" (Is. 53:9, 11). Herein alone is the victory, as the devil knows all too well.

The devil had poked holes and found levers to pull in all who had walked the earth prior to Christ. Moses, David, and all the prophets fell short, but with Jesus of Nazareth the father of cynics was far from amused. The accuser of the brethren had no case against Christ, no hold through sin, and thus no power over Him.[13] Jesus alone met the glorious standard of true holiness, and hence the sinlessness of Jesus' moral character was forever established on earth. He alone could ask His contemporaries and every generation since: "Which of you convicts Me of sin?" (Jn. 8:46a NKJ) "…If I have spoken evil, bear witness of the evil…" (Jn. 18:23). No one else can stand such a test. Christ's sinlessness is paramount to our understanding of what transpired with His advent. Finally, here is a Man without sin, fully submitted to God, aggressively resisting the devil. All Heaven looked on as the Holy One walked the earth, and the greatest drama of the ages unfolded before their very eyes.

The Heavens Now Open

An inescapable principle has stood from the beginning that in relationship to God, sin separates! The problem is not that God's hand is so short that He cannot reach down to save men on earth, nor that His ears are so heavy that He cannot hear their cry.[14] Instead, as Isaiah records:

> But your **iniquities have separated** between you and your God, and your **sins** have **hid His face** from you, that He will **not hear** (Isaiah 59:2).

The Bible calls this condition a closed Heaven. Heaven was shut by Adam's transgression.[15] Later, as part of the curses that would come from disobeying God, are the words, "And thy heaven that is over thy head shall be brass" (Deut. 28:23a). Brass speaks of judgment, and although there were gracious acts from Heaven in Old Testament times, these were the exceptions. Law and judgment rather than grace and mercy were the norm.[16]

Christ established an open Heaven as the order of the day when the Holy Spirit came down at His baptism, and maintained it by His sinlessness in spite of satan's attempts to cut Him off from the Father. All four Gospel accounts of Jesus' baptism refer to the opening of Heaven. Through His baptism Jesus, although without sin, fully identified Himself with sinful humanity and indicated His determination to assault the gates of hell to redeem them.[17] The Father empowered Him to fulfill His mission, pouring upon Him the Holy Spirit in order to bring the Kingdom of Heaven to a world of sinful men.[18] Jesus said to Nathaniel:

> ...**hereafter** you shall see **heaven open**, and the angels of God ascending and descending upon the Son of Man (John 1:51 NKJ).

Before Christ came, Heaven was closed to man, but still open to satan. With His coming, Christ opened Heaven to man and closed it to satan.[19] Miracles unlike any ever seen before both in number and quality became the firstfruits of this newly opened communication between Heaven and earth. Those who teach that the advent of Christ did not affect satan's access to Heaven should read their Bibles again.[20] To argue that nothing changed in respect to satan's position with the advent of Christ ignores the power of His death and resurrection, which is obvious in the spirit world. It's time we recognize this and declare His victory!

The Demons and His Works Declare

When exposed by Jesus during His ministry, demons acknowledged His person and holiness.[21] In one instance in the synagogue, a demon cried out, "Let us alone; what have we to do with Thee, Thou Jesus of

Nazareth? art Thou come to destroy us? I know Thee who Thou art, the Holy One of God."[22] Satan's cohorts knew Jesus and were tormented by His presence because it marked the beginning of the end for them.[23] How did they know who Jesus was? They got their information from head-quarters; they were not in hell, nor even confined to the earth. Aware of the extreme gravity of what was happening on earth, they were on red alert now that the Seed of the woman had arrived.

The casting out of demons and Jesus' other mighty works declared the arrival on earth of God's Kingdom and the impending overthrow of satan's:

> *But if I cast out devils* **by the Spirit of God**, *then the kingdom of God is come unto you. Or else* **how** *can one enter into a strong man's house, and spoil his goods, except* **he first bind the strong man?** *and then he will spoil his house* (Matthew 12:28-29).

Jesus had first to subject satan to the stronger power of the Holy Spirit by which He operated and by which He cast evil spirits out of people. In *Powers of Evil*, Sydney Page writes:

> "It is not that satan is completely powerless, but that because his assault on Jesus in the desert was a failure, he is unable to prevent Jesus from liberating those who are in bondage to him and his min-ions. If satan had been able to deflect Jesus from his messianic task in the desert, satan would have been free to continue to exercise his tyranny over humankind. Satan's defeat in the desert means that, even though he remains active, he cannot stop Jesus from bringing the blessing of the kingdom to those formerly under satan's power. It is not surprising then that the demons characteristically display fear when confronted by Jesus, for they know that Jesus has already worsted their master."[24]

Jesus often appealed to His works as a witness of His divine mission: "The works that I do in My Father's name, they bear witness of Me. ...though ye believe not Me, believe the works..." (Jn. 10:25b,38). Jesus' good works and healing of those who were oppressed of the devil revealed Him as the Messiah. The appointed time had come for the release of God's people from bondage:[25]

> *And ought not this woman, being a daughter of Abraham, whom* **Satan hath bound**, *lo, these eighteen years,* **be loosed** *from this bond on the sabbath day? And when He had said these things,* **all**

His adversaries were ashamed: and all the people rejoiced for all the *glorious things that were done by Him* (Luke 13:16-17).

Jesus, the servant of Jehovah, became the perfect burden bearer. As He moved toward the cross He began bringing to bear the benefits of His atonement, carrying away the infirmities of all who trusted in Him.[26]

This reminds me of an incident in Africa. An old woman climbed aboard a bus carrying a great bag over her shoulders. She stood on the crowded bus, gripping the rail with her free hand while balancing the large bag with the other. The bus conductor tried twice to get her attention, calling loudly the second time, "Woman, set your package down on the floor! The bus is able to carry both you and your package!" Perhaps she felt that the items she carefully carried would not be safe outside her grasp. If only people would understand that they can cast their cares upon Jesus because He cares for them. The nail prints in His feet and hands testify to His trustworthy love and divine ability to bear both our burdens and us, even the weight of the entire human race.

Satan Falls Like Lightning From Heaven

Satan sought to stop Christ by every available means. It wasn't hard for the devil to stir up the religious establishment. Although he could find no fault in Christ to accuse Him before the Father, his slanderous accusations, blasphemous lies, and legalistic claims found ample expression on earth among his children.[27] They ridiculed Him, called Him a glutton and a winebibber, a sinner and a friend of sinners. They accused Him of perverting the nation, of forbidding tribute to Caesar, of speaking blasphemy, of being insane, of having a demon, of breaking the Sabbath, of making Himself a king, and of speaking against Caesar.[28] These are a few of the more notable slanders He endured in His struggle with satan. So what has that devil falsely accused you of? Although he can no longer accuse us to God in Heaven, he does plenty of it on earth. His nature is still that of the accuser of the brethren. It is no wonder Jesus said, "Beware when all men speak well of you."[29]

None of these things moved Jesus off His mission. Instead, making matters worse for the devil, He commissioned 12 disciples, giving "power against unclean spirits, to cast them out, and to heal all manner of sickness and all manner of disease" (Mt. 10:1b). Satan was now not only contending with Jesus, but also with His representatives who were exercising heavenly authority in His name.[30] Applying even more pressure, Christ appointed another 70 disciples whom He sent forth like lambs among wolves, healing the sick and announcing the advent of God's Kingdom.[31] He told them, "Behold, I give unto you power to tread on serpents and scorpions, and *over* all the power of the enemy: and nothing shall by any means hurt you" (Lk. 10:19).

Satan's power was finally being overridden. Desperately trying to hold their defensive positions, satan and his demons had no rest day or night as Christ aggressively opened up a war against them, putting satan's kingdom into an irreversible retreat mode. By advancing the Kingdom of Heaven through His followers, Jesus began repossessing the earth. This can be likened to the turn of World War II: The Allied Forces swiftly advanced against Nazi Germany on multiple fronts. When they invaded the beaches of Normandy, the Allies retook the land and soon drove Hitler's forces back. His evil war machine went from defense to defeat!

When the 70 returned, Jesus shared an important vision with them: "...*I beheld Satan as lightning fall from heaven*" (Lk. 10:18). This was not a vision of a prehistoric fall before the creation of man. No! Jesus envisioned what the prophets Isaiah and Ezekiel had foretold. With the advent of Christ, the accuser's judgment was looming on the horizon and was already in sight. The context and the entire tenor of Scripture will allow for no other interpretation.

Sydney Page's insights here are helpful:

"Since Jesus' comment in Luke 10:18 about the fall of satan was in response to the seventy-two disciples' report concerning the successful exorcisms they performed it is unlikely that the comment is to be understood as referring to satan's original fall from innocence, as some have thought. The context demands a reference to a fall that is the result of being defeated, not a fall which is the result of sinning....Furthermore, this victory is new and unique, something that Jesus views as resulting from a defeat of satan that took place during Jesus' lifetime....The successes of the seventy-two were signs of the arrival of a new era in which satan's position would be significantly different than it had been earlier. The messianic age had arrived."[32]

Satan's fall was sure when Jesus shared His prophetic vision with His disciples, but the accuser's defeat had to be sealed by the blood of Jesus on the cross and guaranteed by the resurrection. This brings us to the cross, which is the watershed of the Bible and the devil's Waterloo! Fulfillment of God's promise of a Seed of the woman to crush the serpent's head was now at hand.

Endnotes

1. See Job 1:7; Ezekiel 28:17b; Genesis 3:15.

2. R.W. Stott, *The Cross of Christ*, a chapter on "The Conquest of Evil" (Downers Grove: IL: InterVarsity, 1986).

3. See 1 Corinthians 15:45.

4. See Matthew 3:16-17.

5. Matthew 4:1ff; Mark 1:12ff; Luke 4:1ff.

6. See 1 Corinthians 15:45,47. The first temptation took place in a garden where Adam was at peace with the whole animal creation, whereas the last Adam was tempted in the wilderness where He "was with the wild beasts" (Mk. 1:13). This is a picture of the ruin caused by sin.

7. See Matthew 13:38; John 8:44; Acts 13:10; Ephesians 2:2; 1 John 3:10.

8. See John 14:30; 2 Corinthians 4:4.

9. See Matthew 26:39; Philippians 2:8.

10. See Isaiah 53:3,7; Matthew 4:2; 16:21; Mark 8:31; 9:12,19; 16:14ff; 17:17; Luke 2:51; 22:28,48,61; John 4:6; Romans 5:19.

11. See Hebrews 1:9; 2:18; 4:15; 5:7-9; 7:26-28; 1 John 2:1-2.

12. On TV, evil is often portrayed as mighty, almost invincible, while righteousness is viewed as insipid and disabled. The rough and tough bad guys shoot the place up with their guns and ride off with impunity, while the wimpy preacher is left to passively bury the dead: *Ashes to ashes, dust to dust.*

13. See John 14:30. Sinful men find it easy to imagine virtually anything except that which is genuinely pure. Movies like *The Last Temptation of Christ* have railed abuse at the character of Jesus and blasphemed His sinless nature. The world has seen great hypocrisy, but who has seen anyone who continually does good and does not sin? There is only One.

14. See Isaiah 59:1-2.

15. Although the Old Testament saints had answers to prayers, miraculous signs and wonders, and the hope of eternal life, they did not possess

the reality of the Kingdom of God. One had to be born again to enter the Kingdom (see Jn. 3:1ff). Therefore, Jesus said that "among those born of women no one is greater than John the Baptist; *yet*, the least in the Kingdom of God is greater than he" (see Mt. 11:11-15; Lk. 7:28).

16. See John 1:16-18; Ephesians 2:7-13; 3:2-10.

17. Dr. C. Peter Wagner points out that Jesus went on the offensive after His baptism and provoked this conflict with the devil by going to the wilderness (satan's stronghold) to pray (*Warfare Prayer* [Ventura, CA: Regal Books, 1992], 514).

18. See John 1:32-34; Mark 1:10; Luke 3:21.

19. Chapter Seven discusses in greater depth the important truth of Christ opening Heaven to mankind by His death and resurrection. The Old Testament saints did not ascend to Heaven at death, but waited in a place called "Abraham's bosom" for the gates of Heaven to be opened by Christ.

20. Clarence Larkin, a dispensationalist, wrote, "Satan had not been cast out of heaven up until that time, A.D. 96, when John wrote the Book of Revelation, and has not been cast out since. Nothing has changed that." (*Dispensational Truth or God's Plan and Purpose in the Ages*, [1920], 112). Chapter Nine of this book looks closely at Revelation chapter 12 to establish the context of this important passage on when satan was cast out of Heaven.

21. Have you ever wondered why in the New Testament (compared to the Old Testament), satan is suddenly exposed all over the place? His work in the Old Testament as the accuser was hidden in heaven and only revealed as the veil was drawn back. When Christ and the Holy Spirit came down, heaven was opened and the veil removed.

22. Mark 1:24.

23. See Matthew 8:29; Mark 3:11; Luke 4:41; Acts 19:15.

24. Sydney H.T. Page, *Powers of Evil* (Grand Rapids: Baker Books, 1995), 106-108. Page observes further that, "In Matthew and Mark, the imagery is that of a domestic robbery; in Luke, it is that of a military conquest. In all three, the point is the same. In order to plunder the strong man's goods, one must first overcome the strong man. Obviously, satan is being compared to the strong man, and the exorcisms, to the despoiling of his possessions. Less certain is exactly how Jesus intended the tying up (Mt. 12:29; Mk. 3:27) or overpowering (Lk. 11:22) of the

strong man to be understood. The analogy of tying up/overpowering the strong man naturally suggests that the exorcisms were preceded by a decisive victory over satan. A number of scholars have found just such a victory in the temptation of Jesus in the desert. This first encounter that Jesus had with satan came at a critical juncture in Jesus' life (after his Messianic investiture at his baptism and prior to his public ministry), and Jesus emerged from the contest as the victor." The principle of the Kingdom as coming and yet already present applies here. "The hour is coming and now is," Jesus reiterated on more than one occasion (see Jn. 4:23; 5:25; 16:32).

25. See Luke 4:17-19.

26. See Isaiah 53:4; Matthew 8:17; John 19:17.

27. See John 8:44; 9:24.

28. See Matthew 9:34; 11:19; 26:64; Mark 3:21; Luke 23:2; John 7:20; 9:16.

29. See Luke 6:26.

30. By means of the Word of God, the power of the Holy Spirit and the authority of Jesus' name, believers are invested with authority and power greater than that of satan. This was taken for granted by the New Testament writers, although they recognized that satan was a real and powerful enemy who could only be overcome in the strength of the Lord and the power of His might (see Eph. 6:10).

31. See Luke 10:1,3.

32. Page, *Powers of Evil*, 109-110. Sydney H. T. Page points out the difficulties associated with the imperfect tense of the verb "saw" which is governed by the leading verb "fall"; he wisely concludes that the simile "fall like lightning" expresses the suddenness of the accuser's fall now that the Messiah has come. Then he ties Jesus' vision into the rest of Scripture, and presents his view of satan's fall. "Some draw a connection to Revelation 12:9, which speaks of satan's being hurled from heaven following a battle in which Michael and his angels fought with satan and his angels. That Luke 10:18 and Revelation 12:10 are referring to the same event is surely correct; however, there is good reason to think that Revelation 12 is describing what happened at the first Advent of Christ" (*Powers of Evil*, 109-110).

Chapter Six

The Accuser and the Cross

As the time for Jesus' death grew nearer, satan and his forces intensified their attacks against Him. Jesus endured the full range of satanic temptation throughout His earthly ministry as the enemy sought to distract Him, sidetrack Him, slander Him, blaspheme Him, turn His friends against Him, bring religious, social, and legal pressure to bear on Him, and even to destroy Him before He could complete His mission. One of satan's strategies was attacking the disciples Jesus had called and was preparing to carry on His work after He returned to the Father. Perhaps the clearest example of this kind of attack is seen in the experience of Simon Peter.

Satan's Request to Sift Peter

The devil had a special hatred for Simon Peter, perhaps because Peter was the first apostle to confess that Jesus was the Messiah or because Peter, being in the center of the inner circle of Christ's apostles, had a motivating influence on the rest of them.[1] Either way, Peter's impulsive temperament certainly made him a target of satan's attack.[2] On the night that Jesus was arrested, satan's position before God's throne as the accuser is revealed once again, but this time Jesus Himself draws the curtain back for us:

> And **the Lord said,** Simon, Simon, behold, **Satan** hath **desired to have you**, that he may **sift** you as wheat: but I have prayed for thee,

that thy faith fail not: and when thou art converted, strengthen thy brethren. And he said unto Him, Lord, I am ready to go with Thee, both into prison and to death (Luke 22:31-33).

Satan desired to cut Peter off from Christ. The Greek word for "desired" means *to make a strong request*, and is often used for prayer. It has even been translated as *demanded*. Where did satan make his influential request to sift Peter? Was it to Jesus on earth? No! Satan made his request to the same One to whom Jesus interceded: God the Father! As in the Book of Job, satan was able to make such a request before God because he still had a place in Heaven and because Peter had given satan an opportunity to accuse him there. Jesus had told His disciples that they would all be scattered, but Peter denied the Lord's words, brashly promising to stay at His side, even to the death. Only a few hours later, before the cock crowed to announce the morning, Peter was snared by the words of his mouth and denied three times that he even knew Jesus. Undoubtedly, satan orchestrated what happened that night to try Peter on the words of his mouth. Imagine the scene in Heaven—satan demanding to examine Simon's claim of being ready to die with Jesus!

By praying that Peter's faith might not fail, Jesus was a step ahead of satan. He is our Advocate and High Priest with the Father, and while He was on earth, He had a position in heavenly places like we now have through Him.[3] It is interesting to note that though satan was granted permission to test the truth of Peter's words, Christ's intercession for Peter was also effective at the same time. Thank God for the Holy Spirit in our lives and for Jesus interceding for us in Heaven! Thank God that satan can no longer accuse us as he did Job, nor demand to sift us as he did Peter! What would our lives be like if he still possessed such heavenly authority? Would we be "more than conquerors"?[4] I think not!

The main road connecting Harare, the capital of Zimbabwe, to the distant cities of South Africa, is one lane in either direction. Passing a slow-moving vehicle on such a two-lane road can be dangerous. One day my family and I were outside Masvingo traveling back to Harare. The sun was setting and I was in a hurry to get home. I approached a slow-moving bus, which was blowing a lot of black smoke out of the exhaust. I then pulled out to pass without fully checking the oncoming lane for sufficient passing clearance. As I began to overtake the bus, one of its passengers threw a carton of red juice that splattered on our windshield. Before I could express my anger through the horn, however, the Lord spoke to my heart: "That could have been the blood of your family on the windshield." Chastened about my reckless driving, my initial anger was replaced by thankfulness for God's intervention. If Christ my Advocate was not interceding for me constantly, devastation and despair would have overtaken me long ago.

The Prince of This World Is Cast Out

Satan's removal from Heaven was predicated by the cross and carried out at the ascension of Christ. Before He went to the cross, Jesus spoke openly of satan's heavenly position and of bringing it to an end through His death and resurrection:

> *And Jesus answered them, saying, The **hour is come**, that the Son of man should be **glorified**. Verily, verily, I say unto you, Except a corn of wheat fall into the ground and **die**, it abideth alone: but if it die, it bringeth forth much fruit. ... Father, glorify Thy name. Then came there a **voice from heaven**, saying, I have both glorified it, and will glorify it again. The people therefore, that stood by, and heard it, said that it **thundered**: others said, An angel spake to Him. Jesus answered and said, This voice came not because of Me, but for your sakes. **Now is the judgment of this world: now shall the prince of this world be cast out**. And I, if I be lifted up from the earth, will draw all men unto Me. This He said, **signifying what death He should die** (John 12:23-24,28-33).*

What did Jesus mean when He said, *"Now* is the judgment of this world: *now* shall the prince of this world be *cast out"*?[5] From where would satan be cast out? Clearly, he was not cast out of the world; he still roams about today like a roaring lion, seeking someone to devour.[6] Satan was cast out of Heaven, from before God's throne, where he accused the brethren. Satan fell from the *third*, or highest Heaven, where God dwells, and he is now confined to the two lower heavens.[7] (The biblical teachings regarding the three heavens will be discussed in more detail in Chapter Eight.)

Jesus said this would happen *now*! There are two Greek words for "now": one means *soon*, the other, *immediately*. The Greek word in this case, *nun*, means *soon*. On my first visit to Zimbabwe I discovered that people there use the colloquial phrases "just now" and "now-now." I was at a birthday celebration, and toward the end of the evening the person who had brought me said, "We are leaving just now." I stood up and prepared to go. He looked at me rather surprised and said, "Not now-now, just now," so I sat down again. Only later did I learn that the phrase "just now" can mean anywhere from 10 to 30 minutes, while "now-now" means immediately. John 12:31b has the Greek equivalent to "just now": "*Soon shall the prince of this world be cast out.*" It would happen as soon as Jesus died, rose, and returned to glory.[8]

When Jesus spoke about His departure and the coming of the Holy Spirit, He said the Spirit would convict the world "of judgment, because the prince of this world is judged" (Jn. 16:11). By crucifying the Lord of glory, satan brought judgment upon himself and the world system that he had instituted. As "the prince of this world," satan's judgment and that of the world are synonymous.[9] The Greek word *krisis* (judgment) denotes a distinct decision, a divine ruling, in which there must be a separation. Satan is separated from Heaven, and forever cast out because of the cross. John uses the same basic Greek word *ballo* (cast out) in both John 12:31 and Revelation 12:9. It specifically means to hurl deliberately, throw out, or expel.

The Garden of Gethsemane and the Cross

Once an artist was at his easel in an open-air market. As he put the final brush strokes on his painting of the crucifixion he noticed a small girl staring at his work. After a few moments, her little face looked up at him as she solemnly said, "He must have been a very bad man to be punished that way!" The painter replied gently, "Not at all, my child. He was the best man who ever lived!"

F.J. Huegel wrote, "The cross of Calvary marked the greatest hour in the entire moral history of Deity."[10] At the cross, God revealed His nature as holy love that hates sin but loves the sinner. By choosing to bear the penalty Himself rather than forcing humanity to face the final consequences of our rebellion, God satisfied His own holy justice and expressed His great loving-kindness in one great substitutionary sacrifice. At the same time, He displayed both His wisdom in dealing justly with sin and His gracious power in nullifying evil.

What a joy it is to see one's children come to an understanding of the cross! Our son Nathan was four when he began to grasp the meaning of Jesus' death. It was Christmas time, and he had attended two powerful performances of a Christmas pageant in which the dramatic opening scene showed Jesus' crucified body in the arms of His weeping mother, Mary, beneath the cross! On the way home he asked a searching question: "Why did Jesus die?" Answering him using the three rules at our home that he knows by heart, "No fussing, no fighting, and you must listen," I explained that Jesus died because at times we have all fussed, fought, and not listened. God still loves us, however, and became a Man, taking our punishment for us. Now we must say we're sorry and through believing on Jesus, God becomes our Father. Nathan was satisfied with that answer.

Love caused Jesus to embrace the cross. He set His face resolutely toward Jerusalem, knowing He would be crucified there.[11] In the garden of Gethsemane, He faced His greatest temptation: to avoid the cross altogether. His holy soul despised the shame of the cross and recoiled at the thought of being spitefully abused at the hands of wicked men.[12] Deeper than the thoughts of enduring great indignities at the hands of sinners was the thought of separation from His Father. On the cross, Jesus would not only *bear* human sin; He would *become* human sin.[13]

His travail in prayer was so heavy that He sweat great drops of blood as He cried out to God, "Father, if Thou be willing, remove this *cup* from Me: nevertheless, not My will, but Thine, be done" (Lk. 22:42). The *cup* represented God's righteous anger against humanity's rebellion. For us, Jesus experienced a sinner's death, a sinner's curse under the Law, and the full cup of God's wrath.[14] Words, however, could never describe what that cup tasted like. Jesus endured the full range of rage, hatred, and abuse that satan and his kingdom could muster. His sufferings went far beyond the pains of the flesh. In the agony of His soul, Jesus drank in and tasted of death, and it was the thought of drinking that cup that made His heart so very heavy and sorrowful in Gethsemane.[15]

What did Jesus endure? He was betrayed by a close friend, arrested in the middle of the night, and seized by force as if He were a criminal. He was abandoned by His friends, falsely accused, unjustly tried, and wrongly convicted. He was rejected by the people He came to save, in favor of a murderer. He was abused, spat upon, beaten, and mocked by the soldiers detailed to execute Him. They ripped out His beard and jammed onto His head a crown of long, sharp thorns. They tore apart His back and legs with the cat-o'-nine-tails, then led Him away to crucifixion, forcing Him to carry the rough, heavy cross on His bleeding shoulders until He fell and was bruised beneath its weight. Arriving at Golgotha, He was stripped naked, laid out on the cross, and huge spikes were driven through His hands and feet.

Those who crucified Jesus and those who abused and mocked Him—soldiers and civilians, common people and religious leaders—

acted out the evil lust of their father, the devil, but they did not know who they were crucifying, "for had they known it, they would not have crucified the Lord of glory" (1 Cor. 2:8b). Jesus Himself prayed from the cross, "...Father, forgive them; for they know not what they do" (Lk. 23:34a). Paul, preaching at Antioch of Pisidia, referred to the religious leaders when he said, "...because they knew Him not, nor yet the voices of the prophets which are read every sabbath day, they have fulfilled them in condemning Him" (Acts 13:27). Satan, however, knew full well w*ho* Jesus was and *what* He came to do, and used every means at his disposal to prevent Jesus from going to the cross.[16] When Jesus refused to be deterred, evil mustered all the might it possessed, and hurled it in His face.

Demons of blasphemy, religious legalism, pride, violence, hatred, racism, enmity, and murder manifested themselves against Jesus through the religious leaders, the soldiers, and the people. They surrounded Him like dogs, encompassing Him about like strong, angry bulls. They beset Him and gaped their mouths as ravening and roaring lions, laughing, shaking their heads, and challenging Him to come down from the cross. Satan and his legions had focused their prior efforts on intimidation, to deter Jesus from the cross; to offer Him another way.[17] Their assaults became increasingly vicious as now they tempted Jesus to come down from the cross. Had He done so, satan would have succeeded, and humanity would have remained trapped in sin's bondage.

Jesus did not come down, however. He chose not to call on the more than 12 legions of angels at His disposal.[18] Instead, He committed His spirit into the just and faithful hands of His Father. He drank unmixed to the last dreg the cup of furious wrath that the wicked should drink.[19] Satan played his hand powerfully to the very last, but exhausted his authority, coming up short as Jesus remained obedient and faithful to the end. Jesus' sinlessness and perfect obedience thus made Him an acceptable offering for sin. In death He neither reviled nor threatened His enemies, but forgave them. When He uttered a loud cry and gave up His spirit on that day when the sun was darkened, the veil of the temple was rent from top to bottom.

The Cherubim Rent in Two

The veil in the temple that separated the Holy Place from the Holy of holies represented a great spiritual reality regarding Heaven, revealing in no uncertain terms that the way into Heaven was closed to humanity. As long as the veil was in place, the high priest alone could enter the Holy of holies once a year on the Day of Atonement.[20] The Holy of holies represented the highest, or third Heaven where God dwells. When Jesus died, the veil was torn from top to bottom, indicating that God had reached down to man and opened once more the way back to His presence in Paradise.

The way was now open for all to enter into God's heavenly presence and approach His throne of grace to obtain mercy and find help in the time of need, free from accusations and all condemnation. God's holy love was on display, visible to all who would look through the eyes of faith. The glory of the true and living God could be seen in the face of the risen Lord Jesus.[21] Indeed, the rending of the veil exposed satan's lies against God's character, because it became plain to see that God had withheld nothing from humanity: "He that spared not His own Son, but delivered Him up for us all, how shall He not with Him also freely give us all things?" (Rom. 8:32)

There is another deep spiritual meaning to the tearing of the veil. According to Exodus 26:31, the inward curtains and veil of the tabernacle (and later temple) were embroidered with cherubim.[22] Consequently, when the veil was torn in two, so were the cherubim. The torn veil signified that the way back to God was now open because the guardian cherub was cut away from his position.[23] The accusing cherub who had veiled the minds of men and accused them before God was torn down from his high place. God's judgment without mercy was measured back to him who had rejoiced in deceiving, accusing, and condemning humanity! Michael and his angels, however, remained at their post on the right side of the mercy seat. Mercy triumphed over judgment.[24]

There is no way to overestimate the importance of the cross of Christ, either for the destiny of mankind or the doom of satan. The cross had an incredible impact for both the heavens and the earth. This impact has been a theme in Christian artistic expression throughout the centuries. As Dr. J. Hastings notes: "Some of the great artists of the Crucifixion have painted the cross as reaching into the skies, exercising a cosmic influence for the world upon which its foot rests, while its top touches and moves the very heavens."[25] Because of the death and resurrection of Christ, we can now approach God and look upon His face without fearing death, and at physical death, enter His very presence. This is why Matthew's Gospel connects Jesus' death with the rending of the veil in the Holy of holies and with the opening of the graves at Christ's resurrection. The departed saints then appeared in Jerusalem on their way to glory. Before that, however, it was necessary for Christ to release them from Abraham's bosom. This required Him descending into hell itself, assaulting the very stronghold of the enemy.

Endnotes

1. See John 6:68-69. Peter often expressed the group's convictions and sentiments at crucial junctions. When Jesus asked the 12, "Will ye also go away?" Simon Peter answered Him, "Lord, to whom shall we go? Thou hast the words of eternal life. And we believe and are sure that Thou art that Christ, the Son of the living God" (Jn. 6:67-69). See also Matthew 14:28; 16:23; John 13:8.

2. As a momentary mouthpiece for satan, Peter even rebuked Jesus for saying He would go to the cross (see Mt. 16:23). His impetuous nature was also seen in refusing at first to have his feet washed by Christ (see Jn. 13:8), in offering to build Christ a tabernacle alongside Moses and Elijah (see Mt. 17:4), and in drawing his sword to defend his Lord in the garden (see Jn. 18:10). No doubt satan wanted him to go the way of Judas Iscariot—if it were possible! Indeed, although satan seeks to cut off every disciple, he concentrates his most severe attacks against those who lead others in Christ.

3. See John 3:13; 15:4-7; Ephesians 2:6.

4. See Romans 8:37.

5. John 12:31. Sydney H.T. Page comments on this verse that, "Whatever power satan has is decisively broken by Jesus, according to John 12:31 and 16:11. In John 12:31-32, Jesus says, 'Now is the time for judgment on this world; now the prince of this world will be driven out. But I, when I am lifted up from the earth, will draw all men to myself.' In this saying, Jesus speaks unequivocally concerning satan's imminent defeat and associates it with the crucifixion. In John's view, the crucial battle between Jesus and the devil takes place not in the desert or during Jesus' public ministry, but on the cross. One might, as the synoptic writers do, speak of earlier conquests of Jesus over his foe, but the Ultimate conflict happens at Calvary. There, satan is vanquished, and as a result, salvation comes to humanity" (*Powers of Evil* [Grand Rapids: Baker Books, 1995], 129).

6. See 1 Peter 5:8.

7. According to Scripture, there are three heavens! Since Paul was caught up to the *"third* heaven," there must be a *second* and a *first* heaven. The Old Testament speaks of the Heaven of heavens. Based on the pattern of the three places in the temple, the Holy of holies is like the third Heaven from which satan was cast out. He still has a place, however, in the first and second heavens: "For we wrestle...against spiritual wickedness in high places." (Eph. 6:12).

8. Using the same Greek word, the context confirms that the meaning is *soon* (see also Jn. 17:11).

9. See 2 Corinthians 4:4.

10. F.J. Huegel, *The Cross Through the Scriptures* (Grand Rapids: Zondervan, 1996), 1.

11. See Luke 9:51.

12. See Mark 8:31; 9:12.

13. See 2 Corinthians 5:21; 1 Peter 2:23-24.

14. See Galatians 3:13.

15. See Matthew 26:37-42.

16. See Matthew 16:21-27.

17. In Matthew 16:23, Jesus rebuked Peter in the strongest possible terms ("Get thee behind Me, satan") because satan was using Peter as a mouthpiece to stop Him from going to the cross: "Never, Lord! This shall never happen to You" (see Mt. 16:22 NIV). Jesus recognized satan's influence immediately. It is enlightening that this "get thee behind Me, satan" contains an echo from the prior temptation in the wilderness where Jesus said, "Away from Me, satan!" Satan assailed Jesus at birth, at the beginning of His public ministry and throughout His ministry until He breathed His last breath on the cross. Several other cases from the Gospels reveal various demonic ploys such as attempting to make Him king by force (see Jn. 6:15).

18. See Matthew 26:53.

19. See Psalm 75:8; Isaiah 51:17.

20. See Hebrews 9:6-9.

21. See 2 Corinthians 3:12–4:6.

22. See also Exodus 26:1; 28:35,43; 36:8.

23. The cherubim are first mentioned in Genesis after the fall of man, where they were placed with a flaming sword to guard the way to the tree of life (see Gen. 3:24). They proclaimed God's just wrath against sin and were the forerunners of the sanctuary where cherubim were on either side of the mercy seat. We have already seen that satan's position in Heaven was represented by one of these temple cherubim.

24. See James 2:13 NKJ.

25. J. Hastings, ed., *The Great Text of the Bible* (New York: Scribner's and Sons, 1915), 11. There is such a painting by Luino at Lugano, and another by Guido Reni at Rome.

Chapter Seven

The Accuser and Christ's Descent Into Hell

Christ's descent into hell, although stated as part of the Apostle's Creed, is shunned or neglected by many believers either because they question its biblical basis, relevance, or importance, or because the whole event seems shrouded in mystery and beyond understanding. As we have already seen, however, much that has been thought hidden with regard to the place and work of satan is revealed clearly through careful study of the Scripture. The same is true concerning the fact and purpose of Christ's descent into hell and the world of the dead between His death and resurrection.

First John 3:8 says that Jesus, the Son of God came to "destroy [lit. undo] the works of the devil." This began when the heavens were opened at Jesus' baptism and continued when He defeated satan in the wilderness of temptation. Throughout His ministry, Jesus put the accuser and his legions on the defensive constantly, as demons manifested and were cast out, as the sick were healed, and as the dead were raised. All these were signs that satan's dominance of humanity's experiences was being nullified and approaching its end. But it was through death that Jesus won the ultimate victory: "that through death He might destroy him that had the power of death, that is, the devil" (He. 2:14). Yes, by the very act of dying, Jesus broke satan's death grip on humanity. In rising from the dead, He destroyed forever satan's power over death.

The tearing of the veil in the temple was one of several unusual occurrences at the time that clearly indicate the spiritual significance of the death of Jesus. Matthew's account makes this plain:

> *And Jesus, when He had cried again with a loud voice,* **yielded** *up the ghost. And, behold, the* **veil of the temple** *was* **rent** *in twain from top to the bottom; and the* **earth did quake**, *and the rocks rent, and the* **graves were opened**; *and many bodies of the saints which slept arose, and* **came out of the graves** *after His resurrection, and went into the holy city, and* **appeared** *unto many* (Matthew 27:50-53).

Jesus' spirit left His body and the veil was torn in two; He rose from the dead three days later, and the earth quaked; the graves of dead saints were opened, and they appeared to many in Jerusalem. The earthquake was a physical reverberation of a trans-dimensional event. Christ's resurrection affected every realm of creation, even opening the gates of hell from the inside. The saints were released from Abraham's bosom (the upper level of Sheol) when Christ ascended from the abode of the dead at His resurrection. To understand why Matthew connects the tearing of the veil at Jesus' death with the opening of the graves and the appearance in Jerusalem of the departed saints at Christ's resurrection, we must look at Jesus's descent into hell.

The Descent Into Hell

During the interval between His death and resurrection, Jesus' spirit descended into hell, where He preached the good news to the spirits in prison; those who had been disobedient in the days of Noah before the Flood. According to the apostle Peter:

> *For Christ also hath once suffered for sins, the just for the unjust, that He might* **bring us to God**, *being put to death in the* **flesh**, *but quickened by the* **Spirit**: *by which also* **He went** *and preached unto the* **spirits in prison** (1 Peter 3:18-19).

> **For for this cause** *was the gospel preached also to* **them that are dead**, *that they might be judged according to men in the* **flesh**, *but live according to God in the* **spirit** (1 Peter 4:6).

Both the appearance of the dead saints in Jerusalem and the preaching of Jesus to the antediluvian spirits in prison create perplexing theological questions. What do these things mean? Obviously, they are part of Scripture, and therefore, God has a reason for including them in His Word. In fact, they are important pieces of the puzzle and fit with the whole of Scripture when accepted at face value.

For one thing, they show that the death of Christ is more than able to bring men to God! The torn veil showed that the way to God was open once more, and Jesus' descent into hell revealed more completely just what His death accomplished: the ultimate sacrifice, paying for the sins of humanity throughout the ages; rescuing from sin, death, and the grave all who would believe. The thief on the cross, confessing faith in Christ even while under the judgment of death, received the promise that he would be in Paradise that very day.

By His descent into hell, Christ demonstrated the good news of life in the Spirit.[1] He died in the flesh, but was alive, "quickened by the Spirit," when He descended.[2] He bore sin in His body on the cross, not in His spirit in hell.[3] Christ did not undergo suffering when He descended into hell; His suffering ended on the cross. Although His physical body lay dead in the tomb for three days, payment for sin was finished on the cross. Ephraim Syrus wrote in an old Nisibene Hymn: "A medicine of life has entered into Hell, and has restored life to its dead...*But now*, in place of deadly visitations of justice, He has wrought in His Son, the quickening of the dead by grace."[4]

Jesus' descent into hell reveals both the seriousness of sin and the success of His redeeming work.[5] All men were dead in sin and required redemption. Their sin held them in the state of death. When Jesus descended into the abode of the dead, "quickened [made alive] by the Spirit," the spirits of those in Abraham's bosom were quickened also by the Spirit. Death's power over them was broken and they were released forever from its domain. As Jesus entered through the earth and back into His body, there was a great earthquake. His tomb opened as did the graves of the saints, who appeared to many in recognizable form. This was a spiritual resurrection (the bodily resurrection still lies in the future, at the return of Christ) and these saints then entered the presence of God in Heaven, where they await the resurrection of the body. With Heaven opened by the atonement of Christ, all saints at death go immediately to God's presence where, like the saints of old, they anticipate the bodily resurrection.

I believe the Bible indicates that there are three heavens as well as three levels of Sheol (Gk., *hades*), the abode of the dead. The first two of these levels are mentioned in Jesus' parable of the rich man and Lazarus, recorded in Luke 16:19-31, while the third is found in Second Peter 2:4:

- *Abraham's bosom*, where Lazarus and the Old Testament saints went at death.[6]
- *Gehenna*, where the rich man and the ungodly went at death.[7]
- *Tartarus*, or the lowest hell where those went who perished in the great Flood.[8]

Abraham's bosom was an intermediate place of comfort and rest for the godly dead while they were awaiting God's deliverance. Below it, and separated from it by a wide gulf, was Gehenna, an intermediate place of torment for the ungodly dead awaiting God's final judgment. Lower still was Tartarus, where the disobedient during Noah's day were taken when they died under the judgment waters of the Flood. They also await the Great White Throne judgment of Revelation 20:11-15. Apparently, all three of these compartments of Sheol were under the earth, as the Old Testament saints spoke of going "down" into the grave, and the dead prophet Samuel "came up" when he appeared to Saul.[9]

Tartarus

Jesus' spirit descended at death into *the lower parts*, the region of the lost,[10] all the way to Tartarus, the lowest hell, where He "preached unto the spirits in prison" (1 Pet. 3:19b). Here the drowned multitudes of the great Flood were confined, imprisoned in a place of sorrow and torment, bound with the chains of their sins, each under a greater or lesser degree of guilt and condemnation. Jesus did not accuse them to the Father nor condemn them to the torments of hell, but demonstrated the hope of life in the Spirit. Many had heard the righteous preaching of Noah warning them of the judgment to come, and yet his message could not save them. Some may have cried out for mercy before the mighty waters overcame them, but only Noah and his family found grace to physically survive the flood. In fact, Noah's faithfulness *condemned the world*.[11]

Gehenna

The rest of the ungodly were confined in Gehenna, the middle level of Sheol, where they suffered the torments of unmet desires and the accusations of their consciences. In *Reflections of Life After Death,* Dr. Raymond Moody relates the near death experiences of his patients, some of whom have had visions of this abode of the dead. At death they watched passing before them three-dimensional images of every event of their lives—not only the major events, but everything they ever said or did, good or bad—and saw the effects they had on others. All the while the question echoed, "What have you done with your life?" The feeling of being exposed with nothing hidden is overwhelming. One patient described his out-of-body experience at death before being revived:

> "I looked down at bewildered people, dull, bent down, sadly depressed. They seemed to shuffle as someone on a chain gang, seemingly getting nowhere, and not knowing where to go or who to follow. With crushed hopeless faces....they seemed bound to some invisible, oppressive force. Some person, object, or habit that they could not get away from. They were utterly perplexed."[12]

Another fundamental difference between this level and the upper level, Abraham's bosom, is demonstrated by the fact that Jesus' parable in Luke 16 describes a great gulf fixed between the two, so that no one can cross over from either side to the other. Even in death, there is separation between believers and unbelievers. In hell, Jesus' spirit was unbound as He moved about freely and crossed the great divide between Tartarus, Gehenna, and Abraham's bosom. No one had ever done this before.

Abraham's Bosom

The saints who lived and died prior to the death and resurrection of Jesus could not immediately enter Heaven because it was still closed to them due to sin. Only Christ's atoning death opened the way. In the meantime, the departed saints went to Abraham's bosom to await the opening of Heaven and the quickening of their spirit.

Until Jesus died no man could ascend to Heaven, because the accuser still had a place there. Jesus said to Nicodemus, "If I have told you earthly things, and ye believe not, how shall ye believe, if I tell you of heavenly things? And *no man hath ascended up to heaven*, but He that came down from heaven, even the Son of man which is in heaven" (Jn. 3:12-13). Before the advent and death of the Messiah, those who died did not ascend into Heaven. Even men like Enoch and Elijah were taken into a place called Abraham's bosom. Christ had to first die, tearing the veil to open the gates of Heaven, and descend to lead the dead out of hell.[13]

By divine intervention, Moses and Elijah were released from Abraham's bosom before Jesus' resurrection so they could meet with Him on the Mount of Transfiguration and discuss with Him what His death at Jerusalem would accomplish.[14] Their early release encouraged Jesus as He set His face toward Jerusalem,[15] anticipating as it did the permanent release from Abraham's bosom His death would accomplish for all those who had faithfully awaited His coming. This fulfilled the age-old expectation of God's people: "For Thou wilt not leave my soul in hell."[16]

Christ Himself was able to come out of death and hell because He had committed no sin. The pains of death could not possibly hold Him.[17] Being "justified in the Spirit," hell had no dominion over Him.[18] As a result, His body saw no corruption, for satan's angel of death had no authority over Christ's sinless flesh. Nor did His body sleep in death for very long: a mere three days.[19]

When He began to ascend from where He had descended, He "led captivity captive." Another translation reads, "He led a host of captives."[20] The phrase *led captivity captive* originated in the days of Deborah and Barak as a song of victory over an oppressive enemy. Sisera was Israel's deadly enemy. As a type of the devil, he had long confined God's people to fearfully hiding in caves and holes in the ground until he was wounded in his head.[21] In Barak's day, the people of the Lord went throughout the land rejoicing at their release from captivity. This foreshadowed Christ's triumph over the grave and the saints' release from death's bondage.

Scripture reveals a threefold purpose of Christ's descent: to demonstrate life in the spirit, to free captives, and to fill all things from the lowest hell to the highest heaven: He that descended is the same also who ascended up far above all heavens, that He might fill all things.[22] Oh, the depth of His love! There is no void He cannot fill, no deep, desolate, empty place that He cannot reach.[23] If we make our bed in hell, He's been there, and He knows the way out![24]

Personally, I find this doctrine of Jesus' descent into Sheol very comforting and useful, and by it, death has lost its dread and mystery. The powers of darkness no longer intimidate me as they did when I was growing up. As a kid, I watched my share of horror movies, and zombies were among the most terrifying. They would come out of the lagoon with seaweed hanging from their partially decomposed bodies. Not even bullets could stop them from taking you back to where they had come from. And that was the point when I would disappear behind the couch! The question of what might be lurking in the dark, in the cupboard, or under my bed caused me more than one sleepless night.

Jesus' descent into hell has delivered me out of these fears! With nightmares a thing of the past, not long ago I found myself in a dream moving boldly through a graveyard at night, into a mausoleum, and through a mortuary. Ending up in a haunted house, I fearlessly opened cupboards like a professional ghost buster, seeking to expose the works of darkness. What would have been a bad dream was now good sport because of what Jesus had accomplished in my timid personality through His resurrection life.

Peter writes that after descending into hell Jesus was exalted to God's right hand in Heaven with "angels and authorities and powers being made subject unto Him."[25] *Christ's descent illustrates His power to bring us to God.* Although some have twisted this into a doctrine of repentance in the grave, it is really a mighty display of Christ through death destroying him who had the power of death.[26] *Christ brought God's rule into the very epicenter of satan's domain, thus revealing even in hell His supreme sovereignty as absolute Lord of "things under the earth."*[27] They too must bow and confess Him accordingly: *"For to this end Christ both died, and rose, and revived, that He might be Lord both of the dead and living"* (Rom. 14:9).

The Firstborn From Among the Dead

The entire Christian faith rests on the doctrine of the person of Jesus.[28] We are complete and secure in Christ because He is Creator and Redeemer—preexistent, incarnate, and resurrected. He is the beginning of all creation, the end of everything, and the power that holds it all together.[29] In Colossians, where Paul superbly articulates the doctrine of Christ, he writes that Jesus is Lord of the first creation because:

> *For by Him were all things created, that are in **heaven**, and that are in **earth**, visible and invisible, whether they be thrones, or dominions, or principalities, or powers: **all things** were created by Him, and for Him* (Colossians 1:16).

Before His incarnation, Christ was already preeminent in the realm of the first creation: "All things were made by Him; and without Him was not any thing made that was made" (Jn. 1:3). Now, because of His resurrection, He is also pre-eminent as the Head of the re-creation. Just as the initial creation was in Him by virtue of the Word spoken by the Father, so the new creation is in Him by virtue of His resurrection: "And He is the head of the body, the church: who is the beginning, the *firstborn* from the dead; that in *all things* He might have the *preeminence"* (Col. 1:18).

Jesus is first in all things: "the firstborn among many brethren"; "the firstfruits of them that slept."[30] Unlike Lazarus and others, He was the first to rise from the dead to die no more. Jesus alone can say, "I am He that liveth and was dead; and, behold, I am alive for evermore, Amen; and have the keys of hell and of death" (Rev. 1:18). Being the firstborn of every creature, He is the absolute Heir and Sovereign Lord of all.

By virtue of His resurrection from the dead, Jesus is also declared to be the Son of God *with power*. Christ was the Son of God from eternity past, being the Logos in the Father's bosom. With the incarnation He became God's Son in the time frame of creation when the Word became flesh in the womb of Mary. Now, through the power of the Holy Spirit, He is God's Son for eternity by His coming forth from the place of the dead.

The Scripture verse, "Thou art My Son; this day have I begotten Thee" (Ps. 2:7b), applies to Christ and His resurrection.[31] God has begotten Christ from the abode of the dead, and thus become His Father and our Father.[32] *"From the dead"* is the key that unlocks the mystery of the redeemed creation. Christ had to go into death in order to make alive those who were dead in sins and trespasses. His resurrection, therefore, cannot be understood merely in terms of His own body being raised to life and immortality, but it must be understood in the larger scope of the beginning of a new creative order.

Christ's identification with us was utterly complete. He became a man and died as our substitute on the cross. By God's grace, He tasted death for every man and removed its stinger. Our union with Him by faith now enables us to receive the powerful effects of His life, death, and resurrection:

> *Forasmuch then as the children are partakers of flesh and blood, He also Himself likewise took part of the same; that **through death** He might destroy him that had the **power of death, that is, the devil;** ... For verily He took not on Him the nature of angels; but He took on Him the **seed of Abraham**. Wherefore in all things it **behoved** Him to be made like unto His **brethren** (Hebrews 2:14,16-17a).[33]*

With Christ, we cross over from death into life! He has the keys of death and hell—the authority to release us from both spiritual and physical death.[34] What He opens no one can shut.[35] Although we were dead in sins and trespasses, His resurrection power has quickened us to life.[36] Jesus is the embodiment of the resurrection and the life, so that all who were dead may hear His voice and *live*.[37] Satan can no longer hold us under the law of sin and death because Jesus' death reversed the process and activated the law of the spirit of life.[38] The result was a new creation: "Therefore if any man be in Christ, he is a *new creature*" (2 Cor. 5:17a).

The apostle Peter wrote that we have been born again to a "lively hope by the resurrection of Jesus Christ from the dead," which causes our faith and hope to be in God.[39] Our faith is in the operation of God, who quickens the dead and calls those things that be not as though they were. We do not say in our heart, "Who shall descend into the deep (that is, to bring up Christ again from the dead)" (Rom. 10:7). It is not our works that justify us and cause us to prevail, but God's work that raised Christ from the dead.[40]

On August 18, 1995, Rachel Mupukuta of Chitungwiza, Zimbabwe, heard her neighbor Dorothy Chabata cry out for help. Dorothy's father-in-law had collapsed and had no pulse. They tried without success to resuscitate him. While Dorothy went to phone her husband, Rachel stayed with the body and in a loud voice began calling on the name of the Lord. Fearlessly, she rebuked the spirit of death, taking the old man's tongue in her hand. When he began slowly breathing again, she used her other hand to remove foam from his mouth. Before long he sat up and asked for some tea. Although they could scarcely believe what had happened, the neighbors excitedly told everyone that Jesus was alive, and that they had witnessed a miracle.

Recent deaths are reported in the obituary column in most newspapers. In our local Harare newspaper, personal memorials are also written for those who have died months or even years ago. When you read them, you can sense the grief of those who have lost someone they love:

"It's been three months since you left us. Time may hide the sadness, smiles may hide the tears, but what can hide the heartache? My love, I miss you so much. No one will ever fill the gap you left. Thanks for the wonderful years we shared. I am now left with memories that I shall always treasure. I miss you so much. R.I.P. Love you always. Wife."

"Alice: Mummy, 8 painful years today. You left a gap none can ever fill. How I miss your love and guidance. This world is so cruel without you, Mummy. Your daughter."[41]

In Africa, death is traditionally accompanied by loud shrieks and wailing. Various burial rites are then observed to appease the spirit of the dead person.[42] At many Shona funerals, bands are tied around the wrists of those participating. When the body is collected, money is placed on the coffin. As the coffin is lowered into the ground, the bands are buried with the body. Beer is brewed on the anniversary of one's death, and a gravesite meeting is conducted to invite the spirit back home. In every culture, death has a way of exposing the ignorance, fear, and guilt of mankind.

Jesus came to "deliver those who through fear of death were all their lifetime subject to bondage" (Heb. 2:15). He has brought immortality to light by His resurrection and has gone ahead to prepare a place for us in the Father's house. The gates of hell are broken down and the gates of Heaven are open wide. The obstacles and opposition to our abiding in the Father's house have been eradicated. Without this knowledge, life would be unbearable! But believers will neither see nor taste death;[43] they have passed from death to life.[44] We know that "to be absent from the body, [is] to be present with the Lord."[45] To depart from this world as a believer is "to be with Christ, which is far better."[46]

In the Old Testament, because believers had to wait in Sheol, it was not *far better.* Heaven was not yet open to man, nor closed to satan. Jesus Christ opened Heaven, freed the Old Testament saints, and prepared the way for all future believers, but before any could enter in, Heaven had to be cleansed by the applying of Jesus' blood on the true, heavenly Holy of holies.

Endnotes

1. The sixteenth century teachings of Johannes Hoch that the soul of Christ descended into hell to suffer punishment, while His body lay in the tomb, is still taught in some circles. This idea has no *valid* scriptural support.

2. See 1 Peter 3:18.

3. See 1 Peter 2:24.

4. *Select Library of Nicene and Post Nicene Fathers of the Christian Church,* Philip Schaff, ed., (Oxford: The Christian Literature Co., 1891), Volume 13, Part 5, "Concerning Satan and Death, A.D. 350."

5. The day is approaching when God, as in the days of Noah, will bring an end to this world. Then death and hell will give up their dead as God in Christ judges the secrets of men's hearts. All those who are in the grave will hear His voice, coming out of their abodes to either the resurrection of life or to condemnation (see Jn. 5:28-29). This will include Jews and Gentiles alike, who will appear at the Great White Throne Judgment, judged according to their works in the light of their conscience (see Rom. 2:14-16). When the books are opened at the Great White Throne judgment, all mankind will be judged in accordance with what is recorded in the books. Anyone whose name is not found in the book of life will be hurled into the lake of fire (see Rev. 20:11-15).

6. Abel, Enoch, Abraham, Moses, David, Elijah, and all other godly people, both Jews and Gentiles, who lived by faith, and "by patient continuance in well doing [sought] for...eternal life" (Rom. 2:7). Those who died before Christ's ascension (or, in the cases of Enoch and Elijah, were translated without physical death) went to Abraham's bosom. It is significant that it was called after Abraham rather than after Moses, because it was full of both Jew and Gentiles and because Abraham is the father of all who believe.

7. In Luke 16:23, the rich man is said to be in torment in hell (Gk., *hades*). *Hades* is the Greek equivalent to the Hebrew *sheol*, and both refer to the abode of the dead in general. *Gehenna*, a second Greek word translated "hell," occurs 12 times in the New Testament, and invariably refers to a place of punishment. For this reason, I refer to the second level of Sheol as Gehenna, to clearly distinguish this abode of torment for the ungodly dead from Abraham's bosom, the abode of peace, comfort, and joy for the godly dead.

8. Angels and men were sentenced to Tartarus when God brought the great Flood waters on the earth (see 2 Pet. 2:4-5). Peter speaks of the angels who sinned being "delivered...into chains" and later uses the same idea of imprisonment for men (see 2 Pet. 3:18-19).

9. See 1 Samuel 28:3-20; Job 7:9; 17:16; 21:13; Psalm 28:1; 30:3,9; 55:15,23; 88:4ff; 115:17.

10. See Deuteronomy 32:22; Psalm 86:13; Proverbs 9:18; Acts 2:31; Ephesians 4:9.

11. See Hebrews 11:7.

12. Raymond A. Moody, Jr. M.D., *Reflections of Life After Death*, (New York: Bantam Books, 1977), "Drawing from other passages in the Bible it is safe to assume that 'the gates of hell'...kept a tight lid on this cosmic grave, and that prior to Jesus' resurrection, the padlock of death kept those gates secure. The whole picture is the epitome of despair—scores of people eternally buried, rotting in their own sins and trespasses, and programmed to follow the course of an evil master" (Edgardo Silvoso, *That None Should Perish* [Ventura, CA: Regal Books, 1993], 108).

13. See John 3:13; 1 Samuel 28:11ff; Psalm 68:18; Ephesians 4:8-9. If Enoch, Elijah, or anyone else could get into Heaven before the death of the Messiah, then all the Old Testament saints should have been admitted at death (unless not seing death was the decisive criteria). Physical mortality, however, is the result of the deeper issue of sin: "In Adam all died" and "by one man's offense death reigned" (see Rom. 5:12-21). Since Enoch and Elijah had sinned, "for all have sinned and come short of the glory of God" (Rom. 3:23), they went to Abraham's bosom. In Second Kings, Elijah was taken by "the chariot of Israel" in to the sky, "a whirlwind," enroute to Abraham's bosom. (See Second Kings 1:10-12; 7:2,19; 17:16; 21:3-5 for heaven as sky, and see in Second Kings 13:14 the same wording for Elisha's translation at death.)

14. See Luke 9:30-31. This was possible prior to Christ's descent into hell because of Michael's successful contention with the devil over Moses' body, and Elijah's translation without normal death and burial.

15. See Luke 9:53.

16. Psalm 16:10. See also Psalm 86:13.

17. See Acts 2:24.

18. See 1 Timothy 3:16; see also Romans 6:9.

19. See Acts 2:27.

20. See Ephesians 4:8 (RSV).

21. See Judges 5:12-13,26.

22. See Psalm 68:18-20; Ephesians 4:8-10.

23. The Jews have an interesting legend about David's immortal lament over Absalom. So moving was David's cry, they felt that in some

way God must honor such immeasurable grief. According to tradition, at each cry of David, "My son, my son, Absalom!" one of the gates of hell opened until the soul of Absalom was admitted to Abraham's bosom. We know, however, that only the death of Jesus, the true Seed of David, can satisfy the Father and make an atonement for sin. Christ can now legitimately rescue those within the gates of death and hell.

24. See Psalm 139:8.

25. 1 Peter 3:22b.

26. See Hebrews 2:14. There is a danger of formulating doctrine from passages that are not easy to understand. The unlearned and unstable sometimes use them to their own demise (see 2 Pet. 3:16). The often quoted Church fathers such as Clement, Cyril of Alexandria, Athanasius, Augustine, and Jerome went further than we have by claiming that the effect of Christ's descent into hell had been to set free some who were condemned to the torments of damnation. They did not, however, interpret this event to teach an on-going doctrine of repentance in the grave.

27. See Philippians 2:10-11.

28. Those who seek to differentiate between the historical Jesus and the Jesus of Scripture have erred greatly. The Jesus Seminar is an example of a present-day Christological heresy.

29. See Colossians 1:15-20.

30. Romans 8:29; 1 Corinthians 15:20; see also Colossians 1:14.

31. See also Acts 13:33; Hebrews 1:5.

32. See Psalm 89:26; John 20:17; Acts 13:33, Hebrews 1:4-6. A person must be born again from above; his spirit needs the Holy Spirit to impart eternal life. This is a creative act of God compared by Paul to the first creation when God said, "Let there be light." Therefore, the human spirits of those who were dead had to be quickened to new life in Christ and recreated in His image if they were to enter the Kingdom of Heaven. The Bible teaches this throughout its pages: Adam died first spiritually, then physically, and men must come alive spiritually. (See John 3:3ff; 5:24-26; 6:47ff; 17:2ff; 20:22; Romans 5:10-21; Galatians 3:21; 5:6; 2 Corinthians 5:17; Ephesians 2:10; 4:18-24; Colosians 3:3-4,10; 2 Timothy 1:10; 1 John 3:14-15; 5:11-12.)

33. See also John 1:12; Romans 8:14; Galatians 4:6.

34. See Revelation 1:18.

35. See Revelation 3:7.

36. See Ephesians 2:5.

37. See John 5:25.

38. See Romans 8:1-3.

39. 1 Peter 1:3; see also 1 Peter 1:21; Romans 5:17; Colossians 2:12.

40. See Romans 10:3-5,8-10.

41. Edited and reconstructed from *The Herald*, Harare, Zimbabwe, Africa.

42. Often when I inquire as to the medical cause of death, I discover there is no natural explanation given because death is considered a spiritual issue: Unbelievers consult a witch doctor as to the cause of death.

43. See John 8:51-52.

44. See John 5:24.

45. 2 Corinthians 5:8b; see 1 Thessalonians 4:14.

46. Philippians 1:23b.

Chapter Eight

The Accuser and the Cleansing of Heaven

When Jesus walked and ministered on the earth, He was the *Word* of God who "was made flesh, and dwelt among us...full of grace and truth" (Jn. 1:14). The sinless Son of God died on the cross as the suffering servant of Isaiah 53, "...a man of sorrows, and acquainted with grief...He hath borne our griefs, and carried our sorrows...He was wounded for our transgressions, [and] bruised for our iniquities..." (Is. 53:3-5). He was "the Lamb of God, which taketh away the sin of the world" (Jn. 1:29b).

Upon His death, Jesus descended into the abode of the dead as Lord "of things in heaven, and things in earth, and things under the earth" (Phil. 2:10), thus demonstrating God's sovereignty over all the created realm. With His resurrection, releasing the Old Testament saints from Abraham's bosom and opening Heaven for them and all who would follow, Jesus revealed Himself as "...He that liveth, and was dead; [who is] alive for evermore, [and who has] the keys of hell and of death" (Rev. 1:18).

As the risen Lord, Jesus entered into a new ministry as our great "high priest...who is holy, harmless, undefiled, separate from sinners, and made higher than the heavens" (Heb. 7:26), and "who is set on the right hand of the throne of the Majesty in the heavens" (Heb. 8:1). There He "ever liveth to make intercession for [us]" (Heb. 7:25b) as our "advocate with the

Father" (1 Jn. 2:1b). When Jesus entered Heaven as the great high priest, satan was cast out, and Heaven was cleansed of his defiled presence. The *accuser* of men was replaced by the *Advocate* of men!

The Ascent to the True Holy of Holies

While the Old Testament saints appeared to many in Jerusalem, Jesus appeared to Mary Magdalene outside the garden tomb just before His initial ascension as our High Priest. This ascension must be distinguished from His ascension 40 days later, at which time He commissioned His followers. Before Jesus appeared or spoke to His disciples, He appeared first to Mary:

> *Jesus saith unto her,* **Mary**. *She turned herself, and saith unto Him, Rabboni; which is to say, Master. Jesus saith unto her,* **Touch Me not***; for I am* **not yet ascended** *to My Father: but* **go to My brethren, and say unto them, I ascend** *unto* **My** *Father,* **and Your Father***; and to My God, and your God. Mary Magdalene came and told the disciples that she had seen the Lord, and that He had spoken these things unto her* (John 20:16-18).

Why did Jesus tell Mary not to touch Him, yet a week later invite Thomas to do so?[1] Our great High Priest, having offered Himself without spot to God, had not yet ascended to apply His blood on the true mercy seat in Heaven! He was not to be touched or delayed until He had presented Himself before God in the true Holy of holies. This was the ultimate fulfillment of the centuries-old ritual that the Jewish priests performed every year on the Day of Atonement:

> *Now when these things had been thus prepared, the priests always went into the first part of the tabernacle, performing the services. But into the second part the* **high priest went alone** *once a year, not without* **blood***, which he offered for himself and for the people's sins...* **But Christ came as High Priest** *of the good things to come, with the greater and more perfect tabernacle not made with hands, that is, not of this creation. Not with the blood of goats and calves, but* **with His own blood He entered the most Holy Place once for all, having obtained eternal redemption** (Hebrews 9:6-7,11-12 NKJ).

Consider the sequence of events: Jesus dies, descends into hell, rises on the third day, leading the Old Testament saints out of Sheol,[2] reveals Himself to Mary while the raised saints appear to many in the city, and ascends to the heavenly Mount Zion, followed by the saints, where, in the true Holy of holies, He performs His high priestly duty as prefigured on the Day of Atonement. He meets the keepers of the gates of Heaven, who ask Him the age-old question, "Who may *ascend* into the hill of the Lord? Or who may *stand* in His holy place?" (Ps. 24:3 NKJ)

The answer is clear: "He who has clean hands and a pure heart, who has not lifted up his soul to an idol, nor sworn deceitfully. He shall receive blessing from the Lord, and righteousness from the God of his salvation" (Ps. 24:4-5 NKJ). The great host of believers waits outside the Most Holy Place as their High Priest proceeds to the gates, saying, "Lift up your heads, O ye *gates*; and be ye lift up, ye *everlasting doors*; and the *King of glory* shall come in. Who is this King of glory? The Lord strong and mighty, *the Lord mighty in battle*" (Ps. 24:7-8).

Christ, triumphantly ascended from a mighty battle, could charge the guardian rulers of the gates of Heaven to admit Him. The prophetic Psalm 24 becomes a celebration of victory as the King of glory enters Heaven.[3] As Christ applies His blood on the mercy seat, a loud voice announces the proclamation of Revelation chapter 12: "...Now is come salvation, and strength, and the kingdom of our God, and the power of His Christ."[4] Our eternal redemption is secured. Heaven is open to us, and our accuser is silenced.

The Cleansing of Heaven

Heaven was cleansed by Jesus as our great High Priest when He applied His blood to the mercy seat—a much better sacrifice than the blood of bulls and goats. Why did Heaven need cleansing? What kept man out of Heaven until Christ came? Basically, there were *three* spiritual realities in Heaven that required cleansing:

- The blotting out of the handwriting of ordinances in Heaven.
- The silencing of the continual accusations of sin against the brethren in Heaven.
- The removal of the accuser himself from Heaven.

1. The handwriting of ordinances had to be blotted out in heaven.

Before men could be released from death's hold and made alive in God's presence, sin had to be blotted out. The apostle Paul explained how Jesus' death cleansed Heaven of the record of our sins before God, thereby disarming the devil and his angels:

Blotting out the handwriting of ordinances that was against us,
which was contrary to us, and took it out of the way, nailing it to
*His cross; **and having spoiled principalities and powers,** He made*
a show of them openly, triumphing over them in it (Colossians
2:14-15).

In first-century economic terms, the handwriting of ordinances were
interest-bearing notes demanding payment; a record of accounts payable.
With the passage of time, the demand to settle such accounts increased.
From a moral standpoint, the laws God gave to Moses constitute a "handwriting of ordinances." Ordained by the disposition of angels, these com-
mandments defined moral obligations in keeping with the conscience of
mankind.[5] Not only did man's conscience *within* accuse him when he did
not keep these laws, but demonic spirits from *without* caused him to experience the consequences of such violations.

It is easy to understand how the accuser used these decrees to gain
permissible grounds before God to exercise authority in measuring out
judgments such as sickness, calamity, and death against men as the
bearer of the bonds. Sinners fell under satan's domain because, as the
author of sin, he had jurisdiction over its realm. Satan was like a prose-
cuting attorney presenting his charges and evidence against the defen-
dant, endlessly accusing men, appealing to the righteousness of God as
revealed in the Law.

Christ fulfilled the Law's demands by living in perfect love and dying
in perfect sinlessness, and therefore is perfectly capable of delivering men
from satan's power.[6] His substitutionary death has settled all the accounts,
and we are forgiven and released. The ordinances against us were nailed to
His cross and stamped, "Paid In Full." Justice has been satisfied and satan
can no longer approach God demanding payment. The strongman's
weapons have been taken out of his hands; he has been disarmed and
stripped of his grounds for accusing us. Sin and its account have been
removed from us as far as the east is from the west. Christ's death alone is
sufficient for our acquittal; there is no other way that God can justify us and
remain just Himself.[7]

2. The continual accusations of sin against the brethren had to be
silenced in Heaven.

Paul recognized that once Christ removed the handwriting of ordinances against us, satan could no longer accuse us to God, and no charge
against us would be received in Heaven:

*...If God is for us, who can be against us? ... **Who** shall bring a* **charge** *against God's elect? It is **God who justifies**. **Who** is he* **who condemns**? *It is **Christ** who **died**, and furthermore is also risen, who is even at the right hand of God, **who** also **makes intercession for us*** (Romans 8:31,33-34 NKJ).[8]

In these verses Paul fires a barrage of questions: "Who can be against us? Who shall bring a charge against God's elect? Who is there to condemn us?" The definitive answer from Heaven is *no one*! Although satan's aim was to condemn—day and night seeking a judgment against us—God has justified us and all accusations are now of no account: "There is therefore now no condemnation to them which are in Christ Jesus..." (Rom. 8:1). This is a reality forever settled in the third Heaven where Christ is positioned to state the case for us in terms that last for time and eternity.[9]

God's Old Testament people longed for the day when they would be established in righteousness far from oppression with no fear or terror. In that day, although adversaries would assemble, it would not be by God's doing. Therefore, they would fall, their slanderous tongues silenced:

*Behold, they shall surely gather together, but **not by Me**: whosoever shall gather together against thee shall **fall** for thy sake. Behold...I have created the waster to destroy. No weapon that is formed against thee shall prosper; and **every tongue that shall rise against thee in judgment** thou shalt condemn. This is **the heritage** of the servants of the Lord, and **their righteousness is of Me**, saith the Lord* (Isaiah 54:15-17).[10]

The waster's weapon is identified as his tongue rising in judgment. No wonder James calls the tongue "...a fire, a world of iniquity...it...setteth on fire the course of nature; and it is set on fire of hell" (Jas. 3:6). Satan's accusatory words are no longer heard in Heaven. Isaiah's prophetic cry has found its fulfillment in Christ:

*He is near that **justifieth Me**; who will **contend** with Me? Let us stand together: who is mine adversary? Let him come near to Me. Behold, the Lord God will **help** Me; who is he that shall condemn Me? lo, **they all shall wax old** as a garment; the moth shall eat them up* (Isaiah 50:8-9).

The devil may contend with you, claiming that God will no longer help you. He may whisper in your ear a lie that the Lord has left you because of your sin. Never forget that although you may hear the accuser's charges, God has declared them null and void in Heaven. An old hymn aptly reads:

"I hear the Accuser roar

Of ills that I have done;

I know them all, and thousands more,

Jehovah findeth none."

In response to such divine favor, what can we say? With Paul we boldly proclaim that nothing the devil does can really be against us. Since God is for us, even the demonic things that appear to be against us—tribulation, distress, persecution, famine, nakedness, peril, or sword—are conquered by God's indestructible love in Christ. The fallen angels, with their principalities and powers, are unable to separate us from Christ's love. Those troubles are merely instruments by which we show ourselves to be more than conquerors. Truly, God works all things together for our good, and so we lovingly trust Him in spite of outward circumstances.[11]

Satan's slanderous lie in the garden against God's character, accusing Him of withholding something good from man, is exposed as utterly false. God freely gave us all things, even His own Son![12] The prosecutor's case against man is also over, dismissed for lack of evidence because the handwriting of ordinances has been blotted out. Moreover, this dignitary of the court has been exposed for what he is: the main culprit of great wickedness. His domain overstepped the mark when it crucified the sinless One. The execution of Jesus was the culmination of all evils, an act of violence against all good; yet by it and because of it, evil is finished, exhausted, and extinguished. The archangel Michael, like a court bailiff, is ordered to eject satan from the courtroom.[13] All the angelic host and the redeemed saints, that great "cloud of witnesses"..."the spirits of just men made perfect,"[14] join in a great offering of praise and adoration to the Lamb. Heaven rejoices because the accuser has been cast down.[15]

3. The presence of the accuser himself had to be removed from Heaven.

After the ascension of Christ, nowhere in the New Testament is satan seen in Heaven. Although some cite Revelation chapter 12 as evidence of the accuser's presence in Heaven, the passage is actually a magnificent vision of satan cast down by Christ's ascension. (That vision is the focus of our next chapter.)

The Three Heavens

Someone might ask, "If satan was cast out of Heaven, why then do we still wrestle against his forces in heavenly places?"[16] The Scriptures do teach that we are engaged in just such a conflict against spiritual wickedness on high. The reason for this is that the Bible teaches that there are actually three heavens.[17] At the Ascension of Christ, satan was cast out of the third, or highest Heaven, where God abides, and is now confined to the first and second heavens, or "the heavenlies." It is here that our struggles take place.

The word *heaven(s)* is used 700 times in the Bible. Invariably, even when translated in the singular as *heaven*, the original word is plural. This is true in both the Hebrew and the Greek. Therefore, the translator and the interpreter must determine whether it should be in the singular or plural depending on the context. If the reference is to God's abode, it is normally translated in the singular. Consider the following brief outline of the three heavens:

First Heaven: *The atmospheric heaven that surrounds the earth.*

The primary meaning of heaven, "that which is above," applies to our atmosphere. The blanket of air around the earth is approximately 20 miles in height. Rain and hail come down from this first heaven, the birds fly here, and so forth. The Bible refers to the sky as "heaven" in several places.[18]

Second Heaven: *The celestial heaven; the sphere or realm in space where the sun, moon, and stars move.*

Referred to often in Scripture, the second heaven is higher and immensely larger than the atmospheric heaven, extending for light years and thus displaying the infinite grandeur of its Creator.[19]

Third Heaven: *The highest Heaven or the Heaven of heavens.*[20]

A Heaven of heavens requires at least three. There are no more than three, however, because Paul was caught up to the highest heaven, which he identified as the third. Paul calls this place *Paradise*. It is a place, not merely a state of being, since he could have been in his body when he was caught up.[21] The third Heaven is a high and holy place where God dwells and from where the angels are dispatched on specific missions, returning there to receive further instructions.[22]

All three heavens are spiritual spheres with differing degrees of unseen influence. Ranging through the atmosphere, satan is called "the prince of the power of the air."[23] There are unseen realms in which he still derives his evil power due to the sinful activity of man.[24] He has been cast out of the third Heaven, but he is still extremely and desperately active in the other two, opposing the people of God. The apostle John graphically depicts the basis of our every victory in every struggle in the twelfth chapter of Revelation. An in-depth examination of that passage reveals some important insights regarding the defeat and casting down of satan.[25]

Endnotes

1. See John 20:17,27.

2. The saints came out of Abraham's bosom like Moses and Elijah had earlier on the Mount of Transfiguration. This was a spiritual and not a physical resurrection. Unlike the resurrection of Jesus, these saints and now the New Testament saints (that's us) await a complete bodily resurrection (see Heb. 11:39-40; Jn. 5:25,28-29).

3. The application of this psalm to the Ascension goes back to apostolic times, and it is found throughout the whole of early Church tradition. Justin, Ireaneus, and Athanasius present the same tradition, and St. Gregory Nazianzen gathers together the whole of this tradition when he writes, "Join with the angels who escort and receive Him. Command the gates to be lifted still higher to receive Him who has grown to a great stature in His Passion...then show them the beautiful tunic of the Body which suffered, how it has grown even more beautiful in His passion and been made to reflect the shining glory of the Godhead, so that He has no equal in beauty and attractiveness." The tradition also says that the heavenly powers were filled with amazement at seeing Him in the flesh, which is why they cried, "Who is this who has won the victory over the spiritual enemy?" Jean Daniélou writes, "The mystery of the Ascension completely amazes the angels of heaven. For what it reveals to them is really a mystery, hidden up to then, an entirely new reality, disconcerting at first glance. The cosmological presentation of the descent and ascent must not deceive us. The true mystery of the nativity is the self-abasement of the divine Person of the Word, a 'little lower than the angels' (Heb. 2:7). And the true mystery of the Ascension is the exaltation of human nature above all the worlds of the angels. That is the real

double mystery, which is dramatically represented by the descent and ascent in the midst of the choirs of angels. But this 'dramaturgy,' as St. Gregory Nazianzen calls it, must not conceal the reality it bears beneath it. It represents an overthrow of the natural order of things resulting from the revelation of a reality absolutely new and unforeseeable (see Heb. 2:5-9). That is why it throws the angels into a state of astonishment. Gregory of Nyssa has admirably explained this revelation which the paradoxes of the Redemption of the Church made known to the angels. 'Indeed it is through the Church that the great and manifold wisdom of God is made known to the Powers above the heavens, this wisdom which works great marvels by means of opposites. For life is produced by death, blessing by curses, glory by dishonor. In the past the heavenly powers were familiar with the simple and uniform wisdom of God...but, they are now instructed by the Church seeing the Word made flesh, life joined together with death, our wounds healed by His stripes, the strength of the adversary overcome by the weakness of the Cross, the invisible manifested in the flesh.' " See Jean Daniélou *Angels and Their Mission: According to the Fathers of the Church* [Westminster, MD: Newman Press, 1957], 39-42.)

4. See Revelation 12:10-11. Chapter Nine is a verse by verse exposition of Revelation chapter 12.

5. See Galatians 3:9; Acts 7:53; Romans 2:13-15; 7:14. Although often distorted and regardless of how deviant, every society has norms for right and wrong behavior. Sydney H.T. Page observes that "if Colossians 2:15 refers to God's or Christ's rendering the powers impotent, the question arises as to how this relates to the canceling of the written code, which is mentioned in the previous verse. There is evidently some connection between the powers and the written code by which humanity stands condemned, but what is it? Perhaps the powers exercised their influence over humanity through legal regulations, that is by promoting the view that the way to please God is to conform to a set of religious and ethical rules. If this is the case, the disarming of the powers could relate to their losing their power to enslave people to a life of constant striving to reach perfection by following prescribed religious rituals and a strict code of conduct. Another possibility is that the powers are seen as sharing satan's role as accuser (see Job 1:9-11; Zech. 3:1; Rev. 12:10). On this view, Christ's death on the cross deprived the powers of their ability to demand a guilty verdict and its accompanying penalty for humanity. Since forgiveness is prominent in the immediate context, the latter explanation is preferable.

The mention of the disarming of the powers is followed in Colossians 2:15 by the statement '...he made a public spectacle of them.' The verb used here, *deigmatizo*, is not found elsewhere in the New Testament, but it seems to refer to exposure to shame" (Sydney H.T. Page, *Powers of Evil* [Grand Rapids: Baker Books, 1995], 253).

6. See Romans 7:14; Acts 26:18; Colossians 1:13.

7. See Romans 3:26. Since the wages of sin is death, God's plan of salvation was totally dependent on Jesus' sinless obedience unto death. Meanwhile, satan's only chance was to persuade Christ of another way or tempt Him to sin.

8. In the language of a courtroom, Paul's rhetorical question uses the Greek word *egkaleo* (charge), a technical, legal term meaning to call in like a debt on demand, to bring to account and thus accuse. Used with the preposition *kata,* meaning against or in opposition to, the verse contains both attributes of the devil (*slanderer*) and satan (*adversary*). Sydney H.T. Page points out that "John 16:11 speaks of the victory (of Christ) in the language of the law court rather than of the battlefield. Jesus says in 16:11 that the Holy Spirit will convict the world 'in regard to judgment, because the prince of this world now stands condemned.' The verb *condemn* (*krino*) appears in the perfect tense, indicating an action that, from the readers' standpoint, is past but has ongoing results. The verdict on satan is in. He has been found guilty and is now awaiting the execution of his sentence" (*Powers of Evil*, 140).

9. See Matthew 22:44; Hebrews 1:3.

10. God fashioned lucifer to function as a waster to destroy when he rebelled in the garden. Because of man's wickedness, this administration of death enabled men to see how bad sin is by experiencing its dreadful consequences. Scriptures that identify God as the Maker of evil [i.e., calamity] convey the sovereign justice of God in confining satan to move in his evil in order that men may justly reap what they sow. (See Isaiah 45:7.)

11. See Romans 8:28-39.

12. See Romans 8:31-32.

13. See Revelation 12:7.

14. Hebrews 12:1,23; see Revelation 3:21; 4:10; 5:4-11.

15. See Revelation 12:10-12.

16. See Ephesians 6:12.

17. See 2 Corinthians 12:2-4.

18. See Genesis 1:26; Deuteronomy 11:11,17; 2 Chronicles 7:13; Isaiah 55:9-11; Psalm 147:8; Zechariah 2:6; Matthew 24:30.

19. See Genesis 1:14; 15:5; Psalm 33:6; Isaiah 14:12; Jeremiah 23:24.

20. See Deuteronomy 10:14; 2 Chronicles 2:6; 6:18.

21. See 2 Corinthians 12:2-4.

22. See Exodus 20:22; Deuteronomy 4:36; Isaiah 57:15; 63:15; Matthew 3:17; 18:10; Luke 2:13-15; 22:43.

23. Ephesians 2:2; See Ephesians 6:12.

24. See Daniel 12:1ff.

25. Dr. C. Peter Wagner outlines three levels of spiritual warfare. Although interrelated, they include: 1) Ground-level warfare, such as the casting out of demons; 2) Occult-level warfare; and 3) Strategic-level warfare with high ranking territorial spirits like those listed in Ephesians 6:12. Since satan has been cast out of the third Heaven and we have been raised up to sit there with Christ, we have power over the evil one and can, in Christ, successfully wage war against him *on any and every level* (*Warfare Prayer* [Ventura, CA: Regal Books, 1992], 16-19).

Chapter Nine

The Accuser Cast Down

And I heard a loud voice saying in heaven, Now is come salvation, and strength, and the kingdom of our God, and the power of His Christ: for the accuser of our brethren is cast down, which accused them before our God day and night (Revelation 12:10).

Shortly after I became a Christian I had two vivid dreams in the space of a week. In the first one, I was in my car, my hands firmly on the steering wheel, moving at high speed. The problem was that it was pitch black all around and I could see nothing, not even in front of me. I had a great fear that I was going to crash at any moment, but there were no brakes at my feet. Suddenly, I cried out, "Jesus!" At that moment, the light went on in my room as my mother woke me up. That dream makes me think of Ephesians 5:14: "Wherefore He saith, Awake thou that sleepest, and arise from the dead, and Christ shall give thee light."

In my second dream, I was again in my car, but this time I could see. It was daylight, and I was reversing out of a dead-end circle with cars closely parked on either side. The tires were screeching, the gravel crunching beneath them, and although my hands were on the steering wheel, an unseen power was rapidly yet perfectly maneuvering the vehicle in reverse. Quickly I backed out of this descending, curving, dead-end road.

I believe that these were God-given dreams with significant meaning concerning my life in Christ. In both dreams, driving the car symbolized the direction my life was heading. The first showed how Christ had intervened in my life to prevent me from blindly rushing into a dead-end eternity; the second, how His control over my life enabled me to back out of bad associations and sinful habits.

Quite often with dreams and visions, dramatic events are conveyed through simple, straightforward symbolism. These symbols must be properly interpreted if the dream or vision is to be understood. Whenever the dream or vision comes from God, the interpretation must come through the Holy Spirit and be in harmony with God's written Word.[1] The classic New Testament example of this is the Book of Revelation. Although questions, mystery, and schemes of interpretation abound, Revelation has much to say to us when interpreted in the light of the rest of Scripture. It is the revelation of Jesus Christ, centering on His triumph, and when considering its message, it is important that we resist the tendency to place the events of the book exclusively in the future. Otherwise, like the first-century Jewish leaders who expected the Messiah to deliver them from Roman rule, or the disciples on the road to Emmaus who failed to recognize Christ, we may miss the message.[2] Because of misplaced expectations, we may fail to recognize the hour of our visitation or simply misinterpret the teaching of God's Word.

Most discussions of spiritual warfare place Revelation 12:10 in the future, but this doesn't fit with the whole tenor of Scripture, and it makes spiritual warfare at the strategic level impossible. If satan is still before the throne of God accusing us, then it follows that (1) he has the same position as the Church in Heaven; (2) he is not really under our feet; and (3) we can only confidently engage in ground-level spiritual warfare—provided we do not sin—for if the accuser were still in Heaven, we could not stand boldly before God's throne.

Charles Haddon Spurgeon, the great nineteenth-century English preacher, may never have presented a chronology of satan's career, but he did preach from the twelfth chapter of Revelation that Christ, through His death and resurrection, defeated the devil in the highest realm of Heaven. This victory over the accuser means that he can no longer bring a charge against us. Recognizing that Heaven has thus been cleansed of his presence is a key to victorious spiritual warfare. If, however, we consider this to be a future event, we may fail to appropriate what is ours right now.

The Woman Israel

Revelation chapter 12 presents one of the most detailed descriptions of the work, defeat, and fall of satan found anywhere in Scripture. The picture begins with a vivid scene portraying the entire history of Israel as a pregnant woman preparing to give birth, to bring Messiah into the world:

*And there appeared a **great wonder** in heaven; **a woman** clothed with the **sun**, and the **moon** under her feet, and upon her head a crown of twelve **stars**: and she being **with child** cried, **travailing in birth**, and pained **to be delivered*** (Revelation 12:1-2).

There is abundant scriptural support to interpret the pregnant woman as representing Israel. First, the mention of *sun, moon*, and *12 stars* is reminiscent of Genesis 37:9-10, where Joseph describes his dream to his brothers. There, the sun represents Joseph's father, Jacob; the moon, his mother Rachel; and the stars, Joseph's brothers. The entire incipient nation of Israel is represented. Another example is the prophet Jeremiah, who repeatedly uses the motif for Israel of "pain as a woman in travail."[3] After centuries of labor and travail, Israel at last brought forth the Christ child.[4]

Other interpretations exist, but none that hold up under careful study of context and Scripture-to-Scripture comparison. Some say the woman is Mary, the mother of Jesus, and the vision is her miraculous Assumption as Queen of Heaven—a far-fetched *assumption*. Mary Baker Eddy, founder of Christian Science, considered the woman to represent herself, the child her "brainchild" of Christian Science, and the dragon the mortal mind trying to destroy her new religion. (Of course, this was *all in her head*!) Still others say that the pregnant woman is the Church. This is unlikely because the Church did not give birth to Christ; on the contrary, Christ founded the Church. Also, in Revelation the Church is pictured not as an expectant mother but as a chaste bride expecting her bridegroom to come. Understanding the woman as representing Israel is the only interpretation that is consistent with the full testimony of Scripture.

The "sun" clothing of the woman also symbolizes the *Sun of righteousness*,[5] "a light to lighten the Gentiles, and the glory of thy people Israel."[6] From the beginning, Israel was clothed with the hope of Christ: Abraham's *Seed*, of the tribe of Judah and the lineage of David. All her prophets foretold the coming Man-child who would break the serpent's power and rule the nations. The "moon" under her feet represents the dispensation of the Law which, like the moon in relation to the sun, was merely a reflection of the good thing to come, not its substance.[7] The Law and the prophets bore witness of Christ, and Israel walked in the Law until she brought forth the Messiah.[8]

Her Adversary the Dragon

As the pregnant woman representing Israel seeks to deliver her Seed, the Messiah, the next character in this great cosmic drama appears: a horrible dragon waiting to devour the child. It is no surprise to find the serpent on the scene with the birth of the promised Seed imminent; from here until his trip to the lake of fire in the twentieth chapter, satan is on center stage in a big way. Satan is increasingly conspicuous in Christian circles and the secular media. Christian authors expose his devices and explain our spiritual warfare, while the secular world often magnifies the powers of darkness in books, magazines, and videos. With all the exposing and telecasting of the devil, it helps to know that when he appeared to devour the Man-child, it was he who was entrapped and bound to the earth by the cross; hence, we now see so much of his angry activity:

> *And there appeared **another** wonder in heaven; and behold a **great red dragon**, having seven heads and ten horns, and seven crowns upon his heads. And his tail drew the third part of the stars of heaven, and did cast them to the earth: and **the dragon stood** before the woman which was ready to be delivered, for **to devour her child** as soon as it was born* (Revelation 12:3-4).[9]

From the time that he was cursed in the garden, satan was behind the scenes trying to destroy the promised Seed: Cain slaying Abel, the pre-Flood decadence, Pharaoh's decree to kill the Israelite male children, Herod's massacre of the male babies in Bethlehem.[10] In his desperate attempt to prevent the coming of the promised Seed, satan employed the Egyptians, the Assyrians, the Babylonians, the Greeks, and finally pagan, imperial Rome (represented by the "seven heads and ten horns" of the dragon) "to devour her child as soon as it was born." Satan knew that if he could stop Christ at His birth he could remain in power, and his throne would be secure for future generations.

Human history is fraught with examples of rulers who have gone to any lengths to stay in power and who have opposed the ways and the people of God. One by one, however, they have fallen and come to nothing. Such is the end for all who would "take counsel together, against the Lord, and against His anointed"[11]: "For they are dead which sought the young child's life."[12] Before Jesus' appointed time, the enemy and his workers could not touch Him; when at last they were permitted to do so, they unwittingly fulfilled God's plan of redemption.

The Man-Child: Christ

The Man-child is the key to history, the One to rule all nations "with a rod of iron."[13] Christ alone is given that divine right and covenant promise.[14]

> *And she brought forth **a man child**, who was to **rule all nations** with a rod of iron: and her child was **caught up unto God**, and to **His throne**. And the woman **fled into the wilderness**, where she hath a place prepared of God, that they should feed her there **a thousand two hundred and threescore days*** (Revelation 12:5-6).

John's vision passes over the Lord's earthly ministry, going right to His ascension to show the onset of satan's judgment and the wrath that follows. Christ's exaltation brings us to the issue of heavenly authority. The unparalleled event of Christ ascending to God's right hand now becomes the notable factor in the rest of the heavenly vision, because no man before Christ was caught up to God's throne.[15]

Another clue identifying the woman as Israel is that she "fled into the wilderness."[16] Israel fled into the "wilderness of the peoples"[17] when, in A.D. 70, Rome under the command of General Titus destroyed Jerusalem and the times of the Gentiles began.[18]Although scattered among the nations, the culture and faith of the Jews were preserved and nourished. Indeed, with her mission as the Christ-carrier complete, the world would never be the same!

There are times in the course of history when a particular person, event, or invention unleashes radical, unalterable change. For example, a new government comes to power via independence from military or minority rule. Elections suddenly elevate a man and his party to the highest office in the land, replacing a former regime. In South Africa for example, after years of apartheid, Solomon's words were again illustrated, this time in the life of Nelson Mandela: "For out of prison he cometh to reign."[19] Similar changes have happened in all nations at one time or another, whether for good or evil.

Nothing in history can compare, however, to the level and scope of the transformation brought about by the ascension of Christ to the throne of God. The exodus, the dividing of the Kingdom, the rise and fall of the Roman Empire, the "conversion" of Constantine, the Reformation, the defeat of the Spanish Armada, the American Revolutionary War, Waterloo, World War II, the atom bomb, the demise of the Soviet Union— nothing, not even the effect of all these things combined, can be weighed in comparison to the ascension of Christ! It ignited a cosmic war in Heaven itself, bringing it down to the earthly arena, thus ushering in the last days and the beginning of the end of evil.

The War in Heaven

After Jesus Christ, Israel's Man-child, ascended, war broke out in the heavens. It was neither a prehistoric rebellion before creation nor a future conflict, but a just and holy war executing judgment against satan and his angels. What the prophets predicted, Christ accomplished:

> *And there was **war in heaven**: Michael and his angels fought against the dragon; and the **dragon** fought and his angels, and **prevailed not; neither was their place found any more in heaven*** (Revelation 12:7-8).

Skirmishes in the heavenlies had occurred even in Daniel's day when kingdoms were rising and falling. The heavenly host on God's right and left hand, Michael and satan, had often contended, but this was something altogether new. Christ had defeated the devil on earth, fair and square, and now He had entered Heaven victoriously! Satan's judgment was official, so all-out war was declared against him.

The order and sequence here is significant: "Michael and his angels" are spoken of first, because they were on the offensive, moving against satan and his angels. On the defensive and resisting fiercely, satan and his legions nevertheless could not hold their positions nor withstand the authority in which Michael moved. Michael was acting mightily upon the Word! Thus, satan and his angels were forcibly removed from their position in the third Heaven which they had occupied since creation. They were decisively removed with no further right whatsoever to be before God's throne. Satan's eviction was carried out at last!

The outcome of this war could not be more accurately summed up than with the words: "Neither was their place found any more in heaven." This was something new: satan was no longer among the host of Heaven, nor could he ever be again. What a victory! When Lord Nelson reported to the British admiralty his tremendous victory over the

French fleet in the Battle of the Nile, he said that *victory* was not a large enough word to describe what had taken place. During the Gulf War more than one commentator seized the phrase, "a victory of biblical proportions," to describe what the U.S.-led coalition achieved in 48 hours against the Iraqi army under Saddam Hussein. Nothing can compare, however, to the victory that Christ won by means of His death and resurrection: a victory beyond words, longed for since Eden, which every elect angel rejoiced in and every demon dreaded.

Satan Cast Down

The great dragon lost the war in Heaven and was cast down. He is no more in Heaven day and night accusing the brethren before God's throne; he can neither ask permission to test us as Job nor to sift us as Peter! Job's cry for an advocate was answered, and Peter's desperate need for a high priest was met when the Seed of the woman broke the serpent's authority! The Lord has broken the staff of the wicked one; He has drawn out leviathan by His cross and bound the strongman by His blood. The anointed cherub has been cast as profane out of the mountain of God:

*And the great dragon **was cast out,** that old serpent, called the Devil, and Satan, which deceiveth the whole world: he was **cast out** into the earth, and his angels were **cast out** with him* (Revelation 12:9).

Lucifer has fallen from Heaven like lightning. The thunderous sound of God's righteous condemnation against his proud rebellion still echoes throughout creation. What Jesus declared has happened: "Now shall the prince of this world be cast out."[20] What He saw in a vision is now reality: "I saw Satan fall like lightning from heaven."[21] Satan hit the earth and climbed skyward in a flash as far as his energy could carry him. The third Heaven, however, was now beyond his reach. Just as thunder draws our attention, all Heaven took note of satan's crackling judgment.[22]

In A.D. 79 the famous eruption of Mt. Vesuvius wiped out the Roman cities of Pompeii and Herculaneum. In a similar fashion, the prophetic rumblings of the promised Seed, the great shakings of His advent, and the explosion of His resurrection erupted in Heaven when the Man-child ascended. Satan and his angels were swept out of God's presence amid the superheated, red-hot, fiery judgment of God![23]

The Proclamation in Heaven

With the ascension of Christ, our victory became assured in Heaven. Christ's salvation, power, and Kingdom have been established in Heaven with full and absolute authority. Jesus overcame the devil and has been awarded all authority at God's right hand. Our power to overcome satan is based on the Man-child's exaltation in Heaven.[24] Having conquered sin, death, and the grave, He rose for our justification, and is now exalted above every name that is named, not only in this age, but also the age that is to come. At His name, every knee must bow and every tongue confess that Jesus is Lord:[25]

*And I heard a **loud voice** saying in heaven, **Now is come** salvation, and strength, and the kingdom of our God, and **the power** of His Christ: for **the accuser** of our brethren **is cast down**, which accused them before our God day and night* (Revelation 12:10).

All Heaven proclaims that the accuser is cast down. Christ has defeated him in the earthly arena, winning the day for us. His victory is ours. Let the church bells ring: It's V-day! What is proclaimed in Heaven, we should shout from the housetops: "Now is come salvation!"

During the Civil War, President Abraham Lincoln issued the Emancipation Proclamation freeing black Americans from slavery. They were free to live where they wanted and to vote and own property. Nevertheless, their previous oppressors used illegal power and illegitimate authority to deny them their rights. As a result, many former slaves failed to realize any of the benefits of emancipation. After the Civil War, some even returned to their places in the slave gangs under their old masters. Outwardly, nothing seemed to have changed as their oppressors, although defeated in the war, appeared as powerful as ever, angry, bitter, and prepared to do anything to remain in control. Although change did come, it was not immediate. As with the children of Israel possessing the promised land, possessing what was promised required a good fight of faith plus endurance! So it is for the Church on earth. Much territory remains to be won; the war is not yet over, but it has moved to its final arena.

War on Earth

Just because Christ ascended to Heaven and satan was cast down does not mean that all is well. Those who dwell in Heaven are told to rejoice, but the earth is in for woe for a while, a short time, while satan's anger is unleashed in the earthly arena:

> *Therefore **rejoice**, ye **heavens**, and ye that dwell in them. **Woe to** the inhabiters of the **earth** and of the sea! for **the devil** is come down unto you, having **great wrath**, because he knoweth that he hath but a **short time**. And when the dragon saw that he was cast unto the earth, he **persecuted** the woman which brought forth the man child. ... And the dragon was **wroth** with the woman, and went to **make war** with the remnant of her seed, which keep the commandments of God, and have the testimony of Jesus Christ (Revelation 12:12-13,17).*

Satan is very angry because he lost his proud position of influence in Heaven. Although he can never again access the throne of God, he still has a place on earth due to the ongoing rebellion of mankind. Herein lies the source of every injustice and tyranny. God does not disregard man's earthly woes. On the contrary, He is engaged in the work of salvation among all nations, not willing that any should perish. Yet, when God executes His eternal judgment against satan and his angels, mankind must also be judged. In this interim of grace, satan wages an angry war against the woman and her seed because Israel brought forth the Man-child (and even now is the divine timepiece for reckoning satan's remaining moments) and also because the remnant of her seed carries the testimony of Jesus. Once the good news of Christ is proclaimed to every nation and people group, and again to Israel, satan's time will be up.

We who carry God's testimony of salvation in Christ must endure hardships as good soldiers. Many missionaries testify that the last onslaught of heathenism is the most ferocious; it is darkest just before dawn. The same is true in an individual's life, as often things gets worse before they get better. Remember the case of the demonized boy: "And they *brought him unto* Him: and *when he saw Him*, straightway the *spirit tare him*; and he fell on the ground, and wallowed *foaming.* ...and he was *as one dead*; insomuch that *many said, he is dead*. But Jesus took him by the hand, and lifted him up; and *he arose*" (Mk. 9:20,26-27). The disciples asked Jesus why they were unable to cast out the spirit. Many believers today wonder why they do not see God's power to deliver. They wonder, *Where is God?* I believe that we will only see such power when we engage the enemy with Jesus' kind of faith. Christ did not ignore the devil in the hope that satan would go away of his own accord. These spirits only depart when we exercise Christ's authority. When the Anointed One comes down from the mount, as He did then, the demons will sorely cry out.[26]

It is vital to stress that Christ's exaltation does not mean peace on earth, but a sword and fire.[27] Before the arrival of a new earth of righteousness and peace will come a final battle on this earth with evil. We need therefore to know the reality of Christ's victory. We must *stand* our ground in these days of intense demonic activity: "And the God of peace shall bruise Satan under your feet *shortly*" (Rom. 16:20a). As we submit to God and resist the devil, he will flee,[28] bruised under our feet as we walk in the Spirit. In this war, faith is a shield to block doubt, fear, and unbelief, and the Word of God is a sword that pierces the works of darkness.

Positionally, satan and his minions are now under our feet as believers. This is a truth too few Christians realize. There are real, practical implications to this truth that can make a significant difference in our daily lives as believers and our engagement in spiritual warfare.

Endnotes

1. See Daniel 2:18-47.

2. Approaching God's Word in a manner that *demands* a certain interpretation can lead to error when certain verses or passages are forced into a preconceived theological mold.

3. See Jeremiah 4:31; 13:21; 22:23; 30:6; 49:24; 50:43.

4. See Genesis 3:15; Isaiah 66:7-8; Micah 4:9-10; 5:2; John 16:21; Romans 9:4-5; Galatians 4:19.

5. See Malachi 4:2.

6. Luke 2:32.

7. See Colossians 2:16-17; Hebrews 10:1.

8. See Galatians 3:19ff.

9. Notice that the word *and* appears in every verse of Revelation 12. The entire chapter is connected as one glorious vision confirming that satan was cast out of Heaven when Jesus ascended.

10. See Matthew 2:16. Herod the Great did everything he could to preserve his throne. He even slew his wife and his sons to preserve his rule. He systematically hunted down the last of the Hasmonean line to

eliminate them from claiming the throne. More than once he ran to Rome to maintain his crown; in 37 B.C. to Antony and in 31 B.C. to Octavian. It was easy for satan to urge Herod to kill the babies in Bethlehem in his attempt to destroy the Christ child.

11. Psalm 2:2.

12. Matthew 2:20b.

13. See Psalm 2:7-9; Revelation 2:26-28; 19:15.

14. See Psalm 2:1ff.

15. See John 3:13.

16. This speaks of the time of the Gentiles, when Israel was led away captive into all nations, and Jerusalem was trodden down of the Gentiles (see Lk. 21:24; Rom. 11:24-26). It is a prolonged period of testing. Also measured in years (as three and one half or *a broken in half seven*, which is the number of fulfillment), it indicates a restless, incomplete period, also referred to as "a time, and times, and half a time," or 42 months (see Rev. 11:11; 12:14).

17. Ezekiel 20:35 NKJ.

18. See Luke 21:24ff; Romans 11:25ff.

19. Ecclesiastes 4:14a.

20. John 12:31b; see John 12:29.

21. Luke 10:18b NKJ.

22. In John's Gospel, the casting down of satan is preceded by what sounded like thunder (see Jn. 12:29,31). In Luke, the metaphor is that of lightning (see Lk.10:18).

23. This guarantees satan's fiery removal from the heavenlies. His time is short, and his casting down has already begun, the phase of his final judgment ending in the lake of fire.

24. See Hebrews 7:25.

25. See Philippians 2:9-11.

26. The wars, murders, robberies, rapes, and various outrageous crimes of our day are indications that the appearing of Christ is at hand. We look at this feature of the accuser and the last days in Chapter Thirteen.

27. See Matthew 10:34.

28. See James 4:7.

Chapter Ten

The Accuser Under Our Feet

Which He wrought in Christ, when He raised Him from the dead, and set Him at His own right hand in the heavenly places, far above all principality, and power, and might, and dominion...and hath put all things under His feet, and gave Him to be the head over all things to the church, which is His body, the fulness of Him that filleth all in all (Ephesians 1:20-23).

I really liked the greeting card I saw once that said on the front in big, bold letters, **"Keep Looking Down!"** The completed message on the inside read, **"For You Are Seated Together With Christ In Heavenly Places!"** Positionally, as believers we are seated with Christ at God's right hand in the highest Heaven where we enjoy a far better and more exalted place than does satan. Someone once boldly declared, "If you have a message for the devil, write it on the soles of your shoes because he is under your feet."

There is a story told about the great evangelist, Smith Wigglesworth, who was awakened one night to find satan in his bedroom. Recognizing the devil for who he was, Wigglesworth said, "Oh, it's only you," and without concern simply went back to sleep. He understood his place in Christ and knew that the devil was beneath his feet.

A Bible teacher I had as a new believer said one time that satan was still before God's throne accusing us! Perhaps in his own conscience, experience, and understanding of eschatology this seemed to be the case.

The Bible, however, teaches that satan is under our feet. In Christ we have been raised "*far above* all principality and power" (Eph. 1:21). Otherwise, how could we "tread on serpents and scorpions, and over all the power of the enemy"?[1] Also, why would Paul tell the Roman believers that "the God of peace shall bruise Satan *under* your feet shortly," if he wasn't under our feet?[2] How can satan be under our feet and at the same time be accusing us to God in Heaven? He can't!

It is difficult to fight a foe you can neither locate nor determine the size of. That is why guerrilla warfare is so dangerous and reconnaissance so essential. Far too many Christians today are unaware of satan's present position and *modus operandi*.[3] To make matters worse, they lack knowledge regarding their true standing in Christ. It is important that we learn to appropriate what is positionally ours: to abide in the high seat Christ has provided for us in Heaven, walking in the Spirit's power so that every place that the soles of our feet tread upon may be given to us. Because of our position in Christ, we can overcome the devil in every area of life.

Far Above From Head to Feet

The apostle Paul says more in Ephesians about our heavenly position in Christ than all the rest of the New Testament writers combined. Let's follow his teaching through Ephesians, beginning with his praise to God the Father "who hath blessed us with all spiritual blessings in heavenly places in Christ" (Eph. 1:3b). Paul states that spiritual blessings originate in a heavenly realm where God "hath chosen us in Him [Christ] before the foundation of the world, that we should be holy and without blame before Him in love" (Eph. 1:4). The Father adopted us in Christ into His family, and from this vantage point we are forever free from the accusations of the accuser.

All fatherhood derives its nature from God, and human fathers naturally desire the best for their children.[4] Provision, nurture, and security are the norms for fathering, even among sinners.[5] Unfortunately, most of the religious world, including many professing Christians, do not know God as Father; yet this is at the heart of what it means to be a child of God.

Jesus told His first, small flock of followers not to fear, "for it is your Father's good pleasure to give you the kingdom."[6] Christ came down from Heaven to reveal God as Father and thus bring many sons to glory.[7] In John's Gospel alone, Jesus calls God "Father" over 100 times.

Madam Sheik, in her book, *I Dared to Call Him Father*, shares how this revelation of God as Father caused her to convert from a strict Muslim family to the household of God. Economically and socially it meant losing everything, even possibly her life, but her Father in Heaven was more than adequate to raise her above such concerns.

Continuing his theme of our position in Christ, Paul writes that God *"hath raised us up together, and made us sit together in heavenly places in Christ Jesus"* (Eph. 2:6). As we come to know God as our Father we will also come to understand what we as His children have in Him: an inheritance so rich that we are "heirs of God, and joint heirs with Christ."[8] Our heavenly Father provides everything we need: both the hope of our calling and the power to fulfill it.[9]

There, at the Father's right hand, Christ as the Head and we as His Body have a heavenly position so exalted that all things are under our feet. In a state far superior to even Moses' covenant blessings, we are united to the head and not the tail, above and not beneath,[10] and we are no longer subject to the spirit of the prince of the power of the air![11]

As we abide in Christ even the lowest place is above that of the principalities and powers.[12] There are many places in the heavenlies, and where we sit is directly related to our response to the Father. God honors those who respond to His love in Christ and sits them in His presence accordingly.[13] The Father offers us an ever-higher realm of living. "Come up higher," He beckons, but we must answer this upward call in Christ Jesus.[14] When we do, He raises us up to higher degrees of glory.[15]

In Ephesians 2:7, Paul speaks of "the exceeding riches of His grace in His kindness toward us through Christ Jesus," and a little later states that "through Him we both have access by one Spirit unto *the Father*," and are citizens of "the household of God" (Eph. 2:18-19). It is important that we understand this, because without an ongoing revelation of the Fatherhood of God, we will fail to fully access and abide in this exalted relationship.[16] We may forget who we are and what our relationship to God means and behave like mere men, rather than like children of God.

Once when I was traveling, I needed money but hadn't used my local money card for several weeks. When I tried to use it, I realized I had forgotten the access number. I knew the money was there, but I couldn't draw upon it. Although my position with the bank was fine, from the practical standpoint it was of no account. We must remain continually conscious of who we are in Christ and remember to access the place we have in Heaven at God's right hand. *Through faith in Christ* and by the Holy Spirit, we can remain day and night before God's throne and continually receive every spiritual blessing. There is no religious formula, nor do we access God's blessings by works of righteousness: "Say not in thine heart, Who shall ascend into heaven?"[17] It is because of the Father's rich mercy and great love.

Further on in his letter to the Ephesians, Paul prays that the saints will grasp the full dimensions of the Father's love: Christ's glorious presence in their lives, producing inward strength, established faith and deep love (see Eph. 3:16-17), so that they will "be able to comprehend with all saints what is the breadth, and length, and depth, and height; and to know the love of Christ, which passeth knowledge, that ye might be filled with all the fulness of God" (Eph. 3:18-19).

We can lay hold of the Father's great love. His love alone can fill us with *all the fullness of God*. This works a power through us *beyond what we can ask or imagine*. It is a love so *wide* that it came to us while we were His enemies and made us His children, so *long* that it began before time and extends throughout all eternity, so *deep* that it brought Christ down from Heaven into the place of the dead, and so *high* that it raises us up to the highest Heaven, even as high as Christ is exalted.[18]

The world may not acknowledge us as God's children; it did not even recognize the *Son of God*.[19] Nevertheless, we are His children right now. That is the kind of love that the Father has bestowed on us, and our lives become a display of His love when we follow Him as dear children (Eph. 5:1-2). This revelation of the Father's love through Christ is now openly declared through the Church.[20] In the past, the nations did not know or enjoy such a relationship with God because Christ had not yet come to reveal the Father and deliver them from the evil principalities.

The Church and the Principalities

Paul concisely defined his mission as "preach[ing] among the Gentiles the unsearchable riches of Christ" (Eph. 3:8b). These same riches are ours as "fellowheirs, and of the same body, and partakers of His promise in Christ by the gospel" (Eph. 3:6). This dramatic advancement in rank relates us in an exciting new way to the principalities and powers in the heavenly places:

> *To the* **intent** [purpose] *that* **now** *unto the principalities and powers in heavenly* **places** *might be* **known** *by* [through] **the church** *the manifold* **wisdom** *of God* (Ephesians 3:10).

For both the evil and the elect angels, God's eternal purpose is revealed in the Church. The "principalities and powers in heavenly places" come to know experientially through us the manifold wisdom of God in at least three ways:

- They see through the Church a fuller, more complete and expansive view of God's character and infinite perfection.
- They experience God for themselves in a new dimension beyond all their past experiences.
- They understand that the consummation of all things in Heaven and in earth is centered in the Church's mission and composition.

1. The principalities and powers see through the Church a fuller, more complete and expansive view of God's character and infinite perfection.

These supernatural beings come to fathom God's absolute holiness *and* His boundless love. As glorious grace follows the preaching of the gospel, with the Holy Spirit sent down from Heaven, there are "things which have now already been made known plainly to you...Into these things [the very] angels long to look!"[21] There are things about God that neither the angels of God nor the angels of satan know, nor can know, except as they are made manifest in the Church. This is mainly because of the great mystery of Christ made one with the Church. It is glorious to think that we are "members of His body, of His flesh, and of His bones" (Eph. 5:30), and "the fulness of Him that filleth all in all" (Eph. 1:23). We are "builded together for an habitation of God through the Spirit" (Eph. 2:22b), and can "be filled with all the fulness of God" (Eph. 3:19b). By faith we can grow "unto a perfect man, unto the measure of the stature of the fulness of Christ" (Eph. 4:13b). This reality amazes Michael and his angels and terrifies satan and his demons.[22]

It thrills me to hear testimonies of what God has done in the lives of people. At times I am amazed to see what our Father has delivered them from: alcoholism, polygamy, wife beating, adultery, you name it! Not only does He deliver them; He also makes them into His children, the purest, kindest people of all! I'm sure the early followers of Christ, like Matthew the tax collector, Simon the Zealot, and Mary of Magdalene, all received angelic attention: "And when the devil was cast out...the multitudes marvelled, saying, It was never so seen in Israel."[23]

At one time, my friend Ron was a drug addict, serving time in a state penitentiary for an armed robbery conviction. Now he is a missionary setting others free in the town of Karoi, Zimbabwe. In the Shona language, Karoi means "little witch," and a witch on a broomstick is on a sign posted as you enter and leave town. The area is well known for its witchcraft and demonic activity. It is no wonder that Ron experienced great opposition as he pioneered a church-planting there. Unable to secure any property in the town, the church was forced to vacate the building it had rented due to slanderous lies.

Ron and I fasted and spent hours in prayer each day before conducting a crusade on a farm. The farm occupied the highest hill on the outskirts of town. As we preached, the power of God mightily manifested and demons shrieked out of people. One woman fell to the ground and spoke in another voice as she moved across the floor like a snake toward the door. There were powerful deliverances. During the evangelistic meetings that week the high ground was taken from the devil in more than one sense.[24] The church was able to purchase that very farm some two years later and today God's people use two large buildings on that hillside for church services. God's grace is truly amazing! What He does in and through people is as astounding as what Christ did for us. No wonder the angels wish to look into these things!

Consider the apostle Paul, who wrote so much concerning the hidden truths of the gospel: a former blasphemer and persecutor of the Church who threw men and women into prison and even consented to Stephen's death. When Paul met Christ, he was gloriously transformed. From the *chiefest* of sinners to the chiefest apostle, he was made a *spectacle* to angels.[25] Fallen and elect angels both cared more about Paul and his whereabouts than they did the Roman emperor. A major concern of the devil was to prevent apostolic men from coming to the Thessalonian church, but he could at best only hinder them. Time and again the angels of God stood with Paul. They were there when he fought with beasts at Ephesus.[26] A Roman ship at sea would have been lost with all her passengers if God had not given His angels a charge concerning Paul.[27]

2. The principalities and powers experience God through the Church in a new dimension beyond all their past experiences.

The angels were never mere spectators, but always active participants in God's cosmic plan. Before the advent of Christ, the principalities and powers were involved in administrating the world, exercising a dominion from Heaven to earth.[28] When the last Adam came down from Heaven and then ascended far above all principalities and powers, a new dispensation began. The world came under a new administration.[29] The Son of Man now rules from the heavenly Mount Zion.

As a result of the exaltation of Christ, the principalities now know God in a new dimension. Jean Daniélou points this out when he writes:

"The Ascension is not only the elevation of Christ in His Body into the midst of the angels; to be more theologically precise, it is the exaltation of human nature, which the Word of God has united to Himself, above all the angelic orders which were superior to it. This is a complete reversal of the regular order, and it affords the angels an 'unheard-of' spectacle. The overwhelming revelation made to the angels in the mystery of the Ascension is not that they are to adore the Eternal Word—that is already the object of their liturgy; but rather that they are to adore the Word Incarnate—and that overturns all of heaven, just as the Incarnation revolutionized all of earth."[30]

St. John Chrysostom developed Paul's thoughts further when he wrote:

"Today we are raised up into heaven, we who seemed unworthy even of earth. We are exalted above the heavens; we arrive at the kingly throne. The nature, which caused the Cherubim to keep guard over Paradise, is seated today above the Cherubim. Was it not enough to be elevated into heaven? Was it not enough to have a place among the angels? Was this not a glory beyond all expression? But He rose above the angels, He passed the Cherubim, He went higher than the Seraphim, He bypassed the Thrones, He did not stop until He arrived at the very Throne of God."[31]

The angels observed new creatures, full of the Holy Spirit and positioned in Christ at God's right hand, exercising heavenly authority. A New Man emerged with a mighty body whose head had been given "all power and authority in heaven and in earth."[32] With delegated authority in Jesus' name and power by His Spirit, the members of this Body exercise His rule on earth, speaking God's Word and delivering men from satan's kingdom.[33] The holy angels ministered to the heirs of salvation and rejoiced when one sinner repented; whereas evil angels plotted their harm.[34] Moreover, the evil principalities sought to hinder the messengers and distort the message whenever possible.[35] Both the angels and demons continue to this hour; the former in cooperation with, the latter in conflict against, the Church on earth.[36]

When my wife Pat and I flew to Zimbabwe in 1986, we discovered that the devil had taken an earlier flight. He was in Madrid to steal our money, at Jan Smuts Airport in South Africa to deny us passage through that country, and he rented an apartment next to ours when we finally arrived in Harare. The night we finished our first church meeting, our upset neighbor banged on our door, screaming, "American crap!" We could have been intimidated or developed a martyr's complex if we had not known who we were, who we served, and who we were wrestling against. People like you and me are made more than conquerors in Christ. We are no mere pawns in this celestial chess match of intelligent spirit beings. Christ transforms men, women, and children into kings, queens, and bishops. Our words and actions are energized with the supernatural powers of the age to come. By faith, we bring to naught the noble, mighty rulers of this age.

Julian the Apostate tried to light again the fires on the altars of the pagan gods. In the year A.D. 363, he was on the march with his army in the campaign against Persia. A Christian was being abused by some of the soldiers. "Where is your carpenter now?" one of them mocked. "He is making a coffin for your emperor," replied the Christian. A few months later Julian received a mortal wound in battle. The rumor quickly spread through the army that a Christian Roman soldier inflicted the wound. According to the story by Theodoret, Julian, realizing that his death was near, dipped his hand in his bloody wound and threw the blood toward heaven, exclaiming as he did so, "Thou hast conquered, O Galilean!"

Yes, exalted to the right hand of God, Jesus of Nazareth has won the day. He has established an everlasting kingdom. Kings and kingdoms come and go. One by one they flourish and are gone, but Christ builds His Church and the gates of hell cannot prevail against her.[37] He is the Rock cut out of the Kingdom of Heaven that has smitten the kingdoms of this world. With Him, we are living stones that beat small every opposing rule. Indeed, we have now become a great mountain that fills all the earth.[38] Around A.D. 150 during a time of intense persecution, a Christian wrote to the Roman emperor that, "we are but of yesterday and we have filled all that belongs to you: the cities, the fortresses, the free towns, the very camps, the palace, the Senate, the Forum. We leave to you the temples only."[39]

God exhibits His purposes and powers through the Church. His purpose of gathering together in Christ "all things which are in heaven and on earth" into one elect *family* where all opposing rule, authority, and power has been put down, makes for quite a cosmic drama,[40] one in which the vested interests of angels and men display the variegated wisdom of God, creating an intricate pattern of mercy and justice, grace and law, spirit and flesh, power and weakness. Paul was so caught up in this marvelous, divine display of fireworks between Heaven and earth that he could say, "Know ye not that we shall judge angels?"[41] Even now, we judge the evil angels as we pull their strongholds down.

*3. The principalities and powers understand that the consumma-
tion of all things in Heaven and in earth is centered in the Church's
mission and composition.*[42]

The angels don't know the final day or hour, but they do know it's
only a short time away.[43] They realize that once all those whom the
Father has given to the Son are His, then the end shall come. The Church
is Christ's Body. He accomplishes world evangelization and discipleship among the nations through her.[44] No wonder the gates of hell seek
to prevent the Church from advancing and wage an angry war against
her.[45] They know that with every conversion to Christ, their kingdom is
weakened, and their end draws nearer. It especially terrifies them when
a new field of evangelism is opened in a nation, that has not yet heard
of Christ's victory and of satan's demise. Therefore, they raise persecutions and problems to halt the spread of the gospel.[46]

After two months in Zimbabwe, Pat and I were denied renewals on our
visitor's visas. The Immigration official gave us seven days to leave the
country. From the day we had arrived in Harare for the great Fire
Conference conducted by evangelist Reinhard Bonnke, we had heard stories of missionaries who could not get work permits. It was nearly impossible, we were told, and everybody seemed to know someone who had to
leave the country. Fellow believers would ask us how we were in the
country. When we said, "On a visitor's visa," they would say, "We hope
you have heard from God." Although we had applied for permits while we
were still in the United States, we had heard nothing from Immigration,
but we believed we had heard from God and entered the country in time
for the conference.

Now, instead of work permits, we were given seven days to leave the
country. When I got off the elevator and walked out of the government
building, satan was on the sidewalk waiting for me. "You've got seven days
to pack and leave!" he shouted. Then he quickly reminded me of what had
happened in 1981. At that time, I was only scheduled for a short-term mission of four months, but the leadership at the church encouraged me to stay
and marry my fiancée, Pat Donohoue, in Zimbabwe. After praying much
about it, I sensed God's direction and confirmation to do so. My fiancée
received the same guidance, and was Rebecca to my Isaac, crossing a
wilderness of water to be my bride.

Both from large families in Cincinnati, we could have married in our
hometown with many guests present. Instead, about 30 people attended
our wedding in Zimbabwe. I hardly knew my best man, and Pat did not

know her bridesmaids. Four months later, all the open doors suddenly closed. The country had gone through a devastating civil war, and many families had left. There was also a shake-up in the church, and we were told that we would have to return to America.

We had planned to spend our lives in Zimbabwe! God had called us here! Had we somehow missed it? Two days before leaving Zimbabwe to return to the United States for Bible school, we received a Temporary Work Permit, which I filed away. I thought I would never see Zimbabwe again. I questioned whether I had really heard from God. It had made no sense to marry in Zimbabwe only to return to the States four months later. That was 1981.

Now in 1986, I felt the same way again. There on the street I said, "Oh God, haven't I heard You? Wasn't it You who spoke to me in so many ways?" I recalled how clearly God had spoken to me during those years from 1983 to 1985 about returning to Zimbabwe. A missionary from South America came to Centerville to do our Bible school's graduation service. He was unaware when he prophesied over me that I was again pondering the mission field in my heart. "God has put something in your heart," he said, "and you are hearing from Him." A couple of weeks before graduation I awoke in the middle of the night with God's presence so tangible in the room. He spoke to me about returning to Zimbabwe. As I asked Him for confirmation, He directed me to open the hymnal on the table: hymn number 154. His Spirit flooded my heart and tears filled my eyes as I read that missionary hymn. I'll never forget its resounding words: "Send forth laborers, Lord, for the harvest is great, but the laborers few." In 1981, I had seen the need for laborers.

Over the space of three years God had spoken to me regularly about returning. On one occasion, when I was working as a hospital orderly, I was taking a woman down to surgery for an emergency operation to stop a hemorrhage. I spoke to her of the woman in the Bible who had an issue of blood, and although she did not know my past short-term mission service or anything about me, this elderly Pentecostal woman began to prophesy and the presence of God manifested in that hospital's room. She said, "The Lord has called you and is sending you to a *faraway place*." There it was again! I wrote it down and carried it in my wallet for two years.

Pat and I had later communicated our call and started a non-denominational missionary society. We canvassed with churches and friends and gradually got things ready for our return to Zimbabwe. As I gave notice at the hospital, we sent out a couple of newsletters and whittled all our belongings down to a few boxes that we sent ahead by boat to Zimbabwe. Then we flew with one-way air tickets to South Africa. Now we had seven days to pack and leave! Customs had not even released the household items we had posted from Cincinnati. The thought of returning in defeat was unacceptable! When I went to the apartment to lock my door and pray, God encouraged me from the Psalms of David. "They that trust in the Lord shall be as mount Zion, which *cannot be removed, but abideth for ever*" (Ps. 125:1), and "Trust in the Lord, and do good; so shalt thou *dwell* in the land, and verily thou shalt be *fed*" (Ps. 37:3).

We desperately needed a Residency Permit and food, but the permit was more urgent. On the fifth day, I decided to go and appeal to Immigration, although I didn't know whom I should see. Jesus was our only contact in high places. So I just got on the elevator and went to a higher floor than on my previous visit. (Obviously, I needed to speak to someone higher up.) When I got off the elevator, I nervously knocked on one of the many doors. The official in this office kindly listened to my appeal and decided to look for my file. When he found my old file, he discovered the work permit that we had been granted in 1981. As a result, he advised me to fill out an application for a Resumption of Residency. With that, our visitor's visas were extended for another two months.

Then the chief Immigration officer and his board considered our application. When we were informed that we were given Resumption Status, making us permanent residents, free even from the confines of a Work Permit, we experienced a glorious resurrection. Being two of the last missionaries to receive permanent residency, we finally understood why we had been married in Zimbabwe. Although five years had expired, God's plan had come to pass. Everyone we knew who heard the news rejoiced!

At times it has been a struggle, but it has been unquestionably worthwhile. Today we are seeing great results in Zimbabwe and the neighboring nations. Many are genuinely turning to Christ and evidences of a grassroots move toward God abound. Time and again, we have seen God's power and favor subdue opposing forces: "Now I want you to know, brothers, that what has happened to me has really served to advance the gospel."[47] Jesus' method is men and His program is witnessing in the power of the Holy Spirit. Hence, satan's attacks against the Church are against individuals.[48] In fact, when we are on the offensive, we actually provoke the principalities in what Dr. C. Peter Wagner has aptly called *power encounters*.[49] Christ's painful death and glorious resurrection are both our victory and our pattern.[50]

Make no mistake about it: satan is now under our feet. He may rant and rave, fuss and fume, and even mount temptations, persecutions, and other attacks against us to intimidate and discourage us and destroy our effectiveness in living for Christ. If we abide in Christ, however, and claim our heritage and true position before God, satan has no power over us. In fact, God will even use satan's tactics against him. *When we faithfully endure the enemy's onslaughts of temptations and trials, the death and resurrection principle of God's Kingdom then operates: the very things that seem dead set against us become the very things God uses for us.*

Endnotes

1. Luke 10:19; see Matthew 10:1.

2. Romans 16:20a.

3. Satan's *modus operandi* is based on a final *modus vivendi* that is outlined for us in Scripture, and which explains how he *now* operates. Throughout this book, the focus is on the clear teaching of Scripture concerning satan's work as the accuser, consciously avoiding anything that cannot be substantiated from a number of Bible passages.

4. See Ephesians 3:15.

5. See Matthew 7:11.

6. Luke 12:32.

7. See Hebrews 2:10.

8. Romans 8:17.

9. See Ephesians 1:16-19.

10. See Deuteronomy 28:13.

11. See Ephesians 2:1-6.

12. The Greek construction of Ephesians 1:21, "far above," conveys the concept of a great distance, completely out of satan's reach. Perhaps there is a parallel between the three levels of Sheol (Hades) and Heaven in that there was a great gulf between the lower two (Tartarus and Gehenna) and the highest abode (Abraham's bosom). So there may be a great gulf between the first two heavens and the third.

13. See Matthew 23:12; Luke 14:7-11; John 12:26.

14. See Philippians 3:14.

15. See Luke 7:47; 2 Corinthians 3:18; Ephesians 5:1; Hebrews 2:10.

16. See Ephesians 1:3,16ff; 3:14ff.

17. Romans 10:6b.

18. See Ephesians 3:14-21.

19. See 1 John 3:1-2.

20. See Ephesians 3:1-9.

21. See 1 Peter 1:12 (AMP).

22. There may be songs that we can sing that the angels cannot, but the Scriptures teach that they have also been affected by what God did in Christ. How could they not be touched when their King laid aside His glory and became flesh? God's grace upon men through Christ is a revelation to all creation. Christ died in our place and raised us up together with Himself.

23. See Matthew 9:33.

24. It is common knowledge in Zimbabwe that every acre of land is claimed by the *mhondoro*, the spirit of the dead chief, which is said to rule over it as his possession. Beyond the local spirits, however, there are also national spirits that are given homage and allegiance through religious rituals and practices.

25. See 1 Corinthians 4:9.

26. See Acts 27:21-44; 1 Corinthians 15:32.

27. See Acts 27:22-25.

28. See Hebrews 2:5ff.

29. See Ephesians 1:10; 3:2; Hebrews 2:2-9.

30. Jean Daniélou, *Angels and Their Mission: According to the Fathers of the Church*, (Westminster, MD: Newman Press, 1957), 36.

31. Cited by Daniélou in *Angels and Their Mission,* 36.

32. See Matthew 28:18.

33. See Matthew 5:13-14; 16:18-19; 18:18.

34. See Hebrews 1:14; Ephesians 5:11.

35. See Luke 15:10; 1 Thessalonians 2:18; Galatians 5:7.

36. See 1 Corinthians 4:9; 11:10.

37. See Matthew 16:18.

38. See Daniel 2:34-45.

39. S.M. Houghton, *Sketches From Church History* (Carlisle, PA: Banner of Truth Trust, 1980), 11.

40. See Ephesians 1:10; 3:15; 1 Corinthians 15:24.

41. 1 Corinthians 6:3a.

42. See Ephesians 5:26-27; Matthew 24:14; 28:19; Revelation 5:9.

43. See Matthew 24:36; Revelation 12:12.

44. See 2 Peter 3:10; Revelation 6:14; 21:11.

45. See Revelation 12:13-17; 13:6-7.

46. The principalities and powers are intelligent, but they are far from all-knowing. Many teach that they were unaware of God's intention of bridging the gulf between Jew and Gentile and creating a new man in which the walls of separation are broken down. Nevertheless, after Christ ascended and poured out the Holy Spirit on the day of Pentecost, men from diverse nations received the gospel. It spread from Jerusalem, Judea, and Samaria to the uttermost parts of the earth. Now as members from every nation, tribe and tongue are added to the Church (in spite of every opposing effort from the principalities), God's intention and proclamation through the Church is made known to the principalities: hell's gates cannot prevail against the Church.

47. Philippians 1:12 NIV; see Romans 8:28.

48. See Mark 1:17; 1 Corinthians 1:21; 2:1-4.

49. *Confronting the Powers* by C. Peter Wagner.

50. Joseph's dream and slavery before his exaltation, Moses' failure and wilderness before the Exodus deliverance, and David's anointing and flight before his reign may have been part of the Emmaus road sermon of Jesus and may be part our experience as His disciples (see Lk. 24:13-27,46).

Part Two

The Cleansing of the Heavens Applied

Chapter Eleven

The Accuser and Spiritual Warfare

Satan and his legions were cast out of the third Heaven with the ascension of Christ, and their activities are now limited to the first and second heavens. Positionally, satan is under our feet as believers because we have been seated with Christ in heavenly places; a transformation that the angels of Heaven observe in wonder and amazement. As children of the Father, and through the power of the Spirit, we have authority over the devil and his minions.

This does not mean, however, that satan cannot cause trouble for us. In his irreversibly corrupt and evil nature, he constantly and actively opposes the work of God and the people of God. He possesses a vast and frightening arsenal of weapons that he wields skillfully and ruthlessly: lust, anger, hatred, bitterness, slander, greed, selfishness, immorality, idolatry, discord, witchcraft, jealousy, murder, ambition, envy, drunkenness, and many others.[1] A state of spiritual warfare exists between satan and his angels and the Kingdom of God.

As believers, we have been equipped with everything that we need to engage successfully in spiritual warfare. Paul describes our spiritual armor in Ephesians 6:10-18, and we must never forget the constant presence and power of the Holy Spirit. One of our greatest weapons is knowledge: of satan's changed status due to the victory and ascension of Christ and of our position in Christ seated in the heavenly places. With all these resources at our disposal, there is no reason why we must experience defeat by satan or be victimized by his schemes. He has no power over us beyond what we allow him to have. That is why knowing his current status and our present position in Christ is so important.

A Heavenly Wrestling Match

When Pat and I came to Zimbabwe, we were not fully aware of the kind of evil spirits that were at work. Nevertheless, we considered it no coincidence when, in the space of about two weeks, both a bat and a snake made their way into our house, and a black goat came onto our property. Sorcery, word curses, and witchcraft are for real, and they were already at work. However, we knew also that these spirits were powerless against us if we gave them no place. They could not stay in our house, but had to return to the place from which they came. Paul wrote, "Neither give place to the devil" (Eph. 4:27). The New International Version translates the verse, "And do not give the devil a foothold." This is an extremely significant admonition, for satan is always seeking a position against us to advance his devices and so gain an advantage over us.

The context of this passage reveals that the foundation of spiritual warfare is morality. The devil seeks a foothold in the Church through anger, bitterness, lying, stealing, unwholesome talk, sexual immorality, and the various works of the sinful nature.[2] The battle is fought in the hearts, minds, and lives of people. As Jesus Himself modeled, when we resist temptation satan flees in defeat and a new opening for the Kingdom of God is prepared and our proclamation becomes more effective.

In the sixth chapter of Ephesians, Paul describes this great spiritual conflict with the principalities and powers in terms of a wrestling match:

*For we **wrestle** not against flesh and blood, but against principalities, against powers, against the rulers of the darkness of this world* [lit. age], *against spiritual wickedness in high* [lit. heavenly] ***places*** (Ephesians 6:12).

These "principalities" and "rulers of the darkness" inhabit the first and second heavens.[3] Satan directs their activities between the heavenlies and the world, and for this reason is called "the prince of the power of the air, the spirit that now worketh in the children of disobedience" (Eph. 2:2b).[4] These spirits act in concert with one another, whether against an individual or a group. Like an airborne disease, they transfer their influence from person to person,[5] purposefully working to enlarge their spheres of influence. I've seen evil spirits of uncleanness, legalism, deception, "religion," etc., try to infiltrate evangelical churches.

These demonic spirits position themselves against our abiding in Christ and our outreach to the lost, using whatever footholds they can gain; whatever distracts, deceives, or dislodges us from receiving or abiding in Christ. Satan obtains access to men in many ways through the sinful nature. He tries to fill our minds with guilt over our sins, weaknesses, and failures, and to keep us from appropriating our position of authority at God's right hand of favor.

An unforgiving spirit at Corinth threatened to give satan such a foothold: "Lest Satan should get an advantage of us: for we are not ignorant of his devices" (2 Cor. 2:11). The word *advantage* is translated elsewhere as "defraud." Satan seeks a foothold against us by attempting to defraud us of what is ours in Christ. Unforgiveness is a demonic device. Forgiveness belongs to the Church; in fact, it was expressly commanded by Christ and is crucial for abiding in Him. It is the same with slander: satan uses it to gain a place among us since God can no longer tolerate a slanderous accuser in His presence.[6]

In this heavenly wrestling match, satan tries to toss the Church back and forth with theological or doctrinal extremes, inspiring a teaching that goes beyond Scripture: carrying us "about with every wind of doctrine, by the trickery of men, in the cunning craftiness of deceitful plotting" (Eph. 4:14b NKJ).[7] Knowing that satan seeks to change the gospel and distort the Scriptures, it is no wonder that he tries to counterfeit and discredit every move of God. Just as when you are mounting a horse, it will try to hinder you if you are hesitant, so satan tries to hinder you from mounting the move of God by "holding onto your leg" and feeding your doubts. On the other hand, if you are moving forward recklessly, he will push you farther and faster until you crash to the ground on the other side.

We might compare this to driving a car down a narrow lane and trying to stay out of the drainage ditch on either side: We must avoid extremes and stay on the "straight and narrow." Jesus used the analogy of leaven in bread: "Take heed, beware of the leaven of the Pharisees, and of the leaven of Herod" (Mk. 8:15). The leaven of the Pharisees is legalism; of Herod, license, an "anything goes" approach. Both extremes are spiritual dangers to the Body of Christ.

The heart of this spiritual conflict is the spread of the gospel.[8] God's Spirit and Word in His people spread out across the world, battled at every step by the rulers of the darkness of this world, who will not give up their dominion in the earth without a fight. The whole world lies in their sphere of influence through the lust of the flesh, the lust of the eyes, and the pride of life. The people of God, however, are not of this world and are kept from its evil by God's power.[9]

Every Christian experiences this spiritual wrestling because the present evil age and the powers of the age to come co-exist briefly in an interim period during which their opposing powers collide. All creation is subject to the intense pressures of this transitional phase. Christians, in particular, feel this pressure because, although the Kingdom of Heaven has come to earth, it has not yet been revealed in its fullness. The Kingdom of Heaven is within us by the Holy Spirit and we are called to declare and manifest God's reign by doing His will on earth as it is in Heaven.

Satan is the god of this age, however, so we struggle not only in this world, but also in our own souls. Unfortunately, many Christians have never understood the nature of the struggle.[10] It is a war between flesh and spirit; between the old that is passing away, and the new that is dawning. It is the tension between who we were before Christ and who we are in Christ; between where we are now and where we will one day be.[11] The old regime is founded on sin and death with demonic powers governing; the new realm is based on righteousness and life in the Holy Spirit.

We must grow up and recognize our strong position in the Lord and in the power of His might.[12] We can overcome every strategy of the devil, withstanding his onslaughts and quenching all his fiery darts.[13] We can draw on the powers of the age to come and boldly speak the truth in love. We can grow up into the full stature of Christ where satan has nothing in us, just as Jesus said in the hour of His temptation on earth: "For the prince of this world cometh, and hath nothing in Me" (Jn. 14:30b). We can proclaim the gospel to every kindred, tongue, people, and nation and stand glorious without spot or wrinkle when we are presented to Christ.[14]

Signs and Abiding in Christ

The first sign of the believer's victory over the devil is the casting out of demons: We can cast them out because satan has been judged and cast down. Jesus said:

*...**Go** ye into all the world, and **preach** the gospel to every creature. He that believeth and is baptized shall be **saved**....And these
signs shall follow them **that believe**; In My name shall they **cast
out devils**...* (Mark 16:15-17).

Most believers settle for less, merely rejoicing that their sins are forgiven and that Heaven is their home. They believe that casting out demons
is a job for the specialist. They do not see themselves as having this kind
of authority.

1. Every believer has much more authority than he imagines.

This is why it is possible to cast out demons in Jesus' name and still
be a worker of iniquity, doomed to damnation.[15] That should not deter
us from exercising authority over demons. We should simply be sure
that we have departed from our iniquities. Jesus wants us to use the
authority that He has given us. He said that we would do the works that
He did, and greater works than His, because He was going to the
Father.[16] The "greater works" of the believer are based on the exaltation
of Christ and our heavenly position with Him.[17]

Jesus said, "In My name...they shall take up serpents...."[18] This
speaks of our authority over the devil; authority not only to *cast out devils*, which entails taking dominion away from him, but also authority to
take up serpents,[19] or in certain cases to give jurisdiction back to evil spirits to fulfill God's purposes. We can take them up from under our feet
when we judge sin among ourselves. Peter, Paul, and others functioned in
such authority when necessary. At various times they turned persons over
to the devil. The New Testament gives us such examples as Ananias and
Sapphira, Simon, and Elymas the sorcerers, an incestuous sinner at
Corinth, Hymenaeous the false teacher, and Alexander the blasphemer.[20]

God used the serpent in the Old Testament to accomplish His just purposes. Now we can do the same. Instead of satan exercising an accusatory
jurisdiction in the presence of God, we can plead before God's throne for
mercy and forgiveness. If needed, however, we can also release retribution
via demonic spirits aimed at an individual's repentance and salvation:
"...for the *destruction of the flesh*, that their *spirit may be saved* in the day
of the Lord Jesus" (1 Cor. 5:5); "That they may *learn* not to blaspheme"
(1 Tim. 1:20b).

Todd and DeAnn Burke present a good example of this authority in
action. Serving as missionaries in Cambodia just before the Khmer

Rouge's reign of terror, they had to exercise this authority to withdraw the anointing from an unrepentant, but gifted, church leader. With much guidance from the Holy Spirit and confirmation from fellow leaders, they rightcously judged and excommunicated a rebellious, immoral man. In a formal way, they released this person from God's Spirit into the hands of satan. Although contrary to the hyper-grace gospel of some churches, Christ revealed to them His pleasure in their obedience. The church was not only preserved, but it flourished. This wayward leader became powerless to adversely influence others. Gifts of healing ceased to operate in his ministry, and tragedy overtook him.[21]

This authority to remit or retain sins is staggering, and like the ability to bind and loose, it operates on more than one level. It applies on both the individual and collective scale. Clearly, such authority given to us aptly reveals our exalted position in Christ.[22] Abiding in Christ is the key both for the proper use of and avoiding the abuse of such awesome authority. Otherwise, we may act in bitter self-vindication or fiery zeal without knowledge.[23]

2. Every believer has direct and continual access to God through Christ.

When Jesus speaks of "many mansions" in John 14:2, some think of a mansion in glory in the sweet by and by. The Greek word *mone*, translated *"mansion"* in the Authorized King James Version, means "abode" or "abiding place." It comes from the same word used in John 15:4: *"Abide* in Me..."* for "in My Father's house are many *abiding places.*" Jesus said, "I go to prepare a place for you." He prepared an abiding place in Heaven by virtue of His shed blood, then came to His disciples by the Holy Spirit as He had promised. He did not leave them homeless orphans.[24] Yes, we have a place in the Father's house. Although this abiding place includes a future residence in the New Jerusalem, it is a present reality in the Holy Spirit now: "But you *have come* to Mount Zion and to the city of the living God, the heavenly Jerusalem...to God...." (Heb. 12:22-23 NKJ).

In Ephesians 3:12, Paul says, "In whom we have boldness and *access* with confidence by the faith of Him." Having immediate access to the Father through Christ sure beats relying on 9-1-1! God has given us many great promises like Jeremiah 33:3: "Call unto Me, and I will answer thee, and show thee great and mighty things, which thou knowest not."

Little did my wife and I know that a flat tire one morning was setting us up for a near disaster in the evening. It was Sunday, and we had just arrived for furlough in the States. Due to this flat, after the morning service we put two new front tires on the car that we had borrowed, not noticing that the back tires were bald. Late that afternoon, my wife, who was six months pregnant, our five-year-old, and I got in the car to head for the evening meeting, leaving the two oldest children with their grandmother. The service was 50 miles north.

It was raining heavily when I got onto a busy five-lane expressway out of Cincinnati. I began to accelerate and move toward the high-speed lane when the car hydroplaned and spun out of control. The next thing I knew we were facing oncoming traffic. Pat cried out the name of Jesus as we saw the startled faces of drivers passing us at 60 miles an hour. We did a full loop from the far-left lane across four lanes to the far right lane, somehow missing all the traffic, while still remaining on the road.

Just as I thought we were coming out of it, we went into another 180-degree spin. Again and again, Pat cried out to Jesus! Again, we crossed four lanes of traffic, miraculously avoiding a head-on or broadside collision. Just as amazing, we somehow stayed on the road without hitting the center concrete divider or going into the bridge on the opposite side.

Several seconds passed before we came to a stop in the far-left lane, completely untouched. A man who had stopped his car shook his head in wonder that we got out of it unharmed. For a week I could not stop thanking God for His deliverance. I was grateful we were still alive. If someone had videotaped this scene from the overpass, it would have qualified for *That's Incredible* and been worth a fortune. Continual access to God, however, is worth more than all the wealth in the world.

God has made provision for us to abide completely with Him for all time. If Christ were to come for His wedding feast right now, or if we died, we would forever be with Him, but God's house is not yet full. In the Father's house there are many abiding places; enough for all who believe. Since there is yet room, we who are alive must compel people to come in before the door is shut. The greatest concern of the Church in the world must be the finishing of our God-given task of presenting the whole counsel of God's Word to the whole world.

We have more than ample authority to fulfill our commission, and more than enough power to shake the nations. May it again be said of us "these that have turned the world upside down are come hither also"

(Acts 17:6). God is in the process of turning the world right side up—180 degrees. This process involves actions in the spiritual realm that have parallels on earth. Now that the accuser has been cast out and Heaven has been cleansed, the next step is the cleansing of the heavenlies: the removal of satan and his legions from the first and second heavens and their final consignment to the lake of fire.

Endnotes

1. See 2 Corinthians 2:11; Galatians 5:19-21; Ephesians 2:1-3; 4:26-32; James 4:1,4,7.

2. See Ephesians 4:28-32. This is not an undermining of spiritual gifts, for the manifestations and gift ministries of the Holy Spirit are vital to effective spiritual warfare. The foundation, however, is morality.

3. See Ephesians 1:21; 3:10.

4. See also 2 Corinthians 12:7; Job 2:7; Hebrews 1:14.

5. The Greek word *topos*, translated "foothold," "place," or "opportunity," is the root for the English word *topography*, which suggests an area of jurisdiction. Wheather an individual or a collective group—church, community, town, city, region, or nation—the effects of giving a foothold to the devil are the same: deception, heaviness, strife, calamity; the list goes on and on.

6. Paul lamented to Timothy that some of the younger widows were in the habit of being idle; going from house to house being busybodies, saying slanderous things that they ought not: "For some are already turned aside after Satan" (1 Tim. 5:15). Words are a primary medium by which spirits express themselves and influence the lives and affairs of men. Words can be spirit and life or they can be a channel to release hell and death (see Prov. 18:21; Jn. 6:63; 1 Cor. 12:3; Jas. 3:6-9; 1 Jn. 4:1-3). E. Silvoso points out that because the victory of Christ and His exaltation is constant and irreversible, the only variable and point of challenge left open to satan is the position of the Church. Satan thus concentrates his attack against the Church and seeks to deceive her regarding her place in Christ, just as the serpent deceived Eve (*That None Should Perish* [Ventura, CA: Regal Books, 1993]).

7. Through deception and the deceitfulness of sin, satan works to rob us of what is rightfully ours (see 2 Thess. 2:9-10; Heb. 3:13). He will try to steal the truth from us through seducing spirits and doctrines distorted

by demons (see 1 Cor. 7:5; 2 Cor. 11:3; 1 Tim. 4:2; 2 Tim. 2:25-26). He appears as an angel of light, proclaiming another Jesus and another gospel. To do his work he must have a mouthpiece that he has robbed of the truth, and perverted with his lies: "...but there be *some that trouble you*, and would *pervert the gospel* of Christ. But though we, or an *angel from heaven*, preach any other gospel unto you than that which we have preached unto you, *let him be accursed*" (Gal. 1:7-8).

8. See Ephesians 6:15,17-20.

9. See John 17:15; 1 John 2:16.

10. See Romans 8:22-23; Galatians 1:3-4; Ephesians 1:21.

11. See Galatians 5:17.

12. See Ephesians 6:10.

13. See Ephesians 6:11,13,17.

14. See Ephesians 5:27; 6:15,19-20.

15. See Matthew 7:22-23.

16. See John 14:12.

17. Jesus had the Spirit without measure, but believers have only a measure of the Spirit. These greater works, therefore, are a result of Christ's exaltation. They apply to the Body of Christ normally as a whole. With a particular gifting, such as healing, an individual member of Christ's Body may do greater works for a season, like Peter's shadow healing the sick. Nevertheless, faith in Christ's ability is the key that unlocks supernatural signs and wonders. Unbelief, on the other hand, is the reason why there are no signs and wonders in many Christian circles.

18. Mark 16:17b-18.

19. Who can interpret Jesus' words literally without justifying the cultic snake handlers? To argue that Paul's experience with a snake at Melita is the fulfillment of Christ's promise is not only too limiting, but also does not answer the Greek construction of Jesus' words, which indicate an active engagement rather than the conditional passive "if you."

20. See Acts 5:9; 8:20; 13:11; 1 Corinthians 5:5; 1 Timothy 1:20.

21. Todd and DeAnn Burke, *Anointed for Burial* (Plainfield, NJ: Logos International, 1977), 167-181.

22. See Matthew 18:15-35; John 20:17-23; 2 Corinthians 2:6-10.

23. "Strike-'em-dead" prayers such as Cindy Jacob discusses in *Possessing the Gates of the Enemy* are far from the heart of God ([Tarrytown, NY: Chosen Books, 1991], 142). The point, however, from the Scripture, "they shall take up serpents," concerns the extent of the believer's authority in Christ. Although some say that believers do not have authority to engage in strategic level spiritual warfare, I believe that the Scriptures clearly teach that the Church can and should confront the devil and his underlings at every level and at all times. Nevertheless, as in all ministry, this must be done in the power of the Holy Spirit and within the framework of Scripture.

24. Our potential influence through intercessory prayer is based on our authority in Christ. Just consider its extent by comparing it to the kind of authority satan exercised in the Old Testament. If satan exercised such authority for a limited time by accusing men, imagine what we can receive from God's throne as we plead for grace in the eternal righteousness of Christ.

Chapter Twelve

The Accuser and the Cleansing of the Heavenlies

And all the host of heaven shall be dissolved, and the heavens shall be rolled together as a scroll: and all their host shall fall down, as the leaf falleth off from the vine, and as a falling fig from the fig tree. For my sword shall be bathed in heaven (Isaiah 34:4-5a).

The ascension of Christ brought about the first installment of the devil's judgment: Heaven was cleansed of the accuser. Christ's blood blotted out the handwriting of ordinances that satan had used to maintain his position before God's throne. Since the court of the Most High has ruled in judgment against the prince of this world, no longer can any charges be made against us in Heaven. Satan's place is no longer there. However, even as Heaven was cleansed of the accuser, the heavenlies must also be purified of his presence. Scripture is not silent on this subject or its sequence in God's chronology.

The process of the cleansing of the heavenlies will be presented here and in the following two chapters as a series of six related end-time portraits illustrating what the Bible teaches on the bringing down of satan and his angels from the first and second heavens. Imagine them as pictures hanging in a gallery in three groups of two, each portrait painting a graphic picture connecting the exaltation of Christ to the degradation of the devil:

1. **The Heavenly Arena: Visualizing What Is Happening in the Unseen Realms**
   - The Footstooling of His Enemies
   - The Shaking of the Heavens
2. **The Earthly Arena: Identifying What Is Occurring on Earth as a Result of the Above**
   - The Restoration of All Things
   - The Coming Down of the Devil
3. **Synthesis: Anticipating the Merging of Heaven and Earth**
   - The Heavens and Earth on Fire
   - The Lake of Fire

The first two portraits provide an interrelated picture of what is presently happening in the heavenlies. The portrait of *Christ waiting until His enemies are made His footstool* is enthroned in the highest place of our heavenly gallery. Immediately beneath it is the decisive *shaking of the heavens.*

The Footstooling of His Enemies

An expectant Christ, exalted over His earthbound enemies, is a foundational doctrine of the end of the age. Psalm 110 is quoted a dozen times by New Testament writers; more often than any other Old Testament passage. However, it is often omitted in end-time teaching despite its strong prophetic nature and prominent place in first-century apostolic preaching:[1]

> *The Lord said unto* **my Lord**, *Sit Thou at* **My right hand**, *until I make* **Thine enemies** *Thy footstool. The Lord shall* **send the rod of Thy strength out of Zion: rule** *Thou in the midst of* **Thine enemies. Thy people** *shall be willing in* **the day of Thy power**, *in the beauties of holiness from the womb of the morning: Thou hast the dew of Thy youth. The Lord hath sworn, and will not repent, Thou art* **a priest for ever** *after the order of Melchizedek. The Lord at Thy right hand shall strike through kings in the day of His wrath* (Psalm 110:1-5).

With the death, resurrection, and ascension of Jesus, the psalmist's prophecy has come to pass. Enthroned with kingly authority, Christ sits in the place of highest honor at the Father's right hand, extending the rod of His strength in the midst of His enemies to strike them down, and empowering His people who willingly offer themselves to Him in this the day of His power.

What did the apostles say? Since Psalm 110 is at the forefront of New Testament preaching, it is enlightening to see what the apostles said regarding its final fulfillment. On the day of Pentecost, Peter declared that Christ's heavenly reign was demonstrated by the outpouring of the Holy Spirit.[2] By quoting Psalm 110, the apostle showed his understanding that the coming of the Spirit would be the means by which Christ would rule in the midst of His enemies. Just as Christ drove out demons and destroyed the works of the devil by the power of the Holy Spirit, so too would His anointed people. The Holy Spirit is the proof and means of extending Christ's dominion on earth.

The writer of Hebrews quotes Psalm 110 seven times, presenting throughout the Epistle a detailed portrait of Christ seated at the right hand of the Majesty on High.[3] Loving righteousness, hating iniquity, and upholding all things by the word of His power, Christ sends forth His ministering spirits to all who shall be heirs of salvation.[4] Twice, in Hebrews 1:13 and 10:13, the writer speaks of Jesus waiting expectantly for His enemies to be made His footstool. The entire letter powerfully drives home the theme of the Lordship of Christ and His heavenly reign.[5]

Paul writes in First Corinthians that Christ must reign until He has "put down all rule and all authority and power" (1 Cor. 15:24b). Although all things are already under His feet, there are demonic forces in the heavenlies and men on earth who oppose His rule: "We will *not* have this man to reign over us."[6] Stretching forth His rod of authority from Heaven, the Lord strikes down and shatters these powerful enemies who are bent on rebellion, forcing them to bow low before Him.[7] This process of footstooling Jesus' enemies, which began with His ascension, will be completed at His return, at which time death itself, the last enemy, will be destroyed.

What does His footstool represent? The Bible teaches that Heaven is God's throne and *the earth* is His footstool.[8] It stands to reason, then, that Christ is waiting until His enemies (satan and his associates) are brought down to the earth. This is the definite and decisive phase of the devil's judgment that was foretold by the prophets.[9]

The Old Testament saints waited until the fullness of time for the advent of the promised Seed. Now that Christ has come, the countdown for satan's casting down has begun: *three, two, one, earth,* and then the lake of fire. His abode is no more in Heaven; now he is being removed from the heavenlies and confined to the earth. Christ's victory is being extended to every realm of creation. Although this takes time, Christ is not passive during this period. No, His authority from Heaven is being carried out by the Holy Spirit in a specific manner.

Legal and military conflicts illustrate the dynamics of this type of waiting and the kind of power that is being brought to bear.[10] In any legal issue of a business or criminal nature, even after the case is tried, the verdict must be executed. The evidence may be watertight, and the forces of justice already at work, but it always takes time for the judgment to be enforced. For example, when an uninsured driver turned in front of my wife on an expressway, our car was a total write-off. Thank God, she and my son were uninjured. Witnesses confirmed the other driver's fault in the accident, the police cited him, and yet we waited six months before restitution was made for the damages (although we were active during that time with the insurance company and lawyers). It could have taken longer.

As with cases on earth regarding the due process of law and its enforcement, so it is in the heavenly realm. Satan has been judged in Heaven, and we on earth eagerly await his execution. It's not easy to wait, but it helps to know the integrity of the forces of justice that are at work. God is not an unjust judge, but He is patiently bearing with His elect during this time as they cry to Him. He will avenge them against their adversary.[11]

Why the waiting? An illustration from modern warfare will also help clarify why God waits instead of using all-out force against the devil. Ever since World War II, the United States, with its powerful arsenal of nuclear weapons, has struggled with the issue of waiting while limited force is applied. Military leaders in Korea, Vietnam, and the Gulf War faced the same basic question: What kind and how much force should be used to achieve the objective? Use of atomic weapons might hasten the end of a war, but civilian casualties and the destruction of property are never legitimate objectives in themselves.

The complexities of the Bosnian conflict in the former Yugoslavian Republic baffled many. The historic, ethnic, and religious roots of the war, the interrelated dynamics of issues and personalities, and the unrelenting campaign of the Serbian combatants were more than most could follow. The U.N. faced the same simple yet difficult question: What force should be used without the needless loss of life? In Bosnia, the U.N. finally decided to use their superior air power in limited strikes against Serb positions around Sarajevo, forcing them to move their heavy guns and abandon their stranglehold on the city.

In like manner, satan does not retreat from his entrenched position in the heavenlies without ample force being brought to bear. Christ has all power but He is also patient, not willing that any should perish, but that all should come to repentance.[12] Nevertheless, when He returns to the earth He will take vengeance on the devil and all who have not obeyed the gospel.[13] Meanwhile, He waits patiently for those who will hear and believe.[14] Christ is wisely exercising His power through the Church against the strongholds of satan. As the Godhead embodied Jesus to break the devil's power, Christ is steadily working through His Body, the Church, to remove satan from the heavenlies.

Christ's ascension brought about satan's dismissal from Heaven, whereas the Church displaces him in the heavenlies. Christ's redemptive work cleansed Heaven and now the Church is His instrument for the cleansing of the heavenlies. We carry on the work of Christ at another level that involves spiritual warfare against the principalities and powers in the heavenly places. After Christ ascended, Michael and his angels evicted satan and his angels from the third Heaven. There is now a war in the first and second heavens, based on what happens in the affairs of men. The Church is the driving influence in this great struggle. What we say and do *in Christ* has the power to bind and loose the forces of Heaven.[15] We do this by appropriating both the finished work of Christ on Calvary and the ongoing ministry of the Holy Spirit. What a great responsibility the Church has, but what a great privilege!

It is extremely nearsighted to speak on the endtimes without emphasizing Christ's elevation over His enemies. The Lord possesses the authority and power of Heaven and is on the move mightily through His Body on the earth. Those who see only tribulation and the power and work of the devil fail to grasp God's purpose and procedure during this period of waiting between His ascension and His second coming. God has already decreed that His enemies be made earthbound; but this declaration, like the Old Testament prophecies of satan being cast out of Heaven, demands corresponding action and not merely the passing of time.

How will this happen? Does the Bible reveal more about how His enemies are made His footstool? What does Christ do to force satan to vacate his occupancy of the heavenlies? The next heavenly portrait reveals what Christ is doing now. This picture, the second in the first set, is also prophesied throughout the Bible. It is positioned below and is the logical result of the first portrait.

The Shaking of the Heavens

This portrait depicts heavy winds, dark storm clouds, bright flashes of lightning, and rumbling peals of thunder. In the distance, great drops of rain are pouring upon the earth. Perspective for this portrait comes from the Old and New Testaments.

> *Whose voice then **shook** the earth: but now He hath promised, saying, Yet once more I shake not the earth only, but **also heaven**. And this word, Yet once more, signifieth the **removing of those things that are shaken**, as of **things that are made**, that those things which cannot be shaken may remain* (Hebrews 12:26-27).

Here we are shown the *heavenly Zion*, the city of the living God, where innumerable companies of angels dwell. As in Psalm 110, the main attraction is Jesus, the Commander in Chief, who directs the work of the Holy Spirit through His people on earth.[16] He speaks from and shakes the heavens. Speaking is mentioned four times because by speaking, Jesus' voice shakes the very heavens! The battle is the Lord's.

The New Testament

From of old, the Lord has spoken judgment on all that would usurp or rebel against Christ's Kingdom.[17] Now, in these last days, His very words are dislodging these evil principalities and defiant powers.[18] These insurgents must be brought down from their entrenched position in the heavenlies. The shaking, however, will not remove us who are part of God's Kingdom, provided we do not turn from the words of Christ. Although we enter His coming Kingdom through much shaking, His grace is sufficient for us to stand in the midst of such a separating judgment in the heavenlies.[19]

In the Mt. Olivet discourse, Jesus spoke of this shaking of the powers in the heavens, connecting it to stars falling from heaven.[20] He then refers to His coming and the end of the age: false messiahs, fake prophets, wars, rumors of wars, famines, diseases, earthquakes, increased lawlessness, persecutions, distress of nations, and commotions.[21] These various signs of tribulation increase like labor pains before delivery and are a result of the powers in the heavenlies being shaken. The *things* that come on the earth literally come down from the heavens:

> Men's hearts failing them for fear, and for looking after those **things** which are **coming on the earth**: for [because] the **powers of heaven** shall be **shaken** (Luke 21:26).

The Old Testament

Isaiah prophesied that the sword of God's Word would finish its work in the heavens. As a result "...all the host of heaven shall be dissolved...and all their host shall fall down, as the leaf falleth off from the vine, and as a falling fig from the fig tree" (Is. 34:4). What an awesome image! Falling figs and leaves refer to satan and his angels coming down from their place in the heavenlies.[22] Alluding to Isaiah, John adds the Spirit's wind to the sword of the Word as the agents causing them to fall: "And the stars of heaven fell unto the earth, even as a fig tree casteth her untimely figs, when she is *shaken of a mighty wind*" (Rev. 6:13).

Like unripe figs shaken to the ground, the stars or principalities fall to the earth because the gospel *strikes them* and the mighty wind of the Holy Spirit *blows on them.*[23] Acts 2:2 says, "And suddenly there came a sound from heaven as of *a rushing mighty wind*, and it filled all the house where they were sitting." Jesus ascended and poured out the Spirit who shook the principalities and powers. The ascension of Jesus and the coming of the Holy Spirit ushered in the period of history the Bible calls "the last days." World evangelism commenced at Jerusalem where men from every nation gathered for the Feast of Pentecost.[24]

When the prophet Haggai speaks of the shaking of the heavens, he also foretells of this glory of the latter house, by which God "will overthrow the throne of kingdoms, and destroy the *strength* of the kingdoms of the heathen" (Hag. 2:22a).

> For thus saith the Lord of hosts; Yet once, it is a little while, and **I will shake the heavens,** and the earth....and I will shake all nations, and **the desire of all nations shall come**: and **I will fill this house with glory,** saith the Lord of hosts (Haggai 2:6-7).

Christ, the "desire of all nations," comes with the preaching of the gospel of the Kingdom of Heaven. After His ascension comes an early and latter day outpouring of the Holy Spirit to empower His people to be witnesses unto the uttermost parts of the earth. The Spirit is filling God's house with greater glory for this final worldwide advance of the gospel. The evil ruling spirits over the nations thus come down in a desperate, defensive move.

These ruling spirits in the heavenly places, terribly disturbed by the spread of the gospel, wreak havoc and all manner of tribulation on earth in an attempt to hinder or halt the Church in her mission. It is not surprising then to find the red, black, and pale horses of war, famine, and death following on the heels of the gospel. History is replete with such examples, beginning in Jerusalem and Judea.[25]

Few would disagree that the world today appears to be going from bad to worse. In reality, satan has come down in an angry, desperate bid to delay the inevitable. Terminally ill, he is throwing at us everything he has, including himself. Remember that satan's desire was to ascend in Heaven, *not* descend into the earth. The coming down of the devil is a reaction to the advance of the Church. The spread of the gospel to every nation is the key sign of the approaching end of the age: "And this gospel of the Kingdom shall be preached in all the world for a witness unto all nations; and then shall the end come" (Mt. 24:14).

The Church proclaims Jesus Christ, the only name under Heaven given to men for salvation.[26] The Body of Christ will thrive and grow to the very end, and God's Kingdom will continue to increase. Just as in Nebuchadnezzar's dream, the stone cut out of the mountain without hands, representing God's Kingdom, will break into pieces and consume every other domain.[27] As these things are being fulfilled, and especially as we see the Church completing the task of preaching the gospel to the entire world, we are to look up because our redemption draws near. Our Redeemer rules over His descending enemies with the whole earth as His Promised Land: "He shall have dominion also from sea to sea, and from the river unto the ends of the earth. They that dwell in the wilderness shall bow before Him; and His enemies shall lick the dust" (Ps. 72:8-9). All things in Heaven, in earth, and under the earth must bow down at the name of Jesus and acknowledge His lordship.[28]

What is happening on earth while the footstooling of Christ's enemies and the shaking of the heavens are taking place in the spiritual realm? The two portraits in the *earthly arena*, "The Restoration of All Things" and "The Coming Down of the Devil" depict what transpires in this world as a result of Christ's exaltation and the shaking of the heavens.

Endnotes

1. See Matthew 22:44; Mark 12:36; Luke 20:42; Acts 2:34-35; 1 Corinthians 15:25; Hebrews 1:13; 10:12-13. Although Christ's humiliating death was prophesied in the Old Testament, the Jewish rulers expected a glorious, earthly Messianic kingdom in Israel. Jesus knew, however, that He would first suffer rejection before entering a spiritual, heavenly reign. Jesus, therefore, asked them a question from Psalm 110. How could David call the Messiah, *Lord*, and the Messiah still be *David's Son* (see Mt. 22:45)? They recognized that this was a Messianic psalm, and yet the scribes could not answer His question. Also from Psalm 110 was Jesus' last answer to His earthly enemies. "Hereafter you shall see the Son of Man seated at the right hand of power" (see Mt. 26:64; Mk. 14:62; Lk. 22:69). Jesus is now reigning from Zion, but there is a process whereby His enemies shall be made His footstool while His rod rules in their midst.

2. See Acts 2:34-35.

3. The Book of Hebrews refers to the exaltation of Christ some 20 times (see Heb 1:3,8,13; 2:9; 4:14; 5:6; 10:19-20; 7:17,21,25-28; 8:1-5; 9:11-12,24-25; 10:12-13,21; 12:2,22-26).

4. See Hebrews 1:3,9,14.

5. See Hebrews 1:3,8,13; 10:13.

6. Luke 19:14b; See Luke 19:27.

7. See Hebrews 1:3,8,13. This picture of Jesus seated on His throne could be broadened to incorporate other visions of Him such as John's on the island of Patmos. He is portrayed in Revelation chapter 1 with "[hair] white like wool, as white as snow; and His eyes as a flame of fire...His voice as the sound of many waters. And He had in His right hand seven stars...His countenance was as the sun shineth in his strength...[having] the keys of hell and of death" (Rev. 1:14-18). In chapter 5, after he was caught up to Heaven, John saw a Lamb as if it had been slain, standing in the midst of the throne, and who came and *"took the book out of the right hand of Him that sat upon the throne"* (see Rev. 5:6-7). *What a marvelous vision* showing all creation under the influence of the Lamb's throne as He opens the seals and reveals the things that must shortly come to pass!

8. See Psalm 132:7-12; Isaiah 66:1; Matthew 5:35; Acts 7:49.

9. Both Isaiah's proverb and Ezekiel's lament, discussed in Chapter Four, outline this installment of the devil's judgment as he is brought down to the ground.

10. By design, this type of waiting anticipates an objective while power is exercised against opposing forces. Every aspect of life involves an element of waiting (see Rom. 8:19-25).

11. See Luke 18:1-8.

12. See 2 Peter 3:9.

13. See 2 Thessalonians 1:8.

14. Why doesn't God just destroy the devil and get it over with? God will not do this for the same reason that He did not execute lucifer when he first led angels and men into rebellion: When God throws the devil into the lake of fire, in His eternal justice He must also throw in people who are still in sin! As an alternative for humanity, God announced a promise of redemption and is still enacting His plan to show mercy on mankind and judgment on the devil (see 2 Pet. 3:9; Jas. 5:7-9).

15. See Acts 12:5-11.

16. As the Captain of the Lord's host, Christ determines the strategy and reveals each phase to His people as He did through Joshua in taking the Promised Land. Beginning with the stronghold of Jericho, dependence on the Lord's leading was essential. These revealed strategies constitute strategic-level spiritual warfare in which faith and testimony are indispensable elements.

17. See Psalm 2.

18. See Hebrews 12:26-29.

19. See Hebrews 12:25. Nevertheless, whoever will not listen to Him will be completely cut off (see Acts 3:23). For us as believers, only that which is *not* of His Kingdom in our lives will be shaken out during these times, provided we abide in Him and His words abide in us.

20. See Matthew 24:29; Mark 13:25; Luke 21:26.

21. Compare Revelation 6:17–7:4 with Matthew 24:29; Mark 13:25; and Luke 21:26.

22. See Luke 21:26-31.

23. J.H. Thayer's *Greek-English Lexicon of the New Testament* adds: "before the harvest the unripe figs fall." The harvest is the end of the age ([Grand Rapids, MI: Baker Book House, 1977], 444).

24. Pentecost was a harvest festival of firstfruits in which God's people were especially told to rejoice.

25. Famine, war, and desolation followed the preaching of the gospel in Jerusalem and Judea when her leaders rejected Christ and pursued nationalistic aspirations against Rome. The pattern holds throughout history. Just in the history of the United States, consider the pattern: the Great Awakening and the Revolutionary War; the second Great Awakening and the Civil War; the Azusa Street Pentecostal revival and World Wars I and II; the Charismatic renewal and Vietnam. These tribulations, a foretaste of the coming day of wrath, actually serve to alert the people of earth. While the awakened Church is purified, God repays satan's kingdom, "seeing it is a righteous thing with God to recompense tribulation to them that trouble you" (2 Thess. 1:6; see 2 Thess. 1:4-12; Rev. 6:1-11).

26. See Acts 4:12.

27. See Daniel 2:34,44-45. Every other domain includes the realm of the beast and the false prophet.

28. See Philippians 2:10.

Chapter Thirteen

The Accuser and the Last Days

Jesus Christ established the Church as His Body on earth to carry out His commission to take the gospel of the Kingdom of God to every people, tribe, and nation, and promised to empower her for the task. That promise was fulfilled on the day of Pentecost when the Holy Spirit came upon the believers, filling them with spiritual power and holy boldness. The age of the "last days," which was ushered in at Pentecost, is also the age of the Church. We are Christ's organism for evangelizing the world and the outworking of His redemptive plan for the ages.

Just as satan dogged Jesus' every step, hounded Him at every turn, and sought to divert, distract, and finally, to destroy Him, so he does with the Church. What we must realize, however, is that the ascension of Christ and the empowerment of the Church have forced satan and his legions into this defensive posture. One of the greatest mistakes many in the Church have made is to conclude that the intensification of evil and demonic activity in the world is the result of satan's *offensive* strategy. In reality, it is the sign of increasingly desperate *defensive* maneuvers by an enemy who knows that he is defeated and running out of time.

Many modern students of eschatology expect little or no major advances of the Church or restoration in this age; only a great falling away and rise of evil against an increasingly embattled Church until the moment Christ returns to bring everything to an end. I believe, however, that the Bible clearly indicates restoration and the greatest harvest of souls in history *before* the second coming. In addition, there is evidence in history and the present day that this is already happening. The portraits in our *earthly arena*, as first shown in Chapter Twelve, illustrate this as they depict what happens on earth as a result of the footstooling of Christ's enemies and the shaking of the heavens.

The Restoration of All Things

Restore is the word that Joel uses to sum up what God does in the last days: "I will *restore* to you" (Joel 2:25). His prophecies contain several important insights regarding this end-time restoration.

> *The earth shall quake before them;* **the heavens shall tremble:** *the sun and the moon shall be dark, and the stars shall withdraw their shining: and the* **Lord shall utter His voice before His army***: for His camp is very great: for He is strong that executeth His word: for the day of the Lord is great and very terrible; and who can abide it? ... And it shall come to pass afterward, that* **I will pour out My spirit upon all flesh***; and your sons and your daughters shall prophesy, your old men shall dream dreams, your young men shall see visions: and also upon the servants and upon the handmaids in those days will I pour out My spirit. ... And it shall come to pass,* **that whosoever shall call on the name of the Lord shall be delivered... Multitudes, multitudes** *in the valley of decision:* **for the day of the Lord is near** *in the valley of decision* (Joel 2:10-11,28-29,32a; 3:14).

As the day of the Lord approaches, the heavens shake when the Lord utters His voice from Zion before His army, who carry out His Word on earth. The moderate former rains of the Holy Spirit precipitate a heavy latter outpouring on all flesh in preparation for a final harvest of souls.[1] Those in the "valley of decision" who call on the name of the Lord are saved. This wonderful portrait in the earthly gallery is another often-overlooked end-time view. The work of restoration before the return of Christ should not be underestimated. It entails *times of refreshing* and *times of restitution*. The apostle Peter announced both when he addressed the people who had come together in amazement after the healing of a man lame from birth:

> **But those things,** *which God before had* **showed by the mouth of all His prophets,** *that Christ should suffer, He hath so fulfilled. Repent ye therefore, and be converted, that your sins may*

*be blotted out, when the **times of refreshing** shall come from the presence of the Lord; and He shall send Jesus Christ, which before was preached unto you: **whom the heaven must receive until the times of restitution of all things**, which God hath **spoken by the mouth of all His holy prophets** since the world began. ... Yea, and **all the prophets** from Samuel and those that follow after, as many as have spoken, have likewise foretold of **these days*** (Acts 3:18-21,24).

In the last days, the Spirit of the Lord will bring *times* (plural) of refreshment and restitution. Some commentators, however, limit refreshment and restitution to the one-time event of Christ's return. Scripture clearly states, however, that the heavens must retain Jesus *until* the Father fulfills what He has promised by the prophets. Just as surely as Christ came to fulfill what the prophets foretold, so too will God fulfill all that He has promised His Son as a result of His coming.

This portrait reveals that the body of prophetic Scripture as a whole, the full context of Peter's sermon in Acts chapter 3, and the history of God's people all testify to the times of refreshing and restitution that will lead up to Christ's second coming.

1. The Prophetic Scriptures

God has promised Christ an inheritance out of every nation, tribe, and tongue. The conversion of multitudes and the growth and triumph of Christ's Kingdom are prophesied throughout the Old Testament: "And it shall come to pass in the last days, that the mountain of the Lord's house shall be established in the top of the mountains, and shall be exalted above the hills; and all nations shall flow unto it" (Is. 2:2); "...the Gentiles shall come to Thy light" (Is. 60:3a); "...the forces of the Gentiles shall come unto Thee" (Is. 60:5c); "...all the kindreds of the nations shall worship before Thee" (Ps. 22:27b); "...for the earth shall be full of the knowledge of the Lord, as the waters cover the sea" (Is. 11:9b).

Christ's Kingdom must *increase* until His dominion includes all people, nations, and languages, even the uttermost parts of the earth.[2] William Carey, the father of modern missions, put it this way: "Yet God repeatedly made known His intention to prevail finally over all the power of the devil, and to destroy all his works, and set up his own kingdom and interest among men, and *extend it as universally as satan had extended his*."[3]

2. The Seed

When Peter speaks in Acts chapter 3 of the restoration of all things, he cites God's promise to Abraham that his seed would bless *all* the families of the earth.[4] This promise is a cornerstone of restoration expectations. Paul also knew the extent of this restoration that comes through the power of the gospel when he said, "...the salvation of God is sent unto the Gentiles, and...they will hear it" (Acts 28:28). He describes this inheritance for Christ from among all the nations as *"the fulness of the Gentiles."*[5] The Kingdom of God grows like the proverbial mustard seed, becoming "greater than all herbs, and shooteth out great branches; so that the fowls of the air may lodge under the shadow of it" (Mk. 4:32b).[6]

Christ possesses the heavens through His Body on earth, His Church. We are seated together with Christ in heavenly places, where He restores to us all spiritual blessings. Such restoration, however, does not come without a fight. Satan and his forces attempt to prevent us from abiding in what is ours. When the Church abides in Christ, however, she exercises tremendous power, forcing satan under her feet as she advances the gospel around the world, raising multitudes to possess the very heavens in Christ Jesus.

3. Israel's History

Israel's campaign to possess the promised land is a shadow and type of the Church's mission to possess the heavenlies. Both cases involve the Lord's people displacing a powerful, well-entrenched enemy. Although at times this enemy seems to hold out or even hold the upper hand, their spiritual fortresses will be torn down.

Jesus leads the way in this campaign. His voice from Heaven brings down the principalities and raises us up to sit in the heavenlies. Our Joshua will bring us into our corporate and personal inheritance. When we abide in His words and obey His commands, we succeed in taking the land because in Christ, every place we walk has already been given to us by covenant promise.[7]

4. The Context of Peter's Message[8]

Peter preached repentance and faith in view of Christ's death and resurrection. These are the keys to restoration. John the Baptist's ministry prepared the way by calling the people to repentance and belief on Him who was to come.[9]

There is a beautiful picture of restoration in the context of Peter's message. A man crippled since birth is now running through the temple courts praising God upon being healed by the Holy Spirit through Peter. An immense crowd of people gathers at the scene of the miracle, looking in wonder at the joyful leaps of the man whom they had seen year after year begging at the temple gate called Beautiful. Through this miracle 5,000 of those who listened to Peter's message were added to the Church. Imagine the anguish of the principalities as these new believers were raised up to sit in the heavenlies!

Without Christ and the power of the Holy Spirit the people of God, both Old Testament and New, were like the crippled man, begging for alms.[10] Crippled by sin, they were unable to move in the spiritual realm or in their apostolic calling as a nation of priests. They had heard much about God's works of old, but they had seen very little. It is the same way today for churches and believers who lack the power of the Holy Spirit, and thus live by maintenance faith. Rather than expecting real restoration, they look only for enough alms to get by—to continue as they are. Yet, God intends to do so much more than we can ask or think. He has the nations in view!

5. The Early Church

Refreshment and restitution are evident in the early Church through her miracle-working power, with signs and wonders bearing witness in Jerusalem of Christ's resurrection. Daily the Lord added to their numbers as the Church met in the temple and from house to house.[11] Even many of the Jewish priests who had opposed Jesus became believers, bowing the knee and confessing His Lordship. Inspired teaching by the apostles, intimate fellowship, joyful breaking of bread, and continual prayers created a holy reverence and awe for the things of God. There was a tremendous liberality in giving and a gift of faith for miracles. In this heady environment, the Church could easily have forgotten about Judea, Samaria, and the uttermost parts of the earth.[12]

Satan did not simply sit back and watch these multitudes go into the heavenlies. He immediately sought to make inroads against the Church: "...there arose a murmuring of the Grecians against the Hebrews...."[13] By appointing deacons, the apostles handled this divisive issue well so that "the word of God increased; and the number of disciples multiplied in Jerusalem greatly."[14] Problems from within, however, were followed by troubles from without: "...And at that time there was a great persecution against the church which was at Jerusalem; and they were all scattered abroad...."[15] The time of relative peace ended abruptly as Saul made havock of the church."[16]

Nevertheless, there would be times of refreshing and restitution in other places such as Antioch, Ephesus, Corinth, Rome, and throughout the world. Even former enemies of Christ, like Saul, who sought to destroy the faith, would carry His name to the nations. Quickening power and revelation would regularly renew the Church in her long campaign to occupy the heavenlies until the return of Christ.

6. Church History

Satan's opposition to the work of restoration is seen throughout the annals of Church history: persecution from without, heresies, factions, and dissensions from within. For two centuries the early Church endured sporadic persecution from the Roman Empire before the Emperor Constantine made Christianity the state religion. By the fourth century, the biggest threat to the Church was no longer affliction from without, but a crisis of truth from within. Multitudes throughout the empire adopted an outward form of Christianity without the power of a new nature, bringing with them their own beliefs, attitudes, and customs. Gradually the Word of God became subservient to their traditions. Paul had prophesied of a *great falling away* from the faith due to seducing spirits and doctrines of devils. Plunged into such errors of legalism and tradition, the lamp of God nearly went out in the house of the Lord.[17] By the thirteenth century the dark ages covered Europe with a cloak of religious ritual.[18]

In 1517, Christ spoke to a little German monk, Martin Luther, who had cried out to Him for the assurance of salvation. He lit the fires of the Reformation by restoring the great truth of the gospel that "the just shall live by faith."[19] The good news of Christ shook the nations and ushered in a new era in Church history. No longer nullified by the traditions of men, the Bible was printed and placed in the hands of the common people. Doctrines such as the priesthood of believers and the sole authority of Scripture were restored to the Church. Although the Church struggled against the principalities, there were great awakenings and visitations in every century. In time, missionary fervor to evangelize the world was rekindled along with a renewed expectation of Christ's return. A call to personal holiness was proclaimed, and an army of salvation saints performed good works to the poor.

Then, in the early 1900's, the windows of Heaven suddenly opened. (It was the rainy season again.) A great outpouring of the Holy Spirit gave birth to a new worldwide Pentecost that flooded the earth with the knowledge of the glory of God. Holy Spirit gifts such as tongues, prophecies, and healings were again experienced while waves of restoration hit the Church. Various signs and wonders followed faith in the promises of God and in-depth Bible teaching. Church growth and mission outreaches gained momentum in a rising tide of revival. New congregations, new denominations, and a non-denominational movement have appeared on the landscape of the Church. Songs of praise have sprung up among the nations. Widespread intercessory prayer, new strategies, real unity, and increased cooperation are also indicative of the Holy Spirit's end-time work.

There is a general consensus that all this constitutes a latter day rain in preparation for a final global harvest.

7. Restoration Expectations

We are now witnessing an in-gathering from the nations as never before: an increasing number of Jewish believers, the gospel penetrating the former Soviet bloc, and a strong missionary church in Korea leading the way in evangelizing the Far East. We can anticipate the door to open soon among the unreached Muslim nations of Northern Africa and the Middle East. As the Iron Curtain fell, so must the Muslim, the Bamboo, and every other. It is only a matter of time until this gospel of the Kingdom is preached in all the world as a witness to all nations.[20] As Dr. C. Peter Wagner has written:

"We now live in a time when Satan is backed up against the wall of the 10/40 window and when the potential fulfillment of Jesus' Great Commission is in realistic sight for the first time in history."[21]

Consider how in our generation alone God's Kingdom has expanded among the nations. For example, it is estimated that in the year 1430, the number of Bible-believing Christians was one percent of the total population of the world. By 1790, it was two percent, and by 1940, three percent. Over the past 25 years, however, the percentage has risen rapidly from five to ten percent. At the present rate of growth, one percent every three to four years, the born-again Church of Jesus Christ will be 20 percent (one-fifth) of the world's population in another 30 years.[22] By 2025, this will mean a total of one and a half billion believers worldwide. Churches will be filled and many new ones established.[23]

The restored "fivefold ministry" gifts will equip the saints to do works of service.[24] Every member will supply what is lacking in the Body of Christ as we move further away from the clerical systems of the past. Adorned with the gifts and fruits of the Holy Spirit, God's people will be prepared: a bride without spot or wrinkle.[25] However, for this to be fully realized, we can expect a final season of fantastic refreshing and restitution, unparalleled in Church history: everything that the early Church experienced plus more glory in God's house. As with the wine at Cana, I believe that Christ has saved the best for last.

This truly will be the Church's finest hour. When God finishes this beautiful portrait of the restoration of all things, the last brush strokes will add details of what eye has not seen nor ear has heard. In this portrait the sun is shining, the rivers flow, and the hills are full of flocks. This landscape portrait is crowded with people, whom God has used in this restoration process through the centuries; if you look closely you will even find yourself amidst its many compelling scenes. What an honor to be a part of what God is doing in this closing hour!

The Greek word *apokatastasis* (restitution) used by Luke in Acts 3:21 describes a unique work: the house of the Lord restored as the people of God return from captivity to enter their inheritance.[26] The post-exilic restoration prophets Ezra, Nehemiah, Haggai, Zechariah, and Malachi offer many insights regarding these exciting days of restoration. When God's people came out of Babylonian captivity to repossess the land before Christ's first advent, there were still many evil enemies to overcome. So it is today: prior to Christ's second advent, powerful, wicked forces are arrayed against the Church. Satan has come down to do battle against the Body of Christ. It is important to recognize that this is due not to his strength and well-being, but to the end-time restitution in the Church.

The Coming Down of the Devil

In the Old Testament, satan is pictured as an unbound strongman walking up and down between the throne of God in Heaven and among men on earth. This accuser of men was bound and cast down from Heaven when the Man-child ascended to God's throne. The war in Heaven is over; the war on earth remains to be won. Victory is certain, but the battles may get worse before the end. Although there was no doubt as to whom would win the war, more soldiers died in the final months of Word War II in Europe than in the early years.[27]

"Satan is enraged by the sure knowledge of his own impending doom, and his countenance and demeanor reflect increasingly the loathsome bile of spite...it is acted out in the beating of an Algerian mission worker, the hanging of an Iranian pastor, the torture of Egyptian teenage converts. Such paroxysms of anger and violence, while undeniably destructive, are also demonstrations of satanic futility. They are the cheap shots inflicted by a frustrated player in the waning moments of a lost contest, the gratuitous massacre ordered from the Führer's bunker as the allies closed in on Berlin."[28]

Judged, bound, and exiled from Heaven, an angry devil comes down:

Therefore rejoice, ye heavens, and ye that dwell in them. **Woe to the inhabiters of the earth** *and of the sea! for* **the devil is come down unto you,** *having* **great wrath,** *because he knoweth that he hath but a* **short time** (Revelation 12:12).

This portrait in the gallery depicts satan's coming down due to aspects of the previous portraits: footstooling, waiting, speaking, shaking, and restoring.

1. Footstooling

The first portrait in Chapter Twelve depicted the enemies of Christ made His footstool, His feet resting upon their necks. In great humility, the Lord of Heaven came down to earth to give His life as a ransom. In contrast, satan's coming down is clearly predicated by his being cast down.[29] Revelation 12:9 uses the phrase "cast out" three times in referring to satan and his angels. Revelation 12:10 uses the phrase "cast down" once, while verse 12 says the devil "is come down." This is significant because, contrary to popular opinion, the coming down of satan is a *defensive* move, *not* an *offensive* one; it denotes his downfall.[30] Thwarted in his desire to ascend in Heaven, he is now compelled to spend his remaining time on earth defending his dying kingdom.

2. Waiting

Now enthroned, Christ is waiting until His enemies are made His footstool. It is only a matter of time. Satan's fateful, final judgment is sealed and fast-approaching. Cast out of Heaven, he knows that he has only a short time remaining. Once he was in the eternal realm, accusing men in Heaven and, at the same time, causing trouble on the earth. He was able to be many different places in an instant because eternity is not bound by time: "But, beloved, be not ignorant of this one thing, that one day is with the Lord as a thousand years, and a thousand years as one day."[31] While in the third Heaven, satan was in a different time zone. He did not know time as we who are bound by gravity do.[32]

Albert Einstein, the great physicist, discovered with his theory of relativity that time slows down as velocity approaches the speed of light, and that it stops altogether at the speed of light. Therefore, space travelers who were moving at that velocity would cease to age. In a reversal of this process, when satan was cast down, he came under the influence of time, and he has been aging quickly ever since, just like in a science fiction thriller.

3. Speaking

In Jesus' parable of the sower and the seed, the birds of the air (the devil's angels) descend to snatch away the seed (the Word of God) as soon as it is sown. The sowing of God's Word in the earth is the reason for their coming down. By sowing His life into the field of the world, Christ forced the enemy to come down. Satan knows that once the gospel is preached in all the world, it will be *curtains* for him! Therefore, he must come down to hinder the spread of the good news. Just as in a chess match where one has lost his queen to his opponent, so satan's every move is a defensive ploy, which only brings him closer to checkmate. His every scheme backfires, causing his kingdom a further binding judgment both in the heavenlies and on earth; thus sending him and his legions further down toward their ruin.[33]

The gates of hell cannot prevail against the advancing Church. No matter what he does, satan cannot stay God's hand. God rules in the armies of Heaven and does whatever He pleases on earth.[34] In these last days, the whole world will be reached with the gospel, and multitudes will be won to Christ. This makes the principalities furious. They rage and scheme against the Lord's anointed as the council of the Jewish rulers did against Jesus. When Jesus' ministry began to shake Jerusalem and Judea, satan's children took counsel to kill Him. They thought it expedient for one man to die for the nation. Their self-preserving decision to crucify Christ brought about the great victory of the atonement and resurrection. Surely satan's final plans will only help accomplish God's purpose in the return of Christ and satan's own fiery judgment.[35]

4. Shaking

Christ our Lord is the One shaking the heavens. It is His powerful word that upholds and brings down. The worlds themselves were framed by the word of God.[36] It is extremely important that we understand what is taking place and not be confused by this great paradox. Jesus has indeed won the victory and is exalted above all; satan has lost and is cast down. Nevertheless, on earth, things appear to be going from bad to worse as all hell breaks loose! Why? Satan did not relinquish his place in Heaven without a fight, and he will not give up the world any more willingly. We need to know this in order to stand in the midst of the evil day.

The Book of Revelation reveals the victory of Jesus Christ, providing a glorious picture of a Heaven cleansed of the accuser, and a world in which he has been judged. The Lamb is upon the throne. Christ controls history, not satan. Jesus alone is worthy to loose the seals of the book. When He does, trumpets announce and bowls pour out His righteous judgment upon satan's realm of unrepentant sinners. At the same time redeemed multitudes from every nation who have come out of great troubles gather around the throne.[37]

We who live at the end of the second millennium after Christ are witnessing advances in world evangelization and an unparalleled outpouring of the Holy Spirit. At the same time, our century has seen two devastating world wars, the Great Depression, and nuclear bombs. Godless philosophies of evolution, Communism, secular humanism, and many other diabolical imaginations have captured the minds of many. Ethnic wars, terrible droughts, devastating earthquakes, changes in weather patterns, and new and deadlier diseases have wracked the earth. The Christian era exhibits not only the blessed achievements of the gospel of Christ wherever it is received, but also the evil malice of an angry enemy who comes down at the end of his wicked rebellion to wreak havoc and who opposes such restoration every step of the way in order to thwart his own destruction.[38]

In the early 1960's, a worldwide wave of Charismatic renewal hit the shores of virtually every Christian denomination; acid rock music, the sexual revolution, race and war riots, and political scandals broke loose at the same time. During a well-publicized Pentecostal church meeting in the 1950's, the congregation was singing high praises when suddenly a teenage girl fell to the ground, writhing in a demonic manifestation. As the elders gathered around to pray for her deliverance she spoke with a harsh male voice, saying, "We're coming down to inhabit this generation."

Satan comes down through whatever medium he can—music, sexual promiscuity, drugs, pornography. For the past American generation, Bible reading, prayer, and Nativity scenes in public schools have been outlawed, while murder via abortion has been legalized. Teachers may no longer spank children, but they can make condoms available. Discipline and restraint are waning, while images of sex, violence, and the occult are broadcast worldwide via television and videos.[39] Cable networks and satellite dishes transmit vain imaginations, blasphemies, and evil images of the beast throughout the earth. As a result we live in days like the days of Noah before the flood: "...the *wickedness* of man was *great* in the earth, and...every imagination of the thoughts of his heart was only *evil continually*."[40] Satan's angels are casting aside restraint and descending in order to hold this world in their evil grip a while longer. No doubt we're in for another cataclysmic end like the great deluge that destroyed the earth, bringing judgment on both evil men and angels.

5. *Restoring*

Satan's casting down from Heaven to earth parallels the work of redemption in our lives. With the coming of Jesus, our spirits are made alive, and our hearts are purified by faith. Christ has entered His rightful place and driven satan out of our spirits, which is like the Holy of holies or the third Heaven. Because the devil is cast down from the exalted place of the inward man, he madly launches his assault against the unrenewed areas of our souls.[41] The mind, will, and emotions of man correspond to the second heaven. As our minds are renewed, satan's only foothold remains in our earthly bodies that await full redemption, a sort of first heaven. Even here, however, in our earthen vessels, God's power is manifested. Although our bodies may die, the final enemy (death) shall be swallowed up when Christ comes again.[42] Our natural, terrestrial bodies will then be transformed in the twinkling of an eye beyond mere restoration.

We should not count it strange if we bear the brunt of satanic attacks. Instead, we should rejoice that we are counted worthy, because satan especially contends with those who understand the times and through whom Christ is working powerfully. Whenever his kingdom is being plundered, satan targets individuals like Peter and Paul, whom he identifies as frontline influences.[43] As someone said, "There is a devil for every level." Each victory in an area, however, gives us greater ascendancy over our adversary:[44] He who is in us is greater than he who is in the world (see 1 Jn. 4:4b).

We are in a transition period in which we are being raised up while satan is being brought down. It is a time of overlapping ages, a time between times, making for quite a drama full of conflict and contradictions.[45] "It was the best of times and it was the worst of times," wrote Charles Dickens at the beginning of his classic novel, *A Tale of Two Cities*. A paradoxical statement, yes, but it relates well to the end of this age. It is the best of times for those who believe and the worst of times for unbelievers. It all depends on where you dwell. For those who abide in Zion, the heavenly Jerusalem, there are shouts of joy: "Rejoice, ye heavens, and you that dwell in them." But for those who remain in Babylon, the city of destruction, there is gnashing of teeth: "Woe to the inhabitants of the earth."

We must, therefore, never lose sight of Jesus. He is exalted over all and is actively involved in causing His enemies to be earthbound. He is extending His mighty scepter from the third Heaven. When we, His troops, have advanced His Kingdom to every people group, Christ will then personally return with His mighty angels to take vengeance on satan. Two final portraits in the gallery depict the merging of the heavens and the earth and the ultimate end of the accuser and all who follow him. *The heavens and earth on fire* and *the lake of fire* portray God's final scenario for the present heavens and earth, and for evil angels and wicked men.

Endnotes

1. See James 5:7-8.

2. See Isaiah 2:2,9; 9:7; 11:9; Daniel 2:44; 7:14; Psalm 2:8.

3. An excerpt from William Carey, "An Inquiry Into the Obligations of Christians to Use Means for the Conversion of the Heathen," *Perspectives on the World Christian Movement, A Reader*, Ralph Winter and Stephen C. Hawthorne, eds. (Pasadena, CA: The Institute of International Studies, 1981), 227-236.

4. See Acts 3:25.

5. Romans 11:25.

6. Like a great tree, God's Kingdom is on the earth and in the heavens via its many branches.

7. See Joshua 1:3-9.

8. See Acts 3:1–4:4.

9. See Matthew 17:9-13.

10. "In Hebrew *sedaqa*, 'righteousness,' is the equivalent for alms (see Ps. 24:5; Prov. 10:2; 11:4; Mic. 6:5)….Almsgiving came to be associated with merit and was looked upon as a means of conciliating God's favor and warding off evil…To be reduced to soliciting for alms was regarded as a curse from God" (Merrill F. Unger, *The New Unger's Bible Dictionary* [Chicago: Moody Press, 1988]).

11. See Acts 2:41-47.

12. See Acts 1:8. Maybe the thoughts of Acts 1:6 still lingered in the disciples' minds.

13. Acts 6:1.

14. Acts 6:7a.

15. Acts 8:1.

16. Acts 8:3a.

17. See 2 Thesalonians 2:3; 1 Timothy 4:1-3; 2 Timothy 3:1,4; 4:4.

18. "Up until this point, from a satanic perspective, things had not gone altogether badly…from the standpoint of global geography and momentum, Christianity was still fairly contained" (George Otis, Jr., *The Last of the Giants* [Tarrytown, NY: Chosen Books, 1991], 144.)

19. See Romans 1:16-17.

20. At the same time, satan works unceasingly to close these effectual doors of ministry (see 1 Cor. 16:9).

21. Dr. C. Peter Wagner, *Confronting the Powers* (Ventura, CA: Regal Books, 1996), 46. Regarding the 10/40 window, "Luis Bush observed that this area is situated between the latitudes of 10 degrees and 40 degrees north as he drew a rectangle on the map, (stretching from the West Coast of Africa to the eastern borders of China). This 10/40 Window is becoming widely accepted by missiologists as the most crucial area for the focus of the forces of evangelism in the 1990's. Within it are the centers of Buddhism, Confucianism, Hinduism, Islam…95 percent of the world's unreached peoples (but it has only .8 percent of the church's global missionary force laboring among them)…Iran and Iraq [are] situated at the epicenter of the Window. [George] Otis, [Jr.] points out that strategic-level spiritual warfare seems to be building up

at the same geographical location where it started, the Garden of Eden" (C. Peter Wagner, *Warfare Prayer* [Ventura, CA: Regal Books, 1992], 151). "Of all the spiritual superpowers facing the church at the end of the twentieth century, the strongest, and certainly most visible of these is Islam" (George Otis, Jr., *The Last of the Giants,* 58).

22. "The Growth of the Gospel," *Missions Frontiers Bulletin,* USCWM, November to December. I believe that these are conservative estimates. "In all human history not another non-militaristic, nonpolitical voluntary human movement has grown as dramatically as the Pentecostal Charismatic movement has grown over the past 25 years from 16 million in 1945 to 391 million by 1991." (C. Peter Wagner, *Warfare Prayer* [Ventura, CA: Regal Books,1992], 48).

23. *The World Almanac,* 1995 world population projections to 2020. "Global Evangelism Overview; Everyday of the year approximately 364,000 people around the world hear the gospel for the first time. Of these, about 70,000 determine to give their life to Christ for the first time...Every year Christianity realizes a net gain of about 44,000 new churches...If these statistics and others could be superimposed on a map of the world and viewed in time-lapse fashion, the impact of the past hundred years would be that of a spiritual blitzkrieg. In fact, so overwhelming has this progress been to date that a growing number of Church and mission leaders are talking seriously about a final push to victory" (George Otis, Jr., *The Last of the Giants,* 145-146).

24. I.e., apostles, prophets, evangelists, pastors, and teachers (see Eph. 4:11ff.). We have only observed a few of the more notable items restored to the Church.

25. See Ephesians 5:27.

26. Found in inscriptions for repairs to ancient temples, Josephus uses this word for the return of the Jews from captivity, while Philo used it for the restitution of inheritances in the year of Jubilee (A.T. Robertson, *Word Pictures in the New Testament* [Nashville: Broadman, 1982], 46-47).

27. Like in urban war, civilians are often caught in the crossfire, and little ones get hurt. The combatants on both sides are pushed to the limits of their ability to endure.

28. George Otis, Jr., *The Last of the Giants,* 143.

29. This portrait of the coming down of the devil also has many details like the beast, 666, mystery Babylon, and the great tribulation. Prophecy

teachers use these often, however, to paint a picture of a world given over to the devil rather than a world that is being taken away from him.

30. The phrase "come down" indicates a purposeful pursuit. It is also used in reference to God's activity on earth after the fall of man. God "came down" to see what was happening at the tower of Babel and to put a stop to it (see Gen. 11:5). The same image is used again when the angels investigate the sin of Sodom and Gomorrah, and by judgment bring it to an end (see Gen.18:21). The Lord did not merely come down through His angels to safeguard His plans, but in the person of His Son to redeem man. Satan and his angels, however, must descend defensively to preserve their life and domain on earth under the weight of God's binding judgment in Christ. Revelation chapter nine describes a star that falls from Heaven and has the key to the abyss. Many have understood this as a reference to satan since the star unleashes the demonic hordes to afflict mankind.

31. 2 Peter 3:8; see also Psalm 90:4.

32. Imagine what it would mean to enter such a time zone. You could stop reading where you are now, go and take care of business for a few days, and come back without a moment of time expiring. In the enemy's camp, this ability to suspend time and surmount space is called astral travel or projection.

33. Lucifer and his angels had proudly exalted themselves in Heaven, but are now being abased in the earth.

34. See Daniel 4:35.

35. See Revelation 19:20.

36. See Hebrews 11:3.

37. See Revelation 7:9-17.

38. See Revelation 6:13; 8:10-12; 9:1-4; 12:4. Evil angels are the stars that increasingly fall to the earth in John's Apocalypse.

39. "Let it also be known that, if Elijah is coming (to war and restore) before Jesus returns, so also is Jezebel. Indeed, do you not see her in our land in the abundance of witchcraft and harlotries?" (Francis Frangipane, *The Three Battlegrounds* [Marion, IA: Advancing Church Publications, 1989], 114).

40. Genesis 6:5.

41. Soon after regeneration, many new believers go through a time where terrible thoughts invade their unrenewed minds.

42. See 1 Corinthians 15:50-54.

43. See 2 Timothy 1:11-2:12.

44. Usually when we battle in an area and receive healing, provision, deliverance, or some spiritual blessing, we are able to walk in victory in that area and minister the same (see Mt. 10:8; 1 Cor. 2:12ff; 2 Cor. 1:3-4).

45. "What will happen in the end times? Some say a great falling away, while others predict a worldwide revival. Again the answer is both. The Bible predicts a polarization of darkness and light at the end of the age" (John Dawson, *Taking Our Cities for God* [Lake Mary, FL: Creation House, 1989], 59). In this polarization, God separates the light from the darkness as He did in the first creation (see Gen. 1:4; 2 Cor. 4:6).

Chapter Fourteen

The Accuser's Ultimate End

Questions and speculation about the end of the world have fascinated believers and unbelievers alike for centuries. There is something about the thought of the complete end to life as we know it that holds our attention. Consider all the novels, movies, and television shows through the years that have dealt with the subject. There can be little doubt: People are interested in what the future holds.

As in every other area of life, the Bible is our best and most reliable source for information concerning the end times. References to the time of the end and the "day of the Lord" are found in both the Old and New Testaments. Probably the most concentrated Scriptures dealing with the endtimes is the Book of Revelation. As we have already seen, satan and his activities occupy center stage through much of the book. Because satan is the "prince of this world"[1] and the "prince of the power of the air,"[2] the destiny of this present world is directly linked to his destiny. John's Apocalypse tells plainly of the ultimate end of satan and all who follow him. The final two portraits in the gallery, the *synthesis*, the merging of the heavens and the earth, reveal satan's final destiny.

Before considering the end of satan's wicked career as depicted in these last two portraits, it is important to discuss for a moment the question of the Millennium. Although it is mentioned only six times in Scripture, all in the twentieth chapter of Revelation, the Millennium has been nevertheless the subject of great debate and the central focus of most studies and schemes regarding the endtimes. Revelation 20:2-7 contains one reference in each verse to "a thousand years." At the beginning of that time, satan is bound for 1,000 years while the saints reign with Christ. At the end of the 1,000 years, satan is released for a short time to deceive the nations. This final rebellion against Christ is answered with fiery judgment from Heaven. Satan is cast into the lake of fire, along with hell, death, and the lost who are condemned at the judgment of the Great White Throne, while the redeemed are ushered into a new Heaven and earth.

Generally, depending on one's prophetic perspective, interpretation of these verses fall into one of three views regarding the Millennium. Theologically, all three are compatible to the chronology of satan's career presented in this book. They differ in their placement of the time of the Millennium as related to the two advents of Christ, and even in the literalness of it:

- **Premillennialism teaches that Christ's *second* coming *precedes* the Millennium.** This view interprets the Book of Revelation and this thousand-year period literally.

- **Amillennialism teaches that Christ's *first* coming *inaugurated* the Millennium.** Interpreters holding this view consider Revelation, including chapter 20, to be symbolic and figurative rather than literal, understanding the binding of satan and the raising of the martyred dead to reign with Christ as happening not on earth but in Heaven.

- **Postmillennialism teaches that Christ's *second* coming *follows* the Millennium**. Popular before World War I, this view is held by few conservative scholars today because it taught that the gospel through the Church would bring about a time of peace and prosperity on the earth.

Essentially, premillenialism and amillenialism are the only major views still generally accepted. The chronology of satan's career as presented in this book can be harmonized with either view. Historically in the Church, one's view on the endtimes has never been a test of orthodoxy, but an issue of interpretation. Whichever view is held, satan's destiny is the same: the lake of fire. And the lake of fire comes after the second coming in both premillennialist and amillennialist views.

The Heavens and Earth on Fire

Like a light shining in a dark place, the sure word of prophecy reveals that this world will end on a fiery note. Both the heavens and the earth are reserved for fire against the day of judgment.[3] What the shaking of the heavens does not remove, the fire will cleanse. Flames dominate this portrait. Indeed, there will be an atomic meltdown of the old creation; only that which is built on Jesus Christ will remain.[4]

The prophet Isaiah asked a thought-provoking question: "Who among us shall dwell with the devouring fire? who among us shall dwell with everlasting burnings?" (Is. 33:14b), then answers it: "He that walketh righteously, and speaketh uprightly.... He shall dwell on high..." (Is. 33:15-16). In the same verses, Isaiah states that sinners and hypocrites are afraid of the everlasting fire that devours. We need to be like the courageous Hebrew children Shadrach, Meshach, and Abednego who would not worship Nebuchadnezzar's golden image. Although thrown into the fiery furnace, they quenched its violence and stood unharmed, while the same fire consumed their enemies.[5] So shall it be at the end of this age.

In his second Epistle, Peter wrote of the coming day of fire:

> But **the day of the Lord will come as a thief in the night**; in the which the **heavens shall pass away** with a great noise, and the elements shall melt with **fervent heat, the earth** also and the works that are therein shall be **burned up**. Seeing then that all these things shall be **dissolved**, what manner of persons ought ye to be in all holy conversation and godliness, Looking for and **hasting** unto the coming of the **day of God**, wherein the **heavens being on fire** shall be dissolved, and the elements shall melt with **fervent heat**? Nevertheless we, according to His promise, look for **new heavens and a new earth**, wherein dwelleth righteousness (2 Peter 3:10-13).

Peter refers to the end of all things as the "day of the Lord" and the "day of God." Elsewhere it is called "the day of the Lord Jesus," "the day of Christ," "the great day, the last day," "the day of wrath," and simply, "that day." Spoken of in both Old and New Testaments, it is a dreadful day of righteous judgment and indignation in which "all the proud, yea, and all that do wickedly, shall be stubble: and the day that cometh shall burn them up...it shall leave them neither root nor branch" (Mal. 4:1b).[6] In other words, there will be nothing left of them, either in the earth or in the skies.

Like a thief in the night, that day will overtake the unrighteous in a moment. When God breaks in on His creation, it will be a noisy affair. Imagine a "big bang" as all the atoms implode and the elements melt with extreme heat, while the heavens and earth ignite in a fire so hot that it will dissolve the physical creation like billions of atomic explosions. Not only the sky, but also the sun, moon, and stars will burn like a rolled up newspaper.

God has thus prepared a large lake of fire for the final stage of judgment for the devil and his angels.[7] As the prophet Ezekiel wrote: "I will bring forth a fire from the midst of thee, it shall devour thee, and I will bring thee to ashes upon the earth in the sight of all them that behold thee" (Ezek. 28:18b). The lake of fire is the prearranged place for satan's final retribution where he and his children shall receive the ultimate punishment.

Despite the fact that the Bible consistently speaks of fiery judgment, hellfire is not a popular subject anymore. The records of a particular *orthodox* church indicated that no sermon had been preached on hell in 40 years. Not only are the concepts of hellfire and brimstone unfashionable, they are even ridiculed. A recent news headline ran, "Hell is not that bad." The article following said, "A church's Doctrine Commission no longer holds to an eternal, tormenting punishment by fire.... Such preaching inflicts 'searing psychological scars.' "[8]

Many liberal scholars today feel that the total annihilation of the wicked is safer theological ground than eternal torment in hellfire.[9] They base this on their view of God's nature, but what do they really know about His nature? The Bible uses the words *judge* or *judgment* more than 1,000 times, and Jesus Himself spoke of hell more than anyone else. Jesus said that the wicked "shall go away into *everlasting punishment*: but the righteous into *life eternal*" (Mt. 25:46). The tendency in our day, however, is to focus on the love, mercy, and compassion of God's gracious nature, while deemphasizing or ignoring His holiness, righteousness, and justice. Paul says, "Behold therefore the goodness and severity of God..." (Rom. 11:22). Blessings and curses, life and death, Heaven and hell; all are real! Those who have their part in the lake of fire will weep and gnash their teeth when they see what they have forfeited and where they are headed due to their own persistent rebellion. C.S. Lewis wrote, "Sin is man saying to God throughout his life, 'Go away and leave me alone.' Hell is God finally saying to man, 'You may have your wish.' "

The Lake of Fire

*And the devil that deceived them was cast into the **lake of fire and brimstone**...and shall be **tormented day and night for ever and ever*** (Revelation 20:10).

The reality of eternal judgment is a legitimate motivation for both proclaiming and receiving the gospel of Jesus Christ. I developed a healthy fear of the Lord when I read the Book of Revelation for the first time. Although I did not understand much of what I read, I did realize that God was going to punish unrepentant sinners. Mark Twain is said to have stated, "It is not what I don't understand in the Bible that troubles me, but the things that I do understand." This fear of the Lord made me wise concerning salvation, and prompted me to tell others. In my early years as a believer, I regularly visited the Newport Jail in Northern Kentucky. Seman Payne, who introduced me to the prison ministry, had received such a searing vision of hell that for 30 years he went every Sunday to preach to the inmates: "Knowing therefore the terror of the Lord, we persuade men."[10]

Only by preaching the gospel in all the world can we hasten the day of the Lord. Because God is patient, not willing that any should perish, the gospel of the Kingdom must be preached to every creature.[11] Nevertheless, the end shall come, and Christ shall say to them on His left hand, "Depart from Me, ye cursed, into everlasting fire, prepared for the devil and his angels" (Mt. 25:41b).

The lake of fire and brimstone is the final and everlasting phase of judgment against satan and all who follow him. The Greek word *gehenna* is the one most often used of four New Testament words for "hell." A terrible, dreadful place, Gehenna was literally "the valley of dead bodies."[12] Located south of Jerusalem, it was a place where carcasses of animals and the bodies of criminals were burned. All that are unfit for the Holy City were cast into Gehenna. With its worms, decaying matter, and perpetual fire, it became the image of a horrible place of God's judgment: the ever-gnawing worm of conscience from within and the unquenchable holy fire from without. Scripture repeatedly teaches both God's abiding wrath upon the wicked and His eternal pleasure with the saved:

*Lift up your eyes to **the heavens**, and look upon the earth beneath: for **the heavens shall vanish away like smoke**, and the earth shall wax old like a garment, and **they that dwell therein shall die in like*** *manner: but My salvation shall be for ever, and My righteousness shall not be abolished* (Isaiah 51:6).

The principalities and the powers, which dwell in the heavenlies, will perish with the heavens. For the redeemed, however, there will be no more sorrow, crying, pain, or death![13] All these things will be consumed in God's awesome presence: "For our God is a consuming fire."[14] With a new heaven and earth, the former heavens and earth shall not even be remembered, nor come to mind; the former troubles will be forgotten and hidden from our eyes.[15]

Two bumper stickers I have seen speak of the certainty of this final judgment. One reads, "God is even now preparing for judgment! Are you?" while the other warns, "Most people who plan to seek God at the eleventh hour, die at 10:45!"

Time is running out. God drove this home to me one day in a powerful way. It was a Monday, a day full of appointments, and I had overslept. I must have knocked the alarm clock off during the night, because it was lying face down on the floor next to my bed with the battery a few inches away, the hands stopped at 1:10 a.m. Instead of picking up the pieces, I rushed to get my clothes on, pausing only long enough to read my daily devotional.

The thought for December 19, my birthday, was, "Lord, teach us to number our days, to make them count, and to redeem the time." The next words really got my attention: "For you do not know when the clock will stop." Immediately I thought of the stopped clock on the floor by my bed. I read the words again: "For you do not know when the clock will stop." Time itself seemed to stand still as the words echoed in my mind: "For you do not know when the clock will stop." When I walked into the kitchen I received another shock. The kitchen clock had stopped at 2:50 that morning! The words continued to tick in my mind, however: "For you do not know when the clock will stop!"

Soon the clock will stop for satan and time will be no more. His short time will run out and God will execute the judgment He wrote long ago. *The heavens and earth on fire* and *the lake of fire* will be seen by all. These final portraits show satan himself once and for all in the lake of fire. The heavens and the earth are then forever cleansed of his presence. Remember the words of Peter, "Nevertheless we, according to His promise, look for new heavens and a new earth, wherein dwelleth righteousness" (2 Pet. 3:13). There we shall experience unimaginable raptures of ecstasies and joys unspeakable and full of glory...and no more devil! Until his end in the lake of fire, it is vital that we know how to overcome him. Our last three chapters help equip us to live a victorious Christian life in spite of satan's final onslaughts.

Endnotes

1. See John 12:31; 14:30; 16:11.

2. See Ephesians 2:2.

3. See 2 Peter 3:7.

4. See 1 Corinthians 3:4-15. The fire will separate the wheat from the tares as these grow alongside each other until the harvest. The Lord doesn't destroy the tares now lest some of the wheat also be ruined in the process, but when they're fully mature He will apply the fire (see Mt. 3:10; 7:19; 13:40-50). John the Baptist said of Jesus: "Whose fan is in His hand, and He will thoroughly purge His floor, and gather His wheat into the garner; but He will burn up the chaff with *unquenchable* fire" (Mt. 3:12). In the Book of Revelation the word *fire* appears 26 times, more often than in any other New Testament book.

5. See Daniel 3.

6. See also Joel 2:11,31; Zephaniah 1:14; Malachi 4:5; John 12:48; Romans 2:5; 1 Corinthians 5:5; 2 Corinthians 1:14; 1 Thessalonians 5:2; 2 Thessalonians 2:2; Hebrews 10:25; Revelation 6:17. Those who consider each of these to be a different day have complicated the simple Word of God.

7. See Matthew 25:41; Revelation 20:10.

8. Ziana-AFP-Reuter, *The Herald*, Friday, January 12, 1996.

9. Annihilationism teaches that the wicked will be reduced to non-existence.

10. 2 Corinthians 5:11a.

11. See Matthew 24:14.

12. Literally, "the valley of the son of lamentation," so called from the cries of little children who were thrown into the fiery arms of Molech. The Jews so abhorred this place after these horrible sacrifices had been abolished by King Josiah (see 2 Kings 23:10), that they cast into it not only all manner of refuse but also the bodies of animals and criminals" (J.H. Thayer, *Greek-English Lexicon of the New Testament* [Grand Rapids, MI: Baker Book House, 1977], 111).

13. See Revelation 21:3-5.

14. Hebrews 12:29.
15. See Isaiah 65:16-17.

Chapter Fifteen

The Accuser Overcome by the Blood

Ken was wayward and rebellious, his life controlled by many unseen forces through drug and alcohol abuse. His godly mother interceded continually for his salvation, pleading the blood of Jesus. The moment that Ken pulled the trigger, sending a bullet through the main artery of his heart, by all accounts his life should have tragically ended! Today, however, he is full of the Holy Spirit and preaching gospel crusades in Third World nations.

Ken's story is only one of many. Although the names and circumstances may vary, the testimonies agree. Numerous as the stars, they give witness to the power of the blood of Jesus to break demonic bondages!

God is giving His people today greater revelation regarding the blood of Christ to quell the final onslaughts of the devil. The early Pentecostals pleaded the blood, not in the sense of begging, but as a legal defense. They saw the blood as the means of subduing their adversary and claiming their covenant rights. If the demonic assault was not quickly surmounted, they would continue to earnestly and steadfastly resist the devil.[1] It was not a mechanical, repetitious exercise,[2] but a speaking of the blood mixed with faith. As a result they experienced many remarkable victories.

Why Believe in the Blood of Jesus?

The writer of Hebrews had no doubts about the power and significance of Jesus' blood:

*How much more shall **the blood of Christ**, who through the eternal Spirit offered Himself without spot to God, purge your conscience from dead works to serve the living God?* (Hebrews 9:14)

As evangelicals, we preach "faith in Christ" for salvation, "faith in the name" for healing, and "faith in the Word" to affirm our confidence in the Bible.[3] The Scriptures repeatedly refer to faith in Christ, His name, and the Word, and yet they also speak of faith in His blood: God has set forth Jesus Christ to be "a propitiation through *faith* in His blood" (Rom. 3:25a). Encouraging us to trust wholeheartedly in the efficacy of the blood and arguing from the lesser to the greater, the writer of Hebrews tells us, "*How much more* shall the blood of Christ...purge" [our]..." consciences (Heb 9:14).

Why is faith in Christ's blood so crucial, and how does it vanquish satan in our lives? What happens when we apply it to our lives by living faith? According to Scripture, the blood of Jesus accomplishes ten powerful things for us, each one crucial to our relationship to God and our victory over the devil.

As we go through these ten benefits of the blood, remember that "[Christ] is the propitation for our sins: and not for ours only, but also for the sins of the whole world."[4] And so there is a wider application. Paul therefore urged intercessory prayers, based on Christ's atoning death, for all men. Christ gave Himself, according to God's will, as a ransom for all men.[5] Faith in Christ's blood is of supreme importance because:

1. The blood of Jesus satisfies God's holiness.

God is holy, but man is sinful. In fact, our sins are a personal insult to God's holiness. The blood of Jesus demonstrates God's amazing love for us in spite of our sin. Jesus' blood is the *propitiation* for our sins:

*Whom God hath set forth to be a **propitiation through faith in His blood,** to declare His righteousness for the remission of sins that are past, through the forbearance of God* (Romans 3:25).

Propitiation (Gk., *hilasterion*) means "atonement" or "expiation." It carries the idea of uniting enemies in peace and turning them from hostility to friendship. Another way to think of atonement is *at-one-ment*: It makes us "at one" with God. The blood of Jesus is the only thing that can create peace between a holy God and sinful humanity.[6] When Jesus died as an offering for sin, His sacrifice satisfied God's holiness. God's indignation against sin was spent, completely exhausted. The fiery anger of God's holiness and judgment burned at the cross.

A group of early American settlers were traveling westward across the great plains, their wagons loaded with family and household belongings, when they encountered the dreaded prairie fire. The wind was whipping the fire across the tall grasslands in their direction at a speed faster than horses could gallop. The river was a full two days' journey behind them. Panic seized the group, and in a frenzy they turned their wagons to flee. The leader shouted at them to stop, then ordered controlled burning of the grass behind them. When challenged by some of the group to explain the reason for this action, the leader simply said, "Where the fire has already burned it cannot burn again!" A barrier of burned grass was their only hope. Likewise, our only hope is based on Jesus' blood and righteousness. At the cross, the Father's judgment fell upon sin. Just as the safest place to be in the midst of a fire is where the fire has already burned, so the safest place to be at God's judgment is where judgment has already passed. By the sufferings of Christ on our behalf, we are saved from fiery indignation as all other ground burns under the judgment of God's wrath.

Before the blood was sprinkled on the mercy seat to atone for our sins, satan had a place from which to accuse us. God's holiness was not satisfied by the blood of bulls, lambs, or goats. None of these could take away sin. Only the blood of Jesus, the sinless Lamb of God, could satisfy the Father's perfect justice and holy love: "He shall see of the *travail of His soul*, and shall be *satisfied*: by His knowledge *shall My righteous servant justify* many; for He shall bear their iniquities" (Is. 53:11). Satan's accusations before God have been silenced by the cry of the blood of Jesus. No further sacrifice is necessary and satan no longer has a hearing in the ears of justice. God can now receive us and still be true to Himself. Jesus is the mediator of a new covenant sealed by His blood that calls out mercy instead of judgment, forgiveness instead of vengeance, and peace instead of wrath. This work of propitiation was accomplished in Heaven where the handwriting of ordinances against us has been blotted out. Christ has stripped the principalities and powers of their age-old weapons.

2. The blood of Jesus justifies us.

Justification proceeds from propitiation. Paul writes in Romans, his great Epistle of justification by faith, that the blood of Christ is sufficient to justify us:

> **Much more** *then, being* **now justified by His blood***, we shall be saved from* **wrath** *through Him* (Romans 5:9).

Faith in the blood expiates our sin, removes God's anger from us, and declares us justified. The Greek word *dikaioo* ("justified") is a legal term meaning to render or regard as innocent. In the biblical context it means to be made right with God. I like the easy-to-remember definition of justified: *Just* as *if I'd* never sinned! Imagine what it would feel like to have never sinned. How would you feel about yourself and your relationship to God? Jesus knew no sin, yet He became sin for us so that we can now stand before God clothed with His perfect righteousness. Just as there is no sin between Jesus and His Father, so there is none between us and our Father. Nothing stands in the way; nothing separates us from right standing with Him. Christ removed our sin by sacrificing Himself,[7] saving us from all the dreaded consequences of separation from God.

A preacher once was criticized after the service for preaching on the numerous benefits of the blood of Christ. "Blood! Blood! Blood!" the critic complained. "Why all this talk about blood? It sounds like slaughterhouse religion!" The preacher gently responded, "Yes, because without the shedding of blood there is no remission of sins."[8] Satan hates the blood of Christ because it blots out our sin. Not only is there no evidence of sin but sin itself is eliminated. The devil is completely vanquished, because the blood destroys his work of sin and the indictment against us that it furnished.

3. The blood of Jesus redeems us from sin.

The Jewish leaders did not like it when Jesus implied that they were in bondage: "...We be Abraham's seed, and were never in bondage to any man: how sayest Thou, Ye shall be made free?"[9] Never in bondage? What denial! That's like the drunk who insists that he doesn't have a problem with alcohol, claiming, "I can stop anytime I want!" The Israelites had been under Assyrian, Babylonian, Greek, and then Roman bondage outwardly due to their slavery to sin inwardly. Jesus explained that whoever commits sin is the servant of sin, but that He could set them free from sin's dominion if only they would recognize their need and acknowledge Him.[10]

> *Forasmuch as ye know that ye were not **redeemed** with corruptible things, as silver and gold, from your vain conversation received by tradition from your fathers; but with **the precious blood of Christ**, as a lamb without blemish and without spot* (1 Peter 1:18-19).

In Heaven, the redeemed community sings to Christ, "...Thou art worthy to take the book...for Thou wast slain, and hast redeemed us to God by Thy blood out of every kindred, and tongue, and people, and nation" (Rev. 5:9). The Greek word *lutroo* ("redeemed") also means "ransomed" or "purchased." It was a term commonly used in the marketplace for business transactions. In the ancient world this word was used for the purchase of a slave, and it signified the price of release whereby one possessed the item purchased. Redemption equals ownership on receipt of payment. Jesus' blood is the receipt of payment proving that we have been purchased by God from out of sin's imprisonment. We were bought with a price and belong to God. We should therefore glorify Him in our bodies.[11]

The precious blood of Jesus is more than enough to cover the cost of all the sins of every man since Adam. Christ's blood was unique in two ways: It was untainted by sin, and it was the very blood of God. I do not presume to understand the biology involved in the miraculous conception of Christ: the chromosomes, DNA, or genetics. That is outside of God's written revelation. I am certain, however, that the incorruptible seed of God's Word became flesh in the womb of the virgin Mary. The blood flowing in His veins was in fact the blood of God, for God "purchased" the Church "with His *own* blood."[12] That alone made it more valuable than all of creation combined, an incomparably rare and priceless possession.

When David Livingstone was preaching to an African tribe about redemption in Christ's blood, he was candidly asked how one man's blood could be worth so many lives. Reaching into his pocket, he pulled out two coins: one copper and one gold sovereign. He proceeded to explain the vast difference in their value in the British Empire, then applied it to the value of Christ's blood in comparison to that of other men.

As believers, we may not fully understand *how* the blood of Christ affects our salvation, but we certainly have experienced its *power* to redeem us. This redemption in the blood is centered in God's forgiveness. He releases us from the debt we owed. Our unmet obligation is pardoned: "In whom we have redemption through His blood, even the forgiveness of sins" (Col. 1:14).[13] We are free because our sins are forgiven. Christ's blood is sufficient payment.

4. The blood of Jesus washes us clean from sin.

Washing is a big part of our lives. We wash our bodies, our clothes, our fruit and vegetables—everything from cars to carpets. We wash to look nice and to guard against contamination. We wash our outer selves, but what about the moral and spiritual areas of our lives? John understood the sin-cleansing quality of Jesus' blood:

*And from Jesus Christ, who is the faithful witness, and the first begotten of the dead, and the prince of the kings of the earth. Unto Him that loved us, and **washed** us from our sins in **His own blood** (Revelation 1:5).*

Jesus challenged the Pharisees, who always meticulously washed their hands and their utensils before eating, to clean not only the outside, but inside their hearts as well. That reminds me of the man who was hired by a department store to wash their display windows. He vigorously rubbed and rubbed at one particularly stubborn spot on the glass, puzzled as to why it would not come off. His supervisor, observing the man's futile efforts, said, "That spot is on the inside. You'll need to wash the inside before you wash the outside."

Since we are continually exposed to sin in this world, whether in thought, word, or deed, we need to wash regularly. Initially, we wash the entire body of sin's defilement at conversion, when the Holy Spirit applies the blood of Christ to our inner man. It alone is able to remove the filthy stain of sin. Thereafter, we need a periodic foot washing for our earthly walk. The importance of this was illustrated when Jesus came to Peter to wash his feet. At first Peter refused, until Jesus said that unless He washed Peter's feet, he would have no part with Him. Peter then requested that Christ wash his whole body as well. Jesus replied that a person who had bathed needed only to have his feet washed, and that they were all clean except the one who was going to betray Him.[14]

*But if we walk in the light, as He is in the light, we have fellowship one with another, and the **blood of Jesus Christ** His Son **cleanseth us** from **all sin**. ... If we confess our sins, He is faithful and just to forgive us our sins, and **to cleanse us** from **all unrighteousness*** (1 John 1:7,9).

As we continue to look in the mirror of God's Word, we should confess any appearance of sin in our lives. Then beelzebub, the "lord of the flies," will not be attracted to us. Our fragrance to God will remain pleasant as we stand before His throne in Heaven spotless and unstained by the world.[15] The ceremonial washings and various sacrifices of the Old Testament foreshadowed both this need and provision for cleansing. We approach and have constant fellowship with Him whose name is holy.[16] Those who stand before God's throne "have washed their robes, and made them white in the blood of the Lamb."[17]

5. The blood of Jesus sanctifies us.

Related to the work of Christ's blood in washing away our sins is its action in sanctification. All the great doctrines of salvation—propitiation, justification, redemption, forgiveness of sin, cleansing, and sanctification—are established and experienced on the basis of faith in the blood.

*Wherefore Jesus also, that He might **sanctify** the people **with His own blood**, suffered without the gate* (Hebrews 13:12).

The word *sanctify* (Gk., *hagiazo*) means "to make holy, or purify; to set apart for God's use." The blood of Jesus separates us unto God and ministers to us its own purity and holiness. The process of sanctification is thus like a spiritual blood transfusion. The holy blood of Christ is a continual life-quickening flow, combating and destroying all the sin-infested corners of our lives. Our daily walk with Christ becomes more and more holy in a process that Peter calls "sanctification of the Spirit, unto obedience and sprinkling of the blood of Jesus Christ" (1 Pet. 1:2b). As a result, grace and peace are multiplied in our lives.

Sanctification has both a positional and a practical dimension. The blood of Jesus provides both. Through faith in Christ and His shed blood, positionally we are perfectly holy and utterly blameless before God, yet practically speaking, we progress in a lifelong process of sanctification. Sins exposed while we walk in the light of God's Word and the conviction of His Spirit must be confessed and purged out of our lives by the blood.

On this point a note of caution is necessary. It is possible for sin to again gain dominion in our lives if we fail to turn diligently from iniquity. We can still yield our members as instruments of sin and uncleanness. The Scriptures are full of sobering examples of those such as Esau who have sold their blood-bought birthrights to enjoy the pleasures of sin for a season.[18] Practical sanctification can not only be hindered but, by willful and continual sin, can even be halted. Extreme cases can result in a loss of positional sanctification and potential damnation.

> For if we **sin willfully** after we have received the knowledge of the truth, there **no** longer remains a **sacrifice** for sins, but a certain fearful expectation of **judgment, and fiery indignation**.... Of how much worse **punishment**, do you suppose, will he be thought worthy who has **trampled** the Son of God **underfoot, counted the blood** of the covenant by which he was sanctified **a common thing**, and insulted the Spirit of grace? (Hebrews 10:26-27,29 NKJ)

Sin can become a habitual practice in two basic ways, both revealing a loss of faith in the blood: making light of sin, thereby esteeming Jesus' blood to be "an unholy thing," or considering our sins to be too great and beyond the saving power of the blood. The first reckons the blood as an agent of uncleanness, giving license to continue in sin rather than separating from it. Such attitudes "turn the grace of our God into lewdness and deny the only Lord God and our Lord Jesus Christ" (Jude 4b NKJ). It is presumptuous for anyone to deliberately pursue sin and yet expect the blood to continue to cover him.[19] The Books of Hebrews and Jude identify this root of apostasy as unbelief. The second type of unbelief is due to guilt over the magnitude of our sins, causing us to draw back from faith in the blood. We grow weary and faint in our struggle against sin, losing faith in the power of the blood to actually purge our lives from sin.[20]

God rejected the temple sacrifices when they became empty rituals. Once devoid of the substance of faith, they were meaningless dead works.[21] In the same way, Christians may parade the cross, wear crucifixes and other Christian jewelry, repeat prayers and outwardly acknowledge the communion of the blood of Christ, and yet deny its wonder-working power. This is due to a sinful manner of life and a lost fellowship with God.[22] In their unbelief, they trample the Son of God underfoot, and "crucify to themselves the Son of God afresh, and put Him to an open shame."[23]

Satan's strategy is to destroy faith. His lies, coupled with the deceitfulness of sin, aim to persuade us to deny, cover up, and say we have no sins rather than to confess and forsake them.[24] Confession expresses faith. If satan can, through unconfessed sin, destroy our faith in the cleansing flow of the blood, he can subject us to sin again with the latter state becoming worse than the former.[25] A guilty conscience and a cycle of unconfessed and unforsaken sin are telltale signs of satan's attempt to cut us off from the blood. In this struggle against sin we must apply the blood *in faith* until we overcome.

Our conscience is a key faculty for an active faith. We must not ignore it or else it will become defiled and malfunction.[26] A man bought a new car with a voice-warning system. At first, he was amused to hear the voice gently remind him that his seat belt wasn't fastened or that the car was low on gasoline: "Your fuel level is now low." On one occasion he thought he still had enough fuel to go another 50 miles, so he kept driving, ignoring the persistent voice of warning. It kept coming over and over, and even seemed to him to begin to sound harsher each time. Finally, after about 20 miles of this, the man stopped his car, crawled under the dashboard, disconnected the appropriate wires, and silenced the aggravating voice. He stopped smiling to himself a few miles later, however, when his car sputtered to a stop, out of gas!

Although we can repeatedly ignore the voice of conscience, we face real consequences when we do. On the other hand, when we respond to the voice of conscience and apply the blood, it keeps us from wrecking our faith.

6. The blood of Jesus purges our conscience.

Victor Hugo, in his great tale of conscience, *Toilers of the Sea*, writes:

"You can no more keep thought from returning to past transgressions than keep the sea from returning to shore after it has gone out. In the sea we call it the tide, but the guilty man calls it conscience. Conscience heaves the soul as the tide does the ocean."

The blood of Christ alone can calm the stormy conscience, purging our souls from both the practice and the guilt of sin:

*How much more shall **the blood of Christ**, who through the eternal Spirit offered Himself without spot to God, **cleanse your conscience** from dead works **to serve** the living God?* (Hebrews 9:14 NKJ)

Serving God with a clear conscience is the fruit of sanctification. When renewed and properly functioning, the conscience is a good barometer for determining spiritual well-being.[27] A wholesome conscience is maintained by a faith-filled application of the blood to any areas where our conscience accuses us. The enemy of our soul can no longer accuse us to God, so he accuses us to ourselves and to each other. Satan may even try to sound like the voice of conscience, but once we have confessed and forsaken our sin, his voice continues to condemn us. We must learn to discern between the voices of satan, our own conscience, and God's Holy Spirit.[28]

A wounded soldier lay dying in the arms of a friend. In despair he cried out, "Oh, I am in great trouble this morning!" For a moment he seemed to lose consciousness, then trembled and called out the name, "Jesus!" When the dying man opened his eyes again, his friend asked what had happened. The wounded soldier replied softly, "I was attempting to climb an immense, steep-sided mountain. After attaining a considerable height, I suddenly lost my hold and fell back to the bottom. Exhausted, I sat down to weep. But when I called the name of Jesus, a drop of blood fell upon the mountain and dissolved it in a moment of time." When the friend asked what all of this meant, the soldier said, "That mountain was all my sin, and the drop which fell upon it was one drop of the precious blood of Jesus. The mountain of my guilt has melted away." He then died in peace.

An old gospel hymn expresses beautifully the blood's power to purge our conscience:

"There is a fountain filled with blood
Drawn from Immanuel's veins,
And sinners plunged beneath that flood
Lose all their guilty stains."

Another songwriter wrote:

"Though the restless foe accuses,
Sins recounting like a flood,
Every charge our God refuses:
Christ has answered with His blood."

7. The blood of Jesus provides access to God.

Just as we cannot maintain a good conscience without the blood, it is impossible to boldly approach the holy presence of God apart from the blood:

*Having therefore, brethren, **boldness** to enter into the holiest **by the blood of Jesus*** (Hebrews 10:19).

A popular worship chorus contains the words, "Only by grace can we enter, Only by grace can we stand; Not by our human endeavors, but by the blood of the Lamb."[29] It is fitting that the saints both in Heaven and on the earth should sing of the blood of the Lamb.[30] We enter and abide in the Holy Place because Christ's blood has opened the way and prepared a place for us.

Rose was only a few days old in the Lord, but she had truly experienced the cleansing power of the blood. In a vivid dream one night, she stood third in line before the gates of Heaven. Two great angels stood guard there to question all who would enter. She listened to the two men ahead of her. The first explained how he had lived a decent life, had never murdered anyone, and had not committed adultery. Before he finished, the angels sadly began to shake their heads, and he vanished into space. The second man spoke of his baptism, church attendance, and various good works, but he too was denied entrance and disappeared. It was now Rose's turn. Standing before the gates she cried from deep within, "I plead the blood of Jesus!" Immediately, the angels stepped to one side saying, "Daughter, be of good cheer. Your faith has opened the way." Then a thunderous voice was heard that shook the very heavens, declaring:

*I, even I, am He that **blotteth out thy transgressions** for Mine own sake, and will not remember thy sins. Put Me in remembrance: let us **plead together: declare thou** that thou mayest be justified* (Isaiah 43:25-26).

It was the blood of Christ speaking in Heaven, pleading on her behalf as she declared her faith in Christ's death. She entered by the only possible way—the blood of the Lamb.

D.L. Moody, addressing his ministerial students, said, "If you will read your Bible in the light of Calvary, you will find there is no other way of coming to Heaven but by the blood. The devils don't fear 10,000 preachers who preach a bloodless religion. A man who preaches a bloodless religion is doing the devil's work, and I don't care who he is."

8. The blood of Jesus brings us near to God.

Not only does the blood of Christ give us boldness to enter, it also brings us near to God, literally drawing us to Him like a magnetic force:

But now in Christ Jesus ye who sometimes were far off **are made nigh by the blood of Christ** (Ephesians 2:13).

Moses anointed Aaron by applying the blood of a goat to his right ear, thumb, and big toe, consecrating Aaron to draw near and minister to God. In like manner Christ anoints us by applying His own blood to the right ear of our conscience, the thumb of our service, and the big toe of our walk, consecrating us to draw near to God and minister as priests in the Most Holy Place.[31] The only mediator we need is Christ, and He has opened equal access to all who will draw near through His blood.

The story is told that before the breakup of the Soviet Union several years ago, a blasphemous comedy entitled, "Christ in Tuxedo," opened to a packed house in one of Moscow's leading theaters. The first act included a scene set in a church sanctuary where the altar was arrayed like a bar with bottles of beer, wine, and vodka. Fat priests sat around raising their arms in drunken toasts while nuns squatted on the floor playing cards. It was a degrading exhibition of atheism that marked the Communist rebellion against the Savior.

Act Two featured a Moscow matinee idol, Comrade Alexander Rostovsev, a dyed-in-the-wool Marxist and a sneering enemy of Jesus. The audience roared when he walked on stage impersonating Christ, dressed in a flowing oriental robe and carrying a large New Testament. The script called for him to read two verses from the Sermon on the Mount, remove his gown, and cry out, "Give me my tuxedo and top hat!"

As rehearsed, Rostovsev began to intone slowly: "Blessed are the poor in spirit, for theirs is the kingdom of heaven. Blessed are they that mourn, for they shall be comforted." Suddenly, Rostovsev stopped as though paralyzed. An uneasy silence gripped the audience as the smooth, suave actor, his whole body shaking, began reading again: "Blessed are the meek, for they shall inherit the earth. Blessed are they who hunger and thirst after righteousness, for they shall be filled. Blessed are the merciful, for they shall obtain mercy." Before a stunned audience, he continued reading until he had finished the entire 48 verses of Matthew chapter 5.

Backstage, the other cast members coughed, called, and stamped to urge the star on with his forgotten blasphemies, but Rostovsev was no longer a blasphemer. Christ had conquered and converted him! There, before the footlights, he who had reviled the Crucified, now made the sign of the cross in the Russian Orthodox tradition, crying out in the prayer of the penitent thief, "Lord, remember me when Thou comest into Thy Kingdom!" That was too much for the management. The curtain fell, the announcement was made that Comrade Rostovsev had suddenly taken ill, and the performance was canceled.

Only the blood of Christ can draw near those who are far from God. Through His death Christ bought our salvation, sealing the purchase with His blood. Since He alone is able to bring us to God, all other religious attempts are futile.

Neither religious traditions nor church rituals have the power to either bring us to God or change the human heart. Even messages on morality are powerless to transform men. The great Scottish preacher Chalmers was reconverted in the midst of his ministry, turning away from preaching mere morality to preaching Christ crucified. He confessed that all his former sermons about man's moral duty had not exerted a feather's weight of influence upon the conduct of his people. It was only when his preaching brought them near to the cross that he noted any changes in their lives.

9. The blood of Jesus reconciles creation.

Reconciliation required cleansing Heaven of wicked spirits. Because the blood of Christ has blotted out mankind's sin, "the creation itself also will be delivered from the bondage of corruption into the glorious liberty of the children of God" (Rom. 8:21 NKJ). Although we await the redemption of our bodies, even now we are free from the sting of death (which now is likened to sleep in the New Testament). A complete reversal of the Adamic judgment is possible because of the blood of Christ!

*And, having made **peace through the blood of His cross**, by Him to **reconcile all things** unto Himself; by Him, I say, whether they be things **in earth**, or things **in heaven** (Colossians 1:20).*

Dennis Fulton tells a tale that illustrates the age-old expectation of creation reconciled by blood. Landing his plane in a Zairean village to do food relief, he was surrounded by an excited knot of villagers. As he was climbing out of the cockpit, he was met by two men carrying a live chicken between them, one gripping its feet, the other, its head. Before either the chicken or Dennis knew what was happening, the fowl's head and body parted company. The man with the flopping chicken corpse began swinging it over his head, round and round, with predictable results! Fresh chicken blood spattered Dennis, in a freshly pressed white shirt, his plane, and the villagers.

When Dennis asked for an explanation, one of the villagers explained that for generations splattered blood had signified an end to suffering. To the people of this village, Dennis' Cessna promised all kinds of help. In like manner Christ came once to shed His blood to deliver mankind caught in the grip of sin. More provisions from Heaven are guaranteed: "...He will appear a second time, not this time to deal with sin, but to bring to full salvation those who eagerly await Him" (Heb. 9:28b, J.B. Phillips translation).

10. The blood of Jesus overcomes the devil.

It is fitting that the last book of the Bible should highlight the overcoming power of the blood. By the blood, satan's authority to accuse us is broken, and he is dethroned and disarmed. There are shouts of joy in Heaven, great rejoicing in the heavenlies, and victory for those on earth who confess Christ. Every realm of creation—Heaven, earth, and hell itself—testify to the wonder-working power of the blood of Jesus.[32]

*And they **overcame him** by the blood of the Lamb...* (Revelation 12:11).

There is an English cathedral that contains two special graves that tell a remarkable story of love. The graves are marked by the figures of a crusading knight and his lady. The statue of the lady has no right hand. According to tradition, the knight, while on crusade, was captured by the Moslem conqueror, Saladin. When the knight besought Saladin to spare his life for the sake of the love that his lady in England bore him, Saladin scoffed. He told the knight that his lady would soon forget him and marry another. Assured that she would never do that, Saladin asked for proof. If the lady sent Saladin her right hand, he would release the knight from the sentence of death. A letter to this effect was dispatched to the lady in England, who promptly had her right hand cut off and sent to the Moslem conqueror. When Saladin saw it, he set the knight free.

Just as the English lady bore on her body for life the sign of her love for her knight, so Christ bears in His body the marks of His sacrificial love. Through His blood we are set free from enemy bondage, accepted by God, justified, redeemed, reconciled, washed clean from our sins, sanctified, and freed from a guilty conscience. Through His blood we boldly enter God's presence and draw near to Him. Through His blood we prevail over satan. Everything depends on the blood!

*Though your **sins be as scarlet**, they shall be **as white as snow;** though they be **red like crimson**, they shall be **as wool*** (Isaiah 1:18b).

We must apply the blood as the Israelites did during the Passover. When the lamb's blood was applied to the doorpost, the destroyer could not touch God's people: "Through *faith* he [Moses] kept the passover, and the *sprinkling of blood*, lest he that destroyed the firstborn should touch them" (Heb. 11:28). We apply the blood by faith through the word of our testimony. Our words are therefore an absolutely essential component to overcoming satan and his forces.

Endnotes

1. See James 4:7.
2. See Matthew 6:7.
3. See John 2:22-23; 4:50; Acts 3:16; Galatians 3:26.
4. 1 John 2:2
5. See 1 Timothy 2:1-6.
6. See Isaiah 53:3-10.
7. See Hebrews 9:12; 10:17-19.
8. See Hebrews 9:22.
9. See John 8:33.
10. See John 8:32-36.
11. See 1 Corinthians 6:20; 7:23.
12. Acts 20:28.
13. See also Psalm 130:3-5,7-8.
14. See John 13:6-11.
15. See 2 Corinthians 2:15.
16. See Leviticus 6:27; 8:6ff.
17. Revelation 7:14b.
18. See Genesis 25:32; Hebrews 12:16.

19. See Hebrews 10:38; Jude 5.

20. There are two opposite reactions, both a result of unbelief: *despise* and *faint* (see Heb. 12:5).

21. See Isaiah 1:11; 66:3; Hosea 6:6.

22. See 1 Corinthians 11:27; 2 Timothy 3:5; Titus 1:16.

23. Hebrews 6:6b.

24. See 1 John 1:6; 2:12.

25. See Matthew 12:45; 2 Peter 2:20-22.

26. See 1 Corintians 8:7; 1 Timothy 4:2; Titus 1:15.

27. See Romans 2:15; 9:1; 2 Corinthians 1:12; 4:2; 1 Timothy 1:5,19; 3:9.

28. See Romans 9:1.

29. "Only by Grace," Song No. 425, *New Songs for Worshipping Churches*, Songbook 5 (Hosanna! Music).

30. See Revelation 5:9

31. See Revelation 1:5-6.

32. See Revelation 12:10-12.

Chapter Sixteen

The Accuser Overcome by the Word of Our Testimony

Let us hold fast the profession of our faith without wavering; (for He is faithful that promised) (Hebrews 10:23).

A secret house-meeting of Chinese believers was just getting under-way when there was a loud knock on the door. Two soldiers stormed into the crowded room demanding that everyone there deny Christ and that the meeting disband. A few people left immediately while the rest remained seated. The soldiers persisted, giving a final warning and waving their weapons in the air. Three more got up and went out into the night. After a moment or two of silence the two soldiers gently placed their rifles in the corner against the wall and removed their helmets. From their backpacks they produced New Testaments and said excitedly, "We can now have an overcomers' meeting with all the holy brethren here!"

George Otis, Jr., has asked, "Is it conceivable that Christianity's failure to thrive in the Muslim world is due to the notable absence of Christian martyrs? And can the Muslim community take seriously the claims of a church in hiding?"[1] I might add "a worldly, self-seeking church" in hiding.

There is no such thing as cheap faith. Many of the early saints held firm to their testimonies without wavering, even unto death: "...and they loved not their lives unto the death" (Rev. 12:11). Because they were prepared to die rather than deny Christ, the next generation had an opportunity to hear the good news. Paul cites the example of Jesus, "who before Pontius Pilate witnessed a good confession."[2] Bearing witness to the truth cost Jesus His life. Like the first saints, we need to settle in our hearts beforehand what we believe and not be afraid to speak. It may not be cozy or convenient to witness, but Christ does empower His disciples by the Holy Spirit.[3] Indeed, such empowerment is the key to our overcoming the accuser.

We have already seen how the blood of Christ was the first agent in cleansing Heaven of the accuser and making us fit for God's holy presence. Now we can understand that even as Christ's blood needed to be applied on the mercy seat in Heaven, it needs to be applied to our lives on earth. This involves appropriating the overcoming power of the blood through the word of our testimony. In John's vision a loud voice from Heaven says, "And they overcame him by the blood of the Lamb, and by the word of their testimony..." (Rev. 12:11). The word *and* makes all the difference in this world. Victory is based on Christ's blood *and* our testimony.[4] When Christ died, He paid in full our sin debt and made forgiveness available, yet at some point, we must believe the good news and confess Christ. Paul said, "If thou shalt confess with thy mouth the Lord Jesus, and shalt believe in thine heart that God hath raised him from the dead, thou shalt be saved" (Rom. 10:9).

The devil's first objective is to destroy our faith; failing that, he tries to silence or discredit our testimonies. Satan saw to it that the early Church was called a sect and spoken against everywhere.[5] Believers were viewed as evildoers and were persecuted and imprisoned. Every possible attempt was made to keep them from speaking or teaching the people in the name of Jesus.[6] Today, the devil has largely succeeded in silencing believers' testimonies in government, schools, and other public places. He wants to keep the Word off our lips and away from the ears of others because he knows that our testimony not only solidifies our faith, but makes it possible for others to believe. For this reason he comes down to make war on those who "have the testimony of Jesus Christ."[7]

Jesus' High Priestly Ministry

By the word of our testimony, we extend Jesus' heavenly authority to our earthly lives. In many churches, the present high priestly ministry of Christ in Heaven is a neglected doctrine, obscure and devoid of meaning. When properly understood, however, it is of immense spiritual benefit, quickening our faith to full assurance, and our testimony to steadfast stability:

> *Seeing* then that we have *a great high priest, that is passed into the heavens, Jesus the Son of God, let us hold fast our profession* (Hebrews 4:14).

Our profession of faith is founded upon *both* the finished work of Christ's death *and* His present ministry of intercession in Heaven. The first bought our pardon; the second appropriates His finished work in our lives. Our acceptance before God is made possible by Christ's mediation on our behalf of the new covenant in His blood. The Book of Hebrews continually affirms Jesus' high priestly role:

> *When He had by Himself purged our sins, sat down on the right hand of the Majesty on high* (Hebrews 1:3b).

> *Whither the forerunner is for us entered, even Jesus, made an high priest for ever after the order of Melchisedec* (Hebrews 6:20).

> *For Christ is not entered into the holy places made with hands, which are the figures of the true; but into heaven itself, now to appear in the presence of God for us* (Hebrews 9:24).

Christ's ministry as our high priest is distinct from His work on the cross. It is performed in Heaven, not earth, for *believers*, not unbelievers, and is a present, continual ministry of intercession, not a past, one-time work. It is also a completely effective work: "Wherefore He is able also to save them to the uttermost that come unto God by Him, seeing *He ever liveth to make intercession for them*" (Heb. 7:25). How does the blood of Christ speaking in Heaven unite with our testimony on earth to make us victorious?

Five interrelated scriptural principles of testimony help us envision how this works.

1. Christ as our high priest unites His blood with our testimony.

Christ is our great high priest and advocate before God's throne, using His blood and the word of our testimony to give us the victory over satan. However, neither Christ's past work on the cross nor His present ministry of intercession are fully operative apart from the word of faith in our mouths. Victory calls for a union of blood and testimony.[8]

The Scriptures connect blood and testimony in the strongest possible terms. Moses, after he had spoken "every precept" of the Law, took blood and sprinkled it, saying, "This is the *blood of the testament* which God hath enjoined unto you" (Heb. 9:20). During the Last Supper Jesus took the cup and said, "For this is My *blood of the new testament* [covenant], which is shed for many for the remission of sins" (Mt. 26:28). Both testaments required blood. Because life is in the blood, the most important testimonies require the death of the testator. The Greek word *martus* ("martyr") is related to *marturia* (which is translated "testimony" in Revelation 12:11), and is used only twice in the New Testament, both times referring to specific individuals who *died* for their testimony to Jesus: Stephen (Acts 22:20) and Antipas (Rev. 2:13).

Blood and testimony carry deep spiritual significance. John emphasizes both in relation to Christ's crucifixion:

> *Instead, one of the soldiers pierced Jesus' side with a spear, bringing a sudden flow of **blood** and water. The man who saw it has given **testimony,** and his **testimony** is true. He knows that he tells the truth, and he **testifies** so that you also may **believe*** (John 19:34-35 NIV).

This union of blood and testimony appears again in John's first Epistle when he addresses the gnostic heresy claiming that Christ was not really human but only appeared to be. This was based on the erroneous Greek notion of dualism, which considered all matter to be evil; only the spirit was pure. The sinless Son of God, therefore, could never take on sinful flesh. John begins his letter by affirming the reality and humanity of Jesus whose death gives us life and is the basis for Christian fellowship (see 1 Jn. 1:1-3). He then condemns the gnostic heresy as the spirit of antichrist (see 1 Jn. 4:1-3) because God's testimony demands that Christ be fully human and pour out the lifeblood of His flesh and die. When we drink of the cup at the Lord's Supper, we figuratively drink His blood, testifying that we have partaken of Christ's death for us.

> *This is He that came by water and **blood**, even Jesus Christ; not by water only, but by water and **blood**. And it is the Spirit that **beareth witness**, because the Spirit is truth. For there are three that **bear record** in heaven, the Father, the Word, and the Holy Ghost; and these three are one. And there are three that bear witness in earth, the Spirit, and the water, and the blood: and these three agree in one. If we receive **the witness of men, the witness***

*of God is greater: for this is the **witness of God** which **He hath testified of His Son**. He that believeth on the Son of God hath **the witness** in himself: he that believeth not God hath made Him a liar; because he believeth not the **record** that God gave of His Son. And this is **the record,** that God hath given to us **eternal life,** and this life is **in His Son*** (1 John 5:6-11).

God was manifested in the flesh and shed His blood on earth.[9] His incarnation and crucifixion forever silenced the accuser in Heaven. Satan's accusations are replaced with the everlasting song of the Lamb that is sung by the redeemed. The Lamb slain before the foundation of the world has come into His creation to redeem it back to Himself. Heaven and earth bear witness that God is true and the devil is a liar. No wonder satan hates the blood and our testimony concerning Christ. He uses man's proud yet darkened mind to speculate against the Word of God, casting doubt on the deity and humanity of Christ. Satan even employs those who profess to serve God but deny Him by their teachings![10]

As a new Christian, I attended a private university where I studied theology under professors who rejected the bodily resurrection of Christ. One lecturer's entire approach involved "demythologizing" the Scriptures: stripping away the myths behind Adam and Eve, Noah, etc., to get to the "real" message. From the start, my faith in God's Word was challenged. I felt like the seminary student who said, "All day long they tore the Bible apart, and all night long I put it back together." The most conservative member of the department taught a class on the end of the world in which he claimed that Jesus and the apostles thought the end of the world would come in their lifetimes. He cited Jesus' own words as evidence: "...There be some standing here, which shall not taste of death, till they see the Son of man coming in His kingdom."[11]

These misguided professors stimulated me to dig deeper into Scripture. It so happened also that I met my wife in that same class! When Pat had first tried to register, the class was full, and she only secured a place at the last moment when another student dropped the course. I was very outspoken in class, and I often stayed afterward to pursue the discussion with the instructor. Many times, Pat stayed as well. One day I asked her in front of the lecturer, "Who do you agree with?" She won my heart when she answered, "You!" When we agree with God's testimony regarding Christ we unite with His heart, and His testimony gives us the victory. Therefore, we must not allow anyone or anything to cast doubt on the testimony of God's Word.

2. Christ as God's testimony is forever settled in Heaven.

Nothing in the Bible contradicts scientific or historical fact. Someone has wittily remarked that criticism of the Bible is like a blind man looking into a dark room for a black cat that isn't there. I like the bumper sticker that says, "God said it. I believe it. That settles it!" When our testimony is Christ Himself, we overcome the lies of satan every time. Why? Jesus Christ is the Rock on which the Church is built, a foundation for our confession of Him, which the gates of hell cannot withstand. He alone opens Heaven to man and binds the evil principalities and powers. Jesus is the One that the prophetic Scripture testified concerning: "For had ye believed Moses, ye would have believed Me: for he wrote of Me" (Jn. 5:46), and "To Him give all the prophets witness" (Acts 10:43a). The testimony of Jesus is thus called the spirit of prophecy.[12]

John the Baptist testified that Jesus was the Messiah: "Behold the Lamb of God, which taketh away the sin of the world. This is He of whom I [and all the other prophets] said, After me cometh a man which is preferred before me: for He was before me" (Jn. 1:29b-30). This was also the testimony of the apostles and other disciples who saw and heard Him. The Father bore witness of Him at the Jordan River and throughout His ministry. The Holy Spirit testified by remaining on Him without measure. Jesus of Nazareth is therefore the test of the Christian faith, and the dividing line between believer and unbeliever, saved and unsaved.

The Greek word for "testimony" contains the idea of a recorder,[13] in the legal sense of a testimony recorded before a judge. God is the judge of all, and what we say and do with His Son is of the utmost consequence. He still asks men, "What do you say concerning Jesus?" One day the books will be opened, and the things written there will judge everyone. Like the 70 disciples, we should rejoice because our names are written in Heaven, and our voices heard on high, testifying to the Lordship of Jesus![14] The answer to the question of *who* Jesus is logically leads to following Him. Submission to Christ authenticates our profession of faith in Him.[15]

When I had been a Christian for about a year, the Lord led me on a prolonged fast. Toward the end of it a sister in Christ, Margie Bush, prophesied: "The Lord is going to send you to a faraway place." Months passed while this prophecy sat on the shelf—until one day a missionary from Zimbabwe came to our church in Cincinnati. Ron testified about the many opportunities to minister there, and after the service, he encouraged me to come for a four-month visit. Although my heart leaped at such a prospect, the $2,000 airfare seemed like a lot of money to me. I could attend a year of Bible school for that amount. As I prayed, I heard God say that I was to go and that the $2,000 was "a drop in a bucket." The next day a friend visited me and read Isaiah 40:15, which says that all the nations on earth are like "a drop in a bucket" in God's sight. My friend had no idea that I had heard the exact same phrase the night before. These words of confirmation quickened my faith for the money to go. The week before I was due to leave, I received the balance of $1,800 that I needed for airfare. There is nothing like hearing from and following Christ. He thus becomes our testimony each and every time.

3. Christ as our Mediator is the meeting place.

Testimony is the meeting place for God and man. In the Old Testament, the place where God met with His people was called the Tabernacle or tent of the *testimony*.[16] Within the veil was the ark of the *testimony*,[17] which contained the two stone tablets of testimony written by the finger of God.[18] Since God fellowshipped there with His people, all the essential elements were depicted. The two cherubim or angelic powers were there, because they responded to the testimony of men. More importantly, God was there and promised to "...meet with thee, and...*commune* with thee...from between the *two cherubims* which are upon the *ark of the testimony*, of all things which I will give thee *in commandment*..." (Ex. 25:22).

Heaven and earth meet in Christ. When our testimony connects with His, we experience overcoming power, because Heaven has come down to earth. Ed Silvoso aptly points out that "we have reduced it (testimony) to merely witnessing to other human beings. Biblically speaking, the scope of our testimony is much broader. It reaches all the way in to the heavenly places."[19] Many examples from Scripture reveal this reciprocal relationship between God's testimony and ours. These passages help us to see the connection between what happens on earth and what transpires in Heaven as a result of our testimony. For example, Jesus says regarding our profession of Him:

> *Whosoever therefore shall* **confess Me before men,** *him* **will I confess also** *before My* **Father** *which* **is in heaven.** *But whosoever shall deny Me before men, him will I also deny before My* **Father** *which is in heaven* (Matthew 10:32-33).

God met me often in the hospital where I worked as an orderly while attending Bible school. It was my first mission field. I had a strong conviction that God had placed me there to be a witness, and opportunities continually presented themselves. I felt a divine responsibility to the patients I shaved, prepared, and transported to the operating room for open-heart surgery. The preparation process took about half an hour, so there was time to talk to these patients. Daily I experienced God's presence and pleasure as I shared Christ's testimony and prayed with men facing major surgery.

During the five years that I worked at the hospital, not one man of the nearly 2,000 whom I prepared for surgery ever complained, yet slanderous opposition still came against me. On one occasion the head nurse in surgery wrote up a formal stage one disciplinary report against me, claiming that a particular patient had been offended by something I had said to him. When I went to apologize to the patient, I discovered that he had made no such complaint. On the contrary, he had appreciated our conversation and had mentioned it to a doctor who had checked him after I had finished.

When this was reported to the head nurse, she had no option; the report was torn up. On another occasion, a hospital chaplain protested against my praying with a patient. When he had come to pray, the patient had simply said, "Don't worry, I've already had a good prayer with a young man. I'm ready to go!" Time and again I experienced the overcoming power of testimony. In the process, I learned the importance of pursuing matters and not leaving them unresolved. As we bring things to the light, satan's works of darkness are exposed and his lies are powerless.

In spite of these and other conflicts, I knew that God had me there to be a witness. Paul's words greatly encouraged me: "Some indeed preach Christ even of envy and strife; and some also of good will: ...whether in pretence, or in truth, Christ is preached; and I therein do rejoice..." (Phil. 1:15,18). The head nurse who opposed me was demoted and replaced. At the same time, God's favor increased until I was like Paul in relation to Julius and those aboard the Alexandrian ship bound for Italy. By the time I finished Bible school and left for Africa, I was an unofficial chaplain at the hospital. My record was unblemished. Christ's blood and His testimony in my mouth silenced the devil.

John's vision in Revelation pictures our prayers as ascending to God like incense, where they are then poured back onto the earth.[20] When

Cornelius' prayers came "up for a memorial before God," God responded by sending an angel to him. This enabled his whole house to hear the gospel from the apostle Peter and receive the gift of the Holy Spirit.[21] Prayer has tremendous influence both in Heaven and on earth: Elijah was a man of like passions such as we are, but when he fervently prayed, he shut the heavens, and it did not rain for three and a half years. When he prayed again, the heavens opened, and it poured rain so that the earth produced a harvest.[22]

> *...Whatsoever ye shall **bind on earth** shall be **bound in heaven**: and whatsoever ye shall **loose on earth** shall be **loosed in heaven**. Again I say unto you, That if **two** of you shall **agree on earth** as touching any thing that they shall ask, it shall be **done** for them of My Father which is **in heaven*** (Matthew 18:18-19).

The giving of our substance is also part of our testimony, and it affects Heaven and earth. With his offering Abel "obtained witness that he was righteous, God testifying of his gifts" (Heb. 11:4b). The prophet Malachi pictures the tithe as the key that unlocks the heavenly windows from where God pours out earthly blessings and rebukes the devourer.[23] Paul in the New Testament bears witness to the giving of the Corinthians: "I bear record...."[24] He declares to the Philippians that their giving is a sweet-smelling sacrifice to God, building up fruit to their heavenly account, and that God will therefore meet all their needs according to His riches *in glory* by Christ Jesus.[25] John, writing to Gaius, said the "brethren came and testified of the truth that is in thee" and "have borne witness of thy charity before the church" (3 Jn. 13b,6a).

God inhabits our praises too. The principalities and powers are greatly affected by this. The Bible says, "Let the *high praises* of God be in their mouth, and a *twoedged* sword in their hand; to execute vengeance upon the...*people*; to bind their *kings* with chains, and their nobles with fetters of iron; to execute upon them the judgment *written*: this honour have all His saints..." (Ps. 149:6-9). Even in the mouths of babes and nursing infants God has *perfected praise*...and *silenced* the enemy and the avenger.[26] These songs of praise to the Lamb that John saw on high affected every creature in Heaven, on earth, in the sea, and in the subterranean world. When we sing His testimonies the whole universe is touched.[27]

4. Christ as our hope of glory imparts His heavenly life.

Our faith-filled testimony of who Christ is and what He has done for us is a channel for establishing these as firm realities in our Christian walk. Paul wrote this to Philemon: "That the communication of thy faith may become effectual by the acknowledging of every good thing which is in you in Christ Jesus" (Philem. 6). We should with heartfelt conviction publicly acknowledge our relationship to Jesus; that He is the source of every blessing in our lives. This opens us to even more of Christ's resurrection life. Jesus told the Gadarene, who was delivered of legions of demons, to go and testify what great things God had done for him.[28] Likewise the lepers, when healed, were to show themselves to the priest as a testimony to them. Even Jesus repeatedly testified regarding His heavenly Father and His mission on earth. He challenged Nicodemus to believe His testimony because only then could he receive new life:

*Most assuredly, I say to you, We speak what We know and **testify** what We have seen, and you do not receive **Our witness**. If I have told you **earthly things** and you do not believe, how will you believe if I tell you **heavenly things**?* (John 3:11-12 NKJ)

By using the plural "We testify," Jesus refers to Himself and His Father. The Father needed a man on earth who would embody His testimony. When we receive Christ as God's testimony, He starts to mold us to His image. "As He is, so are we in this world."[29] Through faith, by hearing and responding to His testimony, we become what would otherwise be impossible.[30]

I was not a very disciplined person while I was growing up. Upon my conversion, Christ immediately began to change me and fashion me according to His image. When He spoke to me about Bible school, I knew it was not an option, but a vital instruction to follow. Although the closest Spirit-filled Bible school was 50 miles from home, I went in faith. It meant two hours in the car, three hours of class each day, plus a full-time job. I really thought it would kill me! One year grew to two years, two years became five. Those were character-shaping years, in which I learned discipline to become what would otherwise have been impossible. Even today I draw upon that impartation of heavenly life. When we pursue the life Christ has for us, there is no stopping place, only a pressing on.

5. Christ as our life communicates through us.

Since Christ is our testimony, every Christian can have a powerful witness. He is what makes our testimony dynamic. We are what God says we are in Christ. We can do what He says we can do. God's Word is like a seed that produces after its own kind. It has creative power. We can meditate on and "babble" what God's Word says about us as believers. It is ours in Christ.

Do you testify regarding your position in Christ? Do you boldly tell others that you are redeemed from sin and a new creature in Christ? Do you confess that you are complete in Him? Do you personally confess Him as your strength and that you are strong in the power of His might?[31] Or do you say that you are tired, burned out, and need a break! Life is challenging enough without wasting our energy by speaking against ourselves. I am not advocating proud, presumptuous, and foolish statements, but simply saying what God says.[32]

Many Christians think that it is presumptuous and smacks of spiritual pride to speak in this manner, but God delights in His children babbling His Word and boasting in Him. Jesus often spoke of Himself in relation to His Father in a way that infuriated the religious community. In John's Gospel there is a running battle between Jesus and the Jews over the words He spoke. They sought to kill Him. Why? In their minds, He made Himself greater than their father Abraham and even equal to God. The officers of the temple summed it up when they said, "Never man spake like this man."[33] Listening to Jesus made it obvious too that He was afraid of nothing.

There were plenty of fears in my life. However, the more I read, studied, and meditated on His Word, the more His life and spirit drove these fears out.[34] For a period of two years a team of three people from our youth group visited once a week a state hospital for the mentally disturbed. Some of the patients heard voices, others were deluded or simply withdrawn. At this hospital, fear had taken a terrible toll. One evening, after a time of breakthrough in ministry, this spirit of fear sought to intimidate me. As I crossed the parking lot and headed for my car, one of the patients shouted from the steps, "Preacher, you had better never come back here!" He was a big man, well over six feet, wearing a long black overcoat. He had never attended our meetings, yet he was now hurling threats of physical abuse. I began to pray in the parking lot. I knew that if I gave in to this spirit and drove away, there would be more trouble on my next visit.

With Holy Spirit boldness, I slowly walked toward him. As I did, he said, "If you cross over onto the grass you've had it!" I simply proceeded and calmly informed him that I was not afraid. When my foot touched the grass it was as if an invisible force hit him. He whimpered in fear, "Don't hurt me!" as he backpedaled for the porch and disappeared inside. After that, I had no more problems with him. I have often observed an important principle: people project what is influencing them, such as fear, lust, and pride, then it is measured back to them more strongly than they measured it out. The principle holds true for the positive fruit of the Spirit as well as for the devil's garbage.[35]

Speaking God's Word is a key to spiritual maturity and self-control.[36] I know that speaking inspired words from Scripture to encourage, exhort, and comfort enhanced my own spiritual development. The apostle Paul called the Corinthians to edify one another through the gift of prophecy because speech that articulates God's Word is very profitable for spiritual growth. Although in the beginning I was not able to express my faith effectively, I became more proficient through practice.

One does not have to be a developmental child psychologist to know that we learn to speak before we learn to do. We communicate before we can even walk. The more words we can speak the more we can do. A child soon learns that if he can say it, it is possible to have and do. Preachers and teachers of God's Word do a disservice to God's children when they call them to do what they cannot yet articulate! Instead of calling them to actions beyond their spiritual development, they should encourage them first to believe, think, and speak God's Word.[37]

A final example from the life of Paul drives home the power of a believer's testimony to silence the accuser. Ananias the high priest of the Jews traveled from Jerusalem to Caesarea with his elders and a professional accuser named Tertullus where they skillfully accused Paul to Felix, the governor, of inciting sedition against Rome.[38] Paul, however, overcame his accusers by sharing the testimony of his conversion to Christ.[39]

Paul went to Jerusalem fully aware of what he was facing there. Like Christ, his words exerted great authority in the spirit, because he had received them from God. He demonstrated an ability to lay down his life as well as to take it up. His guide in all things was God's words to him, spoken and faithfully acted upon. Paul is an example to us that our testimonies direct the course of our lives and enable us to triumph.[40] The blood of Christ and the word of our testimony are the essential elements to overcoming the accuser. With our position and authority in Christ secure, we can now explore what it means to access a Heaven that has been cleansed of the devil.

Endnotes

1. George Otis, Jr., *The Last of the Giants* (Tarrytown, NY: Chosen Books, 1991), 261.

2. see 1 Timothy 6:13b; John 18:37.

3. See Acts 1:8.

4. D.L. Moody was fond of saying that "the blood alone makes us safe, and the Word alone makes us sure."

5. See Acts 28:22.

6. See Acts 4:17-18.

7. Revelation 12:17.

8. See Romans 10:6-10; Revelation 12:11.

9. See 1 Timothy 3:16.

10. See 2 Peter 2:1-2.

11. Matthew 16:28. Jesus is referring to the Mount of Transfiguration. Luke even says, "And it came to pass..." (Lk. 9:28), and Peter, who was on the Mount of Transfiguration, understood Jesus' words to be fulfilled then and there. In his second Epistle, Peter cites this event as a prefiguring of Christ's second coming: "For we have *not followed cunningly devised fables*, when we made known unto you the power and *coming of our Lord Jesus Christ,* but were eyewitnesses of His majesty. ...when we were with Him in the holy mount. We have also a more sure word of prophecy..." (2 Pet. 1:16,18-19).

12. See Revelation 19:10.

13. *Gesenius*, in J.H. Thayer, *Greek English Lexicon of the New Testament* (Grand Rapids, MI: Baker Book House, 1977), 391.

14. See Luke 10:20.

15. See Luke 6:46-49.

16. See Numbers 9:15.

17. See Exodus 16:34; 25:16,22; 30:6.

18. See Exodus 31:18; 32:15; 34:29.

19. Ed Silvoso, *That None Should Perish* (Ventura, CA: Regal Books, 1993), 198.

20. See Revelation 5:8 compared with 8:3-4. We can cry out to God when our adversary tries to steal from us what is ours in Christ, and claim our covenant rights in prayer. God then has every right to speedily avenge us. Ignatius, the Bishop of Antioch, who died as a martyr early in the second century, wrote to the Ephesians: "Therefore be eager to meet more frequently for thanksgiving and glory to God. For when

you frequently come together, the powers of satan are destroyed and his destructive force is annihilated by the concord of your faith" (13:1).

21. See Acts 10:1ff.

22. See James 5:17-18.

23. See Malachi 3:10-11.

24. See 2 Corinthians 8:1,3.

25. See Philippians 4:19.

26. See Psalm 8:2; Matthew 21:16.

27. See Revelation 5:11-14.

28. See Luke 8:39.

29. 1 John 4:17b.

30. See Romans 4:17-18.

31. See Nehemiah 8:10; Psalm 18:2,27; Isaiah 30:15; 40:29,31; Colossians 1:11.

32. See Romans 8:16-17; 2 Corinthians 5:17,21; Ephesians 1:3,20-21; Philippians 4:13; Colossians 1:13-14; 2.10. The most appealing form of testimony is giving thanks to God because it clearly points to God and gives Him, not man, all the credit. We can sing and say who God is through declaring what He does.

33. John 7:46.

34. Guidance, protection, provision, and healing are other areas that we can confess (see Ex. 15:26; Ps. 1; 23:1,3; 32:8; 37:4,23-24; 103:3; 119:105; Prov. 3:6; 6:22; Is. 30:21; 2 Cor. 9:8; 1 Pet. 2:24; Jas. 5:14-15).

35. See Psalm 23:4; 91:10-11; Isaiah 54:17; Matthew 10:13; Ephesians 3:17; 6:10.

36. See James 3:2.

37. There are additional principles that can help us to understand how Christ uses our testimony to overcome the accuser on earth. These five are simply a good starting place.

38. See Acts 24:1-7.

39. See Acts 24:10-21; 25:11-16.

40. See Acts 18:9-11; 22:1-21,30; 9:6,15-16; 20:21-25; 2 Corinthians 1:7-10; 11:24-28; 12:9; 2 Timothy 3:10-12; 4:18.

Chapter Seventeen

The Accuser and Freedom From Guilt and Fear

For Christ is not entered into the holy places made with hands, which are the figures of the true; but into heaven itself, now to appear in the presence of God for us (Hebrews 9:24).

In a Highland village of Scotland lived a shepherd and his little daughter. He always took the young girl with him when he went out to tend the sheep. The thing the daughter liked most of all was to hear her father call the sheep with the shepherd's call, free and beautiful on the wind and over the moors. The girl grew into a beautiful young woman and went off to the great city of Edinburgh to pursue her career. At first her letters came regularly every week. Before long, however, they became less and less frequent, then finally stopped altogether. Rumors circulated in the village that the shepherd's daughter had been seen in bad company and in questionable places. Then one day a lad from the village happened to see her in the city. He spoke to her, but she pretended not to know him. When the shepherd heard this, he immediately set out for the city with his shepherd's staff in hand to find his lost daughter.

Day after day, he sought her in vain on the avenues and in the slums of the great city. Then, remembering how his daughter had loved to hear him call the sheep, he resumed his search, walking the city streets sounding the shepherd's call, loudly and unashamedly. Passers-by looked with astonishment on the rough, plain shepherd with his smock and staff, searching the streets up and down, calling continually. In one of the degraded sections of the city, the daughter, sitting in a room with her companions, looked up with astonishment as she heard the plaintive cry. There was no doubting her father's voice. It was the shepherd's call! Flinging wide the door, she rushed out into the street and into her father's arms. He held her close, then returned with her to their Highland home where with great compassion he loved her back to decency and to God.

Nathaniel Hawthorne tells the story of the Intelligence Officer, presiding over his lost-and-found office in the midst of a great city. Different people come in seeking what they have lost: for one, the costly jewel of virtue, lost through careless wandering in the city; for another, his shining influence for good. Hawthorne knew that in all of us there is a desire to find what we have lost. The greater the value, the more intense the longing and search.

Jesus illustrates this principle in His three parables in Luke chapter 15: the lost sheep, the lost coin, and the lost son. Each narrative tells of the desire and search to recover what was lost and the rejoicing when it was found. The greatest celebration of all was given for the son who returned home, for he was intrinsically and uniquely of greatest value!

The value to Jesus of one human soul far exceeds the entire material wealth of the earth. Jesus Himself said, "For what is a man profited, if he shall gain the whole world, and lose his own soul? or what shall a man give in exchange for his soul?" (Mt. 16:26) No poet, painter, or philosopher could ever express the true impact and meaning of the loss of a human soul. We are of such worth to God that Jesus willingly died to redeem us: "For the Son of Man is come to seek and to save that which was lost" (Lk. 19:10).

What Happened?

Humanity has lost something of infinite and indescribable worth: our relationship with God. Like the prodigal son of Luke 15 and the shepherd's daughter in the story, we have all gone astray and become separated from God in a condition that the Bible calls "lost." We are aware that "something" is missing, but in our spiritual lostness and blindness we don't know what it is. The cry of the lost echoes through the ages in a search as old as mankind.

Since we don't know *what* we have lost, we don't know *where* to find it. We look many places, try many things, yet continue to live unfulfilled lives, dissatisfied and devoid of purpose. We either intensify the search, growing frenzied in the shallow hope that we will recognize what we're looking for when we find it, or in despair, we abandon the search altogether, simply marking time until we die. The words of a song that say "Leave me as you found me, empty as before..." express the heartache of someone who has looked in the wrong places.

How do we find what we are looking for? How do we get back what we have lost? It is necessary to return to the beginning, to Eden, to understand what humanity lost and why. The third chapter of Genesis reveals *five death signals* that describe what mankind lost. Knowledge of these will enable us to recognize the kind of abundant life God intended for us to have and help us identify what we are seeking to regain.

First Indication of Spiritual Death: *An Evil Eye*

*And the eyes of them both were **opened**, and they **knew** that they were **naked**; and they sewed fig leaves together, and made themselves aprons. And **they**...**hid** themselves from the presence of the Lord God.... And [Adam] said, I heard Thy voice in the garden, and I was afraid, because I was **naked**; and I hid myself* (Genesis 3:7-8,10).

What does the phrase mean, "the eyes of them both were opened"? It sounds like a good thing, doesn't it? Why also is this the first and primary manifestation of the loss of spiritual life? To begin with, Adam's and Eve's eyes were opened to *evil*. They looked upon and personally experienced evil.

The account of mankind's fall makes two explicit references to "open eyes." The serpent says in verse 5 that "in the day you eat thereof, then your eyes shall be opened." Verse 7 says that after they ate, "the eyes of them both were opened." In addition, in verse 22 God acknowledged the drastic change of mankind's perspective: "Behold, the man is become as one of Us, to know good and evil...." Open eyes to good *and* evil triggered every other reaction. The evil eye is not merely the first and foremost effect, but the source of all that follows: guilt, shame, fear, hiding, blaming, deceit. The condition of our eyes determines how we view God and ourselves, and that view determines our actions. Jesus said:

*The light of the body is the **eye**: therefore when thine eye is **single**, thy whole body also is full of **light**; but when thine eye is **evil**, thy body also is full of **darkness**. Take heed therefore that the light which is in thee be not darkness* (Luke 11:34-35).

After the disobedience of Adam and Eve, their "opened" eyes filled them with darkness. The rose-colored garden view was gone, replaced by a thick, evil veil of sin that caused them to see God and each other in a *different* light, a *diffused* and *distorted* light that was actually darkness! Innocence died abruptly that day. With the death of their spirits, their souls were stripped bare before God and each other. The glorious covering of God no longer overshadowed them.[1] As a result, they saw their nakedness and were ashamed. Before, they had never looked at themselves that way; now, with their eyes on themselves and away from God, they became self-conscious, self-centered, and self-seeking![2]

Infants and small children enjoy an age of innocence such as our first parents had in paradise, but their dependency and transparency is short-lived. Born with a sinful nature into a corrupt world, their eyes open to evil all too soon.[3] Inhibitions, fear, hiding, and shame soon emerge, creating a sense of loss of love, security, and significance. Feelings of rejection compete with acceptance, while helplessness challenges their sense of security. This loss of innocence and trust can be devastating. The eighteenth-century philosopher Rousseau struck that note in his glorious yet terrible *Confessions*, which vibrates with a deep sense of loss. When his mother died while he was still a boy, from that hour, he later wrote, the gates of Eden were closed against him:

> "Here was the term of the serenity of my childish days. From this moment I ceased to enjoy a pure happiness and I feel even this day that the reminiscence of the delights of my infancy came to an end. Even the country lost in my eyes that charm of sweetness and simplicity which goes to the heart; it seemed somber and deserted, and was as if covered by a veil, hiding its beauties from our sight. We no longer tended our little gardens, our plants, our flowers; we went no more lightly to scratch the earth, shouting for joy as we discovered the germ of the seed we had sown."

No wonder the Kingdom of Heaven belongs to little children! We must become as little children in order to enter the Kingdom of God. Then we can regain an anxiety-free realm where dependence on God justifies us, makes us peacefully content and joyfully occupied.

The story is told that near the ruins of Baalbek a child was kneeling in prayer by a fountain. A man rode up on his horse and dismounted to quench his thirst. His face mirrored a life full of all manner of iniquity, coarseness, and crime. As he stooped to lift the water to his lips, he saw the child kneeling in prayer nearby. In a flash his hard face softened and a tear flowed down his cheek. He recalled the day when he too had been as innocent as that small child; the time when he himself had prayed as this child now was. He cried out mournfully, "I was that child!" What a sad loss!

Second Indication of Spiritual Death: *Concealment*

Adam and Eve heard the voice of God and, due to a guilty conscience, hid themselves. The naked soul will always cover up and hide from God. This is an instinctive, universal reaction to guilt. The law of sin at work in man produces self-consciousness, coupled with guilt that motivates him to conceal himself from the presence of the Lord. "Adam and his wife hid from the presence of the Lord God amongst the trees of the garden" (Gen. 3:8b). The trees, representing legitamate things in creation, are now improperly used by man in his attempt to hide. Imagine trying to hide from God amidst His creation. How deceitful we are!

Nowhere on earth is there a place or people untouched by sin. The movie, *The Gods Must Be Crazy*, humorously imagined a tribe of bush people in southern Africa that was free from the effects of sin. Their completely harmonious lifestyle changes abruptly when an empty Coke bottle thrown from an airplane lands in their village. For this remote tribal group, planes and gods are synonymous. Why would *the gods* give them this strange item? Then the trouble starts as their *true* selves come out and they vie with one another for possession of the treasure!

"Humpty Dumpty sat on a wall; Humpty Dumpty had a great fall. All the king's horses and all the king's men couldn't put Humpty together again." This classic nursery rhyme is over 1,000 years old, and versions have appeared in eight European languages. In its early days, it was a riddle asking the question, "What, when broken, can never be repaired?" As any child knows, it's an egg. Regardless of how hard one tries, a broken egg can never be put back together again. The Humpty Dumpty of the Bible is the human race. In spite of our own efforts, we cannot make ourselves whole. If we think we have it together, we are only deceiving ourselves. All the king's horses and all the king's men can't put man together again, but the King Himself can! The King of creation alone can put together the broken pieces of our lives. He straightens that which is crooked and removes the blight of sin.

Third Indication of Spiritual Death: *Fear*

Biologists say that fear is one of the first emotions we develop. Often, our fears are multiplied by what we see, hear, and experience as we grow up. There are probably more words in our culture to describe various kinds of fear than there are for any other emotion: *horror, phobia, terror, scare, panic, alarm, trepidation, anxiety, worry, apprehension*; the list goes on and on. Like an airborne disease, fears are easily transmitted from one person to another. A spirit of fear literally pervades the world, and its inhabitants live in a sort of mass hysteria. It flares up greatly from time to time due to circumstances or events, but demonic powers lie at the root. No wonder the Bible tells us over and over to "fear not," but have *faith*!

When Adam sinned, a spirit of fear entered his heart and a dark shadow was cast over his life. We have been unable to handle our experiential knowledge of good and evil. The seed of the serpent and his hateful enmity against mankind began to work in Adam's very soul, and continues in our own.[4] In our fear and anxiety, we expect the worst, often because of guilt. The fear of exposure and punishment go hand in hand. This fear is universal and permeates all of creation. Under its dominion, animals instinctively fear, and even intelligent men are held in bondage all of their lives: "...those who through the [haunting] fear of death were held in bondage throughout the whole course of their lives" (Heb. 2:15 AMP).

I grew up in the 1960's during the cold war. The continual stockpiling of nuclear weapons and the ever-present threat of an all-out war between the superpowers created an anxious generation of "gloom and doomers." What the "day after" would bring was the subject of much speculation and more than one movie. Motivated by fear, many planned for doomsday, digging bomb shelters and storing food.

In the early days of the cold war, Senator Joseph McCarthy alarmed the nation by announcing on the Senate floor: "I have here in my hand a list of 205 individuals who are known to the Secretary of State as being members of the Communist Party. They are shaping the policy of the State Department." The media picked up the story, and panic broke across the land as the nation was swept into an era of fear. After nearly five years of investigations and hearings, the McCarthy witchhunt failed to uncover a single Communist. The alleged list turned out to be temporary employees who had not been recommended for permanent State Department employment. Heaven only knows how much good has been prevented and how much harm done by fear's relentless war against faith!

Fourth Indication of Spiritual Death: *Self-Defense*

A minor league baseball manager was so disgusted with his center fielder's performance that he ordered him to the dugout and assumed the position himself. The first ball that came into center field, which should have been played for a single, bounced past the manager and went to the wall for a triple. The next one was a high fly ball, an easy third out, which he lost in the glare of the sun. Next, he misjudged a hard line drive, charging the ball while it went over his head and allowing another run to score. Furious, the manager ran back to the dugout, grabbed the center fielder by the uniform and shouted, "You idiot! You've got center field so messed up that even I can't play it!"

In order to deal with guilt, we accuse and blame. Children blame their parents; wives accuse their husbands, and husband their wives. To evade our own responsibility, we make someone or something a *scapegoat*. Seeing others take the heat makes us feel better about ourselves. We even blame God to ease our pain. Our attempts to deal with our guilt often leads to self-justification. In fact, all the religions of the world are centered in man's efforts at self-justification. Even much of Christendom is based on works, laws, and rituals as men attempt to remove their guilt and save themselves by their religious activities. The result is a pharisaical system similar to the one so strongly condemned by Christ for making individuals like children of the devil.[5]

When the Pharisees brought to Jesus the woman taken in adultery, their aim was either to see the woman stoned to death or Jesus condemned for not upholding the Law of Moses. An old manuscript of John's Gospel has a striking addendum to the text. John 8:6 reads: "...Jesus stooped down, and with His finger wrote on the ground..." while the addendum reads, "...the sins of each one of them." Although we don't know what Jesus actually wrote, it is true that when we point our finger to accuse, there are three of our own fingers pointing back at us. We remind God of our own sins and give place to the tormentors. This iniquitous mechanism of accusing and condemning others to relieve our own guilt is wicked. It is part of the devil's work to criticize and condemn.[6] Self-justification by blaming others also explains why satan is the accuser: he with the greatest guilt is the most condemning, forever calling to mind his own rebellion. His sins are written not in the dust, but in the very heavens! Left without excuse, he will be tormented forever and ever.[7]

Fifth Indication of Spiritual Death: *Disintegration*

When sin is finished, it brings forth death.[8] The whole of creation was subject to decay and disintegration. From birth to death nature was in bondage. Various forms of death sprang up everywhere: The earth produced weeds and thorns, and many animals became carnivorous. Evidence of the fall was pervasive. The devastation and wreckage of life was seen everywhere. Ruin, spoil, and corruption were the order of the day.

Madeleine L'Engle's novel *A Severed Wasp* was inspired by one of George Orwell's essays, and offers a graphic image of a dying world cut in two by sin. Orwell describes a wasp that "was sucking jam on my plate and I cut it in half. The wasp paid no attention and merely went on with its meal, while a tiny stream of jam trickled out of its severed esophagus. Only when he tried to fly away did he grasp the dreadful thing that had happened." This wasp and people without Christ have much in common. Severed from the life of God, people are greedy but unaware of what they have lost. They continue to consume and console themselves with life's sweetness. Only when it's time to fly do they grasp their dreadful condition.

God's command not to eat of the tree of the knowledge of good and evil was not arbitrary. On the contrary, it was ordained to preserve life. God did not want mankind to experience evil; hence the warning: "in the day that thou eatest thereof thou shalt surely die."[9] Spiritually, Adam died the very day he partook of evil. His spirit was separated from God, but only 900 years later did Adam's body stop functioning. Moreover, those who die physically while spiritually alienated from God are liable for the second death. The second death is eternal separation from the life and love of God!

Sent and Driven So As to Return

Why was mankind removed from Paradise? The answer is important and reveals a twofold reason in God's redemptive purpose. This dual aspect is indicated by the two expressions related to man's expulsion, *sent* and *driven out*:

> *Therefore the Lord God* **sent him forth** *from the garden of Eden, to till the ground from whence he was taken. So he* **drove out the man***; and He placed at the east of the garden of Eden* **Cherubims***, and a flaming sword which turned every way,* **to keep the way** *of the tree of life* (Genesis 3:23-24).

The phrases "sent him forth" and "drove out the man" are significant. The reason for the first phrase is clearly stated: "...lest he put forth his hand, and take also of the tree of life, and eat, and live for ever" (Gen. 3:22b). In other words, *God prevented man from living for ever in his sinful condition.* God never desired for mankind to be alienated from Him, either for time or eternity. He intervened therefore by sending man out with the purpose of redeeming him.

Although man was "sent forth" to prevent him from living forever in his fallen state, he was "driven out" so that he would experience the consequences of his lost state. Man could feel the sting of sin. He could see it in the ground as he toiled and would be buried there. Both the sending forth and the driving out were redemptive in God's plan, intended to bring about man's repentance and restoration.

The serpent, on the other hand, was neither sent forth nor driven out of Paradise because God did not plan for his redemption, but for his eternal expulsion, announced beforehand by the prophets. Once Heaven was reopened to man, the serpent would be barred. In the meantime, the fallen *nachash*, a defiled cherub, became the means by which man was barred from returning. He blocked the way to the tree of life, and was the means by which mankind was made to feel the evil effects of his sin. These were experienced in satan's enmity against man and his dominion over death. The inescapable fact of inward death at work in Adam was the death of his body, and his removal from Paradise was an undeniable indication of his lost relationship to God. Paradise and the tree of life are therefore the last domain regained by the redeemed.[10]

Farther Afield

As with the fallen angels, the mystery of iniquity began to work in mankind. Guilt and fear in Adam regressed to unresolved anger and depression in Cain. Before long, the working of spiritual death arrived at its ultimate end: hatred and murder rooted in a lost relationship to the loving Giver of Life. Satan displayed his broken relationship to God when he murdered Adam and Eve in Eden. He became the father of lies and of those who lust as he did, like Cain, "who was of that wicked one, and slew his brother."[11]

Cain must have heard from his father Adam what mankind had lost with God; yet he did not consider it very worthwhile. Maybe the garden had been great, Cain may have reasoned, but a lost relationship with God was no pearl of great price. Such an attitude clearly revealed Cain as a child of the devil. Unrighteousness multiplied. With such a devilish attitude, Cain's spirit was bound to move farther from God. Spiritual death at work in Cain caused him to depart, and yet he felt driven by God:

> *"Surely You have **driven** me out this day from the face of the ground; I shall be **hidden from Your face**; I shall be a fugitive and a vagabond on the earth, and it will happen that anyone who finds me will kill me."* ... *Then Cain **went out from the presence of the Lord** and dwelt in the land of **Nod** on the east of Eden* (Genesis 4:14,16 NKJ).

Cain ran farther afield from God's presence, exemplifying the way of the world. Mankind went from Paradise, a kind of Holy of Holies or third Heaven, to the Holy Place or second heaven, to the outer court, or the land of Nod, which means a place of exile or wandering. Implied is flight and exile from the presence of God! Such are those who go "the way of Cain,"[12] who "separate themselves...having not the Spirit."[13]

As man's relationship to God diminishes, so the signs of his estrangement multiplies.[14] The vacuum caused by the absence of characteristics of God's Kingdom is filled increasingly by more of satan's dark deeds, because when men retreat from the light they move toward the outer darkness. Thus, in the end, the rebellion in creation is nothing but a return to the dark of the abyss. Without God, there is only emptiness! The crucifixion of the Lord of Life was thus the inevitable and ultimate expressions of both man's rebellion and God's redemptive love.

Satan's kingdom was built upon two dark pillars: sin, which separates from God; and death, the logical result of that separation. Samson is a two-edged example for us of this principle. On the negative side, Samson was not aware that the Spirit had departed from him. His spiritual senses had become duller the farther he went from God. As a result, even before he lost his sight, he could not see very far.[15] Because the benefits of his former relationship to God continued for a season, he did not realize what he had lost. Only when the works of the Spirit ceased, enabling the enemy to bind him and pierce his eyes, did he realize that he had lost his relationship with God! We never seem to realize the true value of something until we lose it.

On the positive side, Samson turned back and sought a restored relationship with God. When his spoilers called for mirth in the temple of Dagon, Samson reached into the darkness and laid hold of the pillars of the temple. As he called on the name of the Lord, his strength returned to pull the idolatrous temple down in ruin around him. In a similar manner, our great champion, Jesus of Nazareth, spread His arms out on the cross, seized the pillar of sin with one hand and the pillar of death with the other, and pulled them down, toppling satan's evil kingdom into irretrievable ruin.

Jesus now lives to restore to us what we lost in Adam: an open, accessible, close relationship with God. The value of this relationship is indescribable, because with God comes everything that pertains to life and godliness!

Much More Restored

The good news is that what we lost in Adam is "much more" restored in Christ. The words *much more* appear three times in the fifth chapter of Romans where, in a series of contrasts, Paul considers what we lost through Adam's transgression, and regained through Christ's obedience. In Christ we have an abundance of favor, a free gift of righteousness, forgiveness for many offenses, and a grace that rules and declares us not guilty. As sin had reigned and abounded unto death, now grace reigns and abounds unto life.[16] This gracious call of the gospel goes out to the land of Nod. Mankind can return to the Father's house.

> *And their **sins and iniquities** will I remember **no more**. Now where **remission** of these is, there is **no more** offering for sin. Having therefore, brethren, **boldness** to enter into the holiest by the blood of Jesus, by a **new and living way**, which He hath consecrated for us, through the veil, that is to say, His flesh; and having an high priest over **the house of God**; let us **draw near** with a true heart in **full assurance of faith**, having our hearts sprinkled **from an evil conscience**, and our bodies **washed** with pure water* (Hebrews 10:17-22).

Here is a complete reversal of what was lost in Eden: remembrance of sin no more, complete remission and restoration, and a relationship to God that is the antithesis of the effects of sin! The five signs of spiritual death are reversed and removed completely:

- *Our hearts are sprinkled from an evil conscience!*
- *We have **boldness to draw near** with a **true heart,** free from guilt and shame, with absolutely no reason to cover and hide from God's presence!*
- *We have **the full assurance of faith** in place of fear and anxiety!*
- *There is **no more remembrance of sin** and so no self-justification!*
- *We have a **new and living way,** not an old, dead, decaying one!*

The way to Paradise is now open.[17] We are brought near and have access (Gk., *prosagoge*) to God with freedom and confidence. At home with the Father, our childhood innocence has been restored.[18] We have "received the Spirit of adoption, whereby we cry, Abba, Father."[19] Guilt and fear are abolished, sorrow and crying flee away!

In our time of need, we find grace to help.[20] Jesus, our merciful high priest, who can be touched with the feelings of our infirmities, is also able to keep us from falling and to bring us into our glorious inheritance. Full of grace and truth, He ministers grace upon grace. He does for us and in us what the Law could never do.

The Shadow of the Law

The Law had only a shadow of these good things to come, not the substance.[21] An example of this is seen in the avenger of blood and the cities of refuge. The Law made provisions to preserve the life of a person who committed manslaughter. That person could flee to any of six designated cities of refuge and remain there until the death of the high priest. The avenger could not touch the one who had sought refuge. The guilty person experienced the mercy of God, who was a fortress and strong tower in the day of trouble.[22] Although they had transgressed the Law, God provided a way for them to halt the retributive process. This was a shadow of the good things to come, but was not the very substance.

In the Old Testament, a person in desperate need could also go into the Holy Place and take hold of the horns of the altar.[23] The four horn-shaped projections on the corners of the altar were used to bind the sacrificial offering as a substitute for the guilty party. The horns were touched with the substitute's blood. These horns represented the mighty salvation and security that Jehovah offered His worshipers. By faith, the transgressor could lay hold of God's strength and salvation and escape the wrath of man. These visible, tangible horns of the altar pointed to an unseen, nonmaterial reality.

It is significant that there were two altars in the sanctuary, both with a set of horns. The brazen altar symbolizing judgment was in the Holy Place, while the golden altar of grace was within the veil. The brazen altar "was a figure for the time then present," a time in which judgment often rejoiced over mercy.[24]

Adonijah and Joab, in their time of need, were able only to enter the Holy Place to lay hold of the brazen altar. Entering the Holy of holies to hold onto the golden altar was not possible; certain death would result. When Joab would not come out willingly, he was slain at the brazen altar for his past sins and forcibly removed.[25] Adonijah also sought refuge there from Solomon due to his plot to obtain the king's throne. When he grabbed the brazen horns, he pleaded for the king to promise not to put him to death.

These men, however, could not find the very essence of what they sought, since they could not enter within the veil and lay hold of the horns of the golden altar. Only once a year on the Day of Atonement could the high priest touch the golden horns with blood.[26] Because of this, the nation of Israel could not completely prevail over their adversaries nor utterly silence their accusers. They continually sacrificed, because those sacrifices did not purge the conscience of the worshipers.[27] Neither did they provide open, bold access to God.[28]

Praise God that in Christ, the way is now open and fully manifest. Jesus Himself is the Way. By faith, we lay hold of Him who is our perfect sacrifice, our great high priest, our refuge, our fortress, and our golden altar! He forever silences the accuser and the avenger. No devil can pull us out of God's presence!

The Heavenly Reality

The Book of Revelation shows Christ, the golden altar, in Heaven.[29] He is the reality that fulfills the Old Testament type.[30] He has perfected the strength of God's salvation as depicted in His seven horns.[31] Although

Solomon could not give his brother Adonijah an oath of life at the horns of the altar, God has sworn with an oath to save us through Christ!

> *For men indeed swear by the greater, and **an oath for confirma-tion** is for them an end of all dispute. Thus God, **determining to show more abundantly** to the heirs of promise the immutability of His counsel, confirmed it by **an oath**, that by **two immutable things**, in which it is **impossible for God** to lie, we might have strong consolation, who have **fled for refuge to lay hold of** the hope set before us. This hope we have as an anchor of the **soul**, both sure and steadfast, and **which enters the Presence behind the veil**, where the forerunner has entered for us, even **Jesus**, having become **High Priest forever** according to the order of Melchizedek* (Hebrews 6:16-20 NKJ).

God was determined to give us complete, blessed assurance. He willed that we who have fled to Him for refuge have no doubt about His salvation in Christ. So He provided us with a sure and steadfast anchor for our souls: His irrevocable oath. He has sworn by Himself that He will save whoever will trust in Christ. To settle the issue, Jesus Christ also sits in His presence as a guarantee and witness for us. God cannot lie, and yet, for our sakes, He backs His Word to us with an oath. What more could we ask for than the death of God's Son and His own sworn testimony to save us? We have every reason to continue in faith, and no reason whatsoever to draw back in unbelief: "For He is faithful that promised."[32]

The Bible concludes with complete restoration, the "much more" than what was lost in Paradise.[33] Our relationship to God is restored beyond breakage, because the time of choice has expired, and the lost substance has been fully found: "...the tabernacle of God is with men, and He will dwell with them, and they shall be His people, and God Himself shall be with them, and be their God" (Rev. 21:3).

With the way open, the gates are never shut, allowing the glory and honor of the nations to enter. Nothing that defiles can enter, only those whose names are written in the Lamb's book of life: "Blessed are they that...enter in...."[34] We shall never shrink back from His presence, but forever enjoy the light of His countenance. No darkness of night is there, for it is always perfect light. There is need of the sun or moon, for God and the Lamb are the light. Since God is all in all, there is no more curse of death nor sorrow and crying. Neither sickness nor anything that causes harm can ever again overshadow the Lamb's throne of mercy: "Let Israel now say, that His mercy endureth for ever."[35]

"He shall be the end of our desires who shall be seen without end, loved without cloy, praised without weariness. This outgoing of affection, this employment, shall certainly be, like eternal life itself, common to all."[36] Within the veil we come, for we have believed in His great love and everlasting mercy. We find what we lost within the veil, and within the veil we can never be lost again!

Found Inside the Veil[37]

Through Thy precious body broken—
Inside the Veil.
Oh! What words to sinners spoken—
Inside the Veil.

Precious as the Blood that bought us;
Perfect as the Love that sought us;
Holy, as the Lamb that brought us
Inside the Veil.

Lamb of God, through Thee we enter,
Inside the Veil.
Cleansed by Thee we boldly venture
Inside the Veil.

Not a stain: a new creation;
Ours is such a full salvation;
Low we bow in adoration
Inside the Veil.

Soon Thy saints shall all be gathered
Inside the Veil.
All at home—no more be scattered—
Inside the Veil.

Naught from Thee our hearts shall sever:
We shall see Thee, grieve Thee never:
"Praise the Lamb!" shall sound forever
Inside the Veil.

Endnotes

1. See Psalm 91:1,4.
2. See Psalm 25:15.

3. Just as Adam and Eve were introduced to evil by satan, children are exposed and subjected to sinful practices by siblings, classmates, friends, and even their own parents and guardians.

4. See Galatians 5:16-17; Ephesians 2:3.

5. See Matthew 23:2-15,25,33.

6. See Matthew 6:2,16; 12:2; 15:1; 23:13; Luke 18:9-14.

7. See Romans 2:1.

8. See James 1:15.

9. Genesis 2:17b; see Romans 7:10-24.

10. See Revelation 2:7; 22:2,14.

11. 1 John 3:12a.

12. Jude 11.

13. Jude 19.

14. See James 4:4-8.

15. See 2 Peter 1:9.

16. See Romans 5:12-21.

17. See Hebrews 9:8.

18. See Ephesians 2:13,17-18; 3:12; 1 Peter 3:8.

19. Romans 8:15b.

20. Hebrews 4:15-16

21. See Hebrews 10:1.

22. See Numbers 35:9ff.

23. See 1 Kings 1:50.

24. Hebrews 9:9a.

25. See Exodus 21:14; 1 Kings 2:29ff.

26. See Exodus 30:10; 37:25-26; 38:1-2; Leviticus 16:18,34.

27. See Hebrews 10:1; 11:4.

28. See Hebrews 9:7-9.

29. See Revelation 9:13.

30. See Hebrews 9:4; 13:10.

31. See Revelation 5:6.

32. Hebrews 10:23b. We are certain of our salvation because we come to God by Christ. To those who come by faith, the way is open, and no devil in the heavenlies can close it off. No wonder the writer to the Hebrews spends the entire next chapter on the subject of faith. This faith draws near, and receives the promise. It never fails, for it is energized by the inseparable love of Christ, a love that constrains us and conforms us to His image!

33. See Revelation 21:3.

34. Revelation 22:14; see Revelation 22:15.

35. Psalm 118:2.

36. St. Augustine, *The City of God*, Book XXII (New York: The Modern Library, Random House, Inc. 1950), 865.

37. Author unknown.

Bibliography

References, Systematic Theology, Commentaries, and Topical Studies

Alexander, P.S. "The Targumim and Early Exegesis of 'Sons of God' in Gen. 6." *Journal of Jewish Studies* 23 (1971).

Anderson, Neil T. *The Bondage Breaker.* Eugene, OR: Harvest House Publishers, 1990.

Anderson, Neil T. and Charles Mylander. *Setting Your Church Free.* Ventura, CA: Regal Books, 1994.

Arnold, Clinton E. *Ephesians: Power and Magic.* Grand Rapids: Baker Book House, 1992.

___. *The Powers of Darkness.* Downers Grove, IL: InterVarsity Press, 1992.

Bancroft, Emery H. *Christian Theology.* Ronald B. Mayers, ed, Grand Rapids: Zondervan Publishing House, 1981.

___. *Elemental Theology.* Ronald B. Mayers, ed. Grand Rapids: Zondervan Publishing House, 1982

Barden, Karl A. *The Enlightened Church, Satan Who?* Shippensburg, PA: Destiny Image Publishers, 1994.

Beeson, Ray. *The Real Battle: Understanding the Darkness.* Wheaton, IL: Tyndale House Publishers, 1988.

Bernal, Dick. *Come Down Dark Prince.* Shippensburg, PA: Companion Press, 1989.

___. *Curses: What They Are and How to Break Them.* Shippensburg, PA: Companion Press, 1991.

___. *Storming Hell's Brazen Gates.* San Jose, CA: Jubilee Christian Center, 1988.

Birch, George A. *The Deliverance Ministry.* Beaverlodge, Alberta: Horizon House Publishers, 1988.

Bloesch, Donald G. *The Struggle of Prayer.* San Francisco: Harper & Row, 1980.

Bonnell, John Sutherland, *Heaven and Hell, What You Can Believe About Them.* New York: Abington Press, 1954.

Boshold, Frank S., ed. *Blumhardt's Battle: A Conflict With Satan.* New York: Thomas E. Lowe, Ltd., 1970.

Bounds, E.M. *The Complete Works of E.M. Bounds on Prayer.* Grand Rapids: Baker Book House, 1990.

Bright, Vonette and Ben A. Jennings, eds. *Unleashing the Power of Prayer.* Chicago: Moody Press, 1989.

Brooks, Pat. *A Call to War With Prayer Power.* NC: New Puritan Library, 1985.

Bryant, David. *Concerts of Prayer.* [revised edition] Ventura, CA: Regal Books, 1988.

Bubeck, Mark I. *The Adversary: The Christian versus Demon Activity.* Chicago: Moody Press, 1975.

___. *Overcoming the Adversary.* Chicago: Moody Press, 1984.

Burke, Todd and DeAnn. *Anointed for Burial.* Plainfield, NJ: Logos International, 1977.

Carter, Harold A. *The Prayer Tradition of Black People.* Baltimore, MD: Gateway Press, 1976.

Cho, Paul Yonggi. *Prayer Key to Revival.* Waco, TX: Word Books, 1984.

___. *Praying With Jesus.* Altamonte Springs, FL: Creation House, 1987.

Christenson, Evelyn. *Battling the Prince of Darkness.* Wheaton, IL: Victor Books, 1990.

___. *What Happens When God Answers.* Waco, TX: Word Books, 1986.

___. *What Happens When Women Pray.* Wheaton, IL: Victor Books, 1975.

Cobble, James F., Jr. *The Church and the Powers.* Peabody, MA: Hendrickson Publishers, 1988.

Cornwall, Judson. *Praying the Scriptures.* Lake Mary, FL: Creation House, 1990.

___. *The Secret of Personal Prayer.* Altamonte Springs, FL: Creation House, 1988.

Cowie, Linda E. and LaPrelle Martin. *Reaching Your City With God.* Kailua-Kona, HI: University of the Nations, 1990.

Crist, Terry. *Interceding Against the Powers of Darkness.* Tulsa, OK: Terry Crist Ministries, 1990.

Daniélou, Jean. *Angels and Their Mission: According to the Fathers of the Church.* Westminsier, MD: Newman Press, 1957.

Dawson, John. *Taking Our Cities for God.* Lake Mary, FL: Creation House, 1989.

___. *Healing America's Wounds.* Ventura, CA: Regal Books, 1994.

Dawson, John and Linda Cowie. *Strategy for Cities.* Sunland, CA: Youth With a Mission 1988.

Dickason, C. Fred. *Demon Possession and the Christian.* Chicago: Moody Press, 1987.

Duffield, Guy P. and Van Cleave, N.M. *Foundations of Pentecostal Theology.* CA: L.I.F.E. Bible College, 1983.

Duewel, Wesley L. *Touch the World Through Prayer.* Grand Rapids: Zondervan Publishing House, 1986.

Eastman, Dick. *The Hour That Changes the World.* Grand Rapids: Baker Book House, 1978.

___. *The Jericho Hour.* Orlando, FL: Creation House, 1994.

Eerdman, Alexander, ed. *Eerdman's Handbook of the Bible.* Grand Rapids: William Eerdmans, 1973.

Efird, James M. *Daniel and Revelation.* Valley Forge, PA: Judson Press, 1978.

Eller, Vernard. *The Most Revealing Book of the Bible.* Grand Rapids: William Eerdmans, 1975.

Exell, Rev. Joseph S.M.A., and Rev. Thomas H. Leale, A.K.C. *The Preacher's Complete Homiletic Commentary on the First Book of Moses Called Genesis.* Grand Rapids: Baker Book House, 1986.

Famighetti, Robert, ed. *World Almanac and Book of Facts 1995.* NJ: Funk and Wagnalls Corp., 1994.

Fausset, A.R. *Fausset's Bible Dictionary.* Grand Rapids: Zondervan Publishing House, 1949.

Frangipane, Francis. *The House of the Lord: God's Plan to Liberate Your City From Darkness.* Lake Mary, FL: Creation House, 1991.

___. *The Three Battlegrounds.* Marion, IA: Advancing Church Publications, 1989.

Garrett, Susan R. *The Demise of the Devil.* Minneapolis, MN: Fortress Press, 1989.

Gasson, Raphael. *The Challenging Counterfeit.* Plainfield, NJ: Logos Books, 1966.

Gay, Robert. *Silencing the Enemy.* Orlando, FL: Creation House, 1993.

Graham, Billy. *Angels: God's Secret Agents.* London, UK: Hodder and Stoughton, 1975.

___. *Approaching Hoofbeats.* Waco, TX: Word Books, 1983.

Green, Michael. *I Believe in Satan's Downfall.* Grand Rapids: William Eerdmans, 1981.

Gromacki, Robert C. *Worthy Is the Lamb.* Schaumburg, IL: Regular Baptist Press, 1986.

Grubb, Norman. *Rees Howells: Intercessor.* Fort Washington, PA: Christian Literature Crusade, 1973.

Habershon, Ada R. *The Study of the Types Priests and Levites.* Grand Rapids: Kregel Publications, 1981.

Halley, H.H. *Halley's Bible Handbook.* Grand Rapids: Regency R. L., Zondervan, 1927.

Hammond, Frank D. *Demons and Deliverance in the Ministry of Jesus.* Plainview, TX: The Children's Bread Ministry, 1991.

Hammond, Frank D. and Ida Mae Hammond. *Pigs in the Parlor.* Kirkwod, MO: Impact Books, 1973.

Harper, Michael. *Spiritual Warfare: Recognizing and Overcoming the Work of Evil Spirits.* Ann Arbor, MI: Servant Books, 1984.

Hastings, J. *The Great Text of the Bible.* New York: Scribner's and Sons, 1915.

Hawthorne, Steve and Graham Kendrick. *Prayerwalking.* Orlando, FL: Creation House, 1993.

Hayford, Jack W. *Prayer Invading the Impossible.* New York: Ballentine Books, 1983 (first printing 1977).

Houghton, S.M. *Sketches From Church History.* Carlisle, PA: Banner of Truth Trust, 1980.

Huegel, F.J. *The Cross Through the Scriptures.* Grand Rapids: Zondervan, Publishing House, 1966.

Hunt, T.W., ed. *Church Prayer Ministry Manual.* Nashville, TN: Sunday School Board of the Southern Baptist Convention, 1992.

Hybels, Bill. *Too Busy Not to Pray.* Downers Grove, IL: InterVarsity Press, 1988.

Hyde, John. *Praying Hyde.* South Plainfield, NJ: Bridge Publishing, 1982.

Ironside, H.A, Litt.D. *Lectures on the Revelation.* Neptune, NJ: Loizeaux Brothers, 1978

Jacobs, Cindy. *Possessing the Gates of the Enemy.* Tarrytown, NY: Chosen Books, 1991.

Jacobus, ed. *New Standard Bible Dictionary.* Philadelphia: Blankiston Co, Funk and Wagnalls, 1925.

Kelsy, Morton. *Encounter With God.* Minneapolis, MN: Bethany, 1972.

Kinnaman, Gary D. *Angels: Dark and Light.* Ann Arbor, MI: Servant Publications, 1993

___. *Overcoming the Dominion of Darkness.* Old Tappan, NJ: Chosen Books, 1990.

Koch, Kurt E. *Christian Counseling and Occultism.* Grand Rapids, MI: Kregel, 1972.

Koch, Kurt E. and Alfred Lechler. *Occult Bondage and Deliverance.* Grand Rapids, MI: Kregel, 1971.

Kraft, Charles F. *Genesis—Beginnings of the Biblical Drama.* New York: Woman's Division of Christian Service Board of Missions, The Methodist Church, 1964.

Kraft, Charles H. *Defeating Dark Angels.* Ann Arbor, MI: Servant Publications, 1992.

Larkin, Clarence. *Dispensational Truth or God's Plan and Purpose in the Ages.* 1920.

Larson, Bob. *Satanism: The Seduction of American Youth.* Nashville, TN: Thomas Nelson Publishers, 1989.

Lawson, Stephen J. *When All Hell Breaks Loose, You May Be Doing Something Right.* Colorado Springs: NavPress, 1993.

Lea, Larry. *Could You Not Tarry One Hour?* Altamonte Springs, FL: Creation House, 1987.

___. *The Weapons of Your Warfare.* Altamonte Springs, FL: Creation House, 1989.

Lewis, C.S. *The Screwtape Letters.* New York: MacMillan, 1961.

Lindsey, Hal. *Satan Is Alive and Well on Planet Earth.* Grand Rapids: Zondervan Publishing House, 1972.

Lockyer, Herbert. *Satan: His Person and Power.* Waco, TX: Word Books, 1946.

MacDonald, Hope. *When Angels Appear.* Grand Rapids: Zondervan Publishing House, 1982.

MacMullen, Ramsay. *Christianizing the Roman Empire.* New Haven, CT: Yale University Press, 1984.

MacNutt, Francis. *Deliverance From Evil Spirits.* Grand Rapids: Chosen Books, 1995.

Mallone, George. *Arming for Spiritual Warfare.* Downers Grove, IL: InterVarsity Press, 1991.

Marocco, James. *Closing the Forbidden Door.* Kahului, HI: Bartimaeus Publishing, 1992.

___. *Winning the Invisible War.* Kahului, HI: Bartimaeus Publishing, 1992.

Marshall, Alfred. *N.I.V. Interlinear Greek-English New Testament.* Grand Rapids: Zondervan Publishing House, 1976.

Matthew Henry. *Matthew Henry's Commentary on the Whole Bible.* McLean, VA: MacDonald Publishing Company, 1706.

Mayhue, Richard. *Unmasking Satan.* Wheaton, IL: Victor Books, 1988.

McAll, Kenneth. *Healing the Family Tree.* London, UK: Sheldon Press, 1982.

McAlpine, Thomas H. *Facing the Powers: What Are the Options?* Monrovia, CA: MARC, 1991.

McClung, B.W. *The History of the Devil.* Printed by Warner at the Black Bay in Patemoster, 1726.

Merck, Bobbie Jean. *Spoiling Python's Schemes.* Toccoa, GA: A Great Love, 1990.

Michaelsen, Johanna. *The Beautiful Side of Evil.* Eugene, OR: Harvest House, 1982.

Miller, Madeleine and J. Lane. *Harper's Bible Dictionary.* New York: Harper and Brothers. 1952.

Montgomery, John Warwick, ed. *Demon Possession.* Minneapolis, MN: Bethany House, 1976.

Moody, Raymond, Jr., M.D. *Life After Life.* New York: Bantam Books, 1975.

___. *Reflections of Life After Death.* New York: Bantam Books, 1977.

Murphy, Ed. *The Handbook for Spiritual Warfare.* Nashville: Thomas Nelson, 1992.

New Layman's Parallel Bible. Grand Rapids: Zondervan Publishing House, 1981.

Otis, George, Jr. *The Last of the Giants.* Tarrytown, NY: Chosen Books, 1991.

___. *Spiritual Mapping Field Guide.* Lynwood, WA: The Sentinel Group, 1993.

___. *Strongholds of the 10/40 Window.* Seattle, WA: YWAM Publishing, 1995.

Owen, Valarie. *In the Beginning God...* Dallas: Word of Faith, 1983.

Page, Sydney H.T. *Powers of Evil.* Grand Rapids: Baker Books, 1995.

Peretti, Frank. *Piercing the Darkness.* Westchester, IL: Crossway Books, 1989.

___. *This Present Darkness.* Westchester, IL: Crossway Books, 1986.

Powlison, Gordon. *Principalities and Powers.* San Jose, CA: Fellowship Ministries, Inc., 1983.

Price, Stanley. *The Giants of Noah's Day.* Oklahoma City: Southwest Radio Church, 1988.

Reddin, Opal L., ed. *Power Encounter: A Pentecostal Perspective.* Springfield, MO: Central Bible College Press, 1989.

Robison, James. *Winning the Real War: Overcoming the Power of Darkness.* Lake Mary, FL: Creation House, 1991.

Rumph, Jane. *Stories From the Front Lines.* Grand Rapids: Chosen Books, 1996.

Russell, Jeffrey Burton. *The Devil: Perceptions of Evil From Antiquity to Primitive Christianity.* Ithaca, NY: Cornell University, 1977.

Schaff, Phillip, ed. *Select Library of Nicene and Post Nicene Fathers of the Christian Church,* Oxford: The Christian Literature Co, 1891.

Shaw, Gwen. *Redeeming the Land.* Jasper, AK: Engeltal Press, n.d.

Sherman, Dean. *Spiritual Warfare for Every Christian.* Seattle, WA: Frontline Communications, 1990.

Sherrer, Quin. *The Spiritual Warrior's Prayer Guide.* Ann Arbor, MI: Servant Publications, 1992.

Silvoso, Edgardo. *That None Should Perish.* Ventura, CA: Regal Books, 1993.

Sjoberg, Kjell. *Winning the Prayer War.* Chichester, England: New Wine Press, 1991.

Smith, William, L.L.D. *Smith's Dictionary of the Bible.* Nashville: Thomas Nelson Publishers, 1979.

Stanford, Peter. *The Devil, A Biography.* New York: Marian World Books, Henry Holt & Co., 1996.

Stedman, Ray. *Expository Studies in Genesis 2 and 3: Understanding Man.* Waco, TX: Word Books, 1975.

Stott, R.W. *The Cross of Christ.* Downers Grove, IL: InterVarsity Press, 1986.

Subritzky, Bill. *Demons Defeated.* Chichester, England: Sovereign World, 1985.

Sumrall, Lester. *Demonology and Deliverance, Vols. 1 and 2.* South Bend, IN: Lester Sumrall Evangelistic Publ. Co., 1983.

___. *Demons: The Answer Book.* South Bend, IN: LeSEA Publ. Co., n.d.

___. *Exorcism.* Green Forest, AR: New Leaf Press, 1991.

Thiessen, Henry Clarence. *Lectures in Systematic Theology.* Grand Rapids: William Eerdmans, 1949.

Thompson Chain Reference Bible, KJV. Fifth Improved Edition, Indianapolis: BB Kirkbride Bible Co., Inc., 1988.

Unger, Merrill F. *Demons in the World Today.* Wheaton, IL: Tyndale Press, 1971.

___. *The New Unger's Bible Dictionary.* Chicago: Moody Press, 1988 (Revised and Updated).

Upchurch, T. Howell. *Strategy for Spiritual Warfare.* Columbus, GA: Brentwood Christian Press, 1987.

Vine, W.E. *Expository Dictionary of New Testament Words* Old Tappan, NJ: Fleming H. Revell Company, 1940.

Virkler, Mark. *Dialogue With God.* S. Plainfield, NJ: Bridge Publishing, 1986.

Wagner, C. Peter, *Breaking Strongholds in Your City.* Ventura, CA: Regal Books, 1993.

___. *Churches That Pray.* Ventura, CA: Regal Books, 1993.

___. *Prayer Shield.* Ventura, CA: Regal Books, 1991.

___. *Warfare Prayer.* Ventura, CA: Regal Books, 1992.

Wagner, C. Peter, ed. *Engaging the Enemy: How to Fight and Defeat Territorial Spirits.* Ventura, CA: Regal Books, 1991.

Wagner, C. Peter and F. Douglas Pennoyer, eds. *Wrestling With Dark Angels.* Ventura, CA: Regal Books, 1990.

Warner, Timothy M. *Spiritual Warfare: Victory Over the Powers of This Dark World.* Wheaton, IL: Crossway Books, 1991.

White, Thomas B. *The Believer's Guide to Spiritual Warfare.* Ann Arbor, MI: Servant Publications, 1990.

___. *Breaking Strongholds.* Ann Arbor, MI: Servant Publications, 1993.

Whitelaw, Rev. Thomas, M.A., D.D. *The Preacher's Complete Homiletic Commentary on the Books on the Acts of the Apostles.* Grand Rapids: Baker Book House, 1986.

Wink, Walter. *Engaging the Powers.* Minneapolis: Fortress Press, 1992.

Witcomb, John C., Jr., and Henry M. Morris. *The Genesis Flood.* Grand Rapids: Baker Book House, 1976.

Young, Robert. *Young's Literal Translation of the Holy Bible.* Grand Rapids: Baker Book House, 1897.

About Uttermost Missions and the Author of *The Cleansing of the Heavens*

Uttermost Mission (U.M.) is committed to evangelism, church planting, and discipleship. With the growth of nondenominational churches and a movement toward cooperation within the Body of Christ, U.M. addresses the vital need for empowering missionaries who are without denominational resources and traditional qualifications. The Lordship of Jesus, the guidance of the Holy Spirit, the knitting of hearts, and the role of senders are the foundational principles of this mission society.

Areas in which Uttermost Missions is currently involved:

- Conducting crusades and evangelistic outreaches.
- Planting strong local churches.
- Running a four-year Bible college.
- Equipping leaders at both the regional and congregational level.
- Supporting relief work to children and orphans.
- Training in entrepreneurship and self-help programs.
- Publishing books, manuals, and teaching materials.
- Hosting guest ministries and missionaries for conferences.

- Building halls and providing equipment.
- Encouraging participation in mission work via speaking in local churches.

A monthly newsletter is available free of charge.

For more information, please write to 1232 East Kemper Road, Suite 179, Cinncinnati, OH 45240. In Europe or Africa, write to #7 Rolf Avenue, Chisipite, Harare, Zimbabwe, Africa. Our e-mail address is utmost@pci.co.zw. For other materials available from Mark Roser, such as manuals and cassette tape series, please write to the U.S.A. address. You can also visit our website: www.uttermost.org.

Mark Roser also visits the U.S.A. to teach at seminars, minister at conferences, and share at local churches. It you would like Dr. Roser to minister at your conference, church, or Bible school, you can contact him in Zimbabwe through the above e-mail address.

A teacher's manual of *The Cleansing of the Heavens* is available for use in Bible schools, Sunday school classes, and Bible studies. It contains the full unedited text with footnotes at the bottom of each page and study questions at the end of each chapter. Please request it at the above U.S. addresss and enclose a gift of $20.

Exciting titles
by Dr. Bill Hamon

PROPHETS AND PERSONAL PROPHECY
This book defines the role of a prophet or prophetess and gives the reader strategic guidelines for judging prophecy. Many of the stories included are taken from Dr. Bill's ministry and add that "hands on" practicality that is quickly making this book a best-seller.
ISBN 0-939868-03-2 $10.99p

PROPHETS AND THE PROPHETIC MOVEMENT
This sequel to *Prophets and Personal Prophecy* is packed with the same kind of cutting instruction that made the first volume a best-seller. Prophetic insights, how-to's, and warnings make this book essential for the Spirit-filled church.
ISBN 0-939868-04-0 $10.99p

PROPHETS, PITFALLS, AND PRINCIPLES
This book shows you how to recognize your hidden "root" problems, and detect and correct character flaws and "weed seed" attitudes. It also can teach you how to discern true prophets using Dr. Hamon's ten M's.
ISBN 0-939868-05-9 $10.99p

Other
Destiny Image titles
you will enjoy reading

THE HIDDEN POWER OF PRAYER AND FASTING
by Mahesh Chavda.
How do you react when overwhelming defeat stares you in the eye? What do you do when faced with insurmountable odds? God has provided a way to turn certain defeat into awesome victory—through prayer and fasting! An international evangelist and the senior pastor of All Nations Church in Charlotte, North Carolina, Mahesh Chavda has seen firsthand the power of God released through a lifestyle of prayer and fasting. Here he shares from decades of personal experience and scriptural study principles and practical tips about fasting and praying. This book will inspire you to tap into God's power and change your life, your city, and your nation!
ISBN 0-7684-2017-2 $9.99p

THE LOST ART OF INTERCESSION
by Jim W. Goll.
The founder of Ministry to the Nations, Jim Goll has traveled the world in a teaching and prophetic ministry. All over the globe God is moving—He is responding to the prayers of His people. Here Jim Goll teaches the lessons learned by the Moravians during their 100-year prayer Watch. They sent up prayers; God send down His power. Through Scripture, the Moravian example, and his own prayer life, Jim Goll proves that "what goes up must come down."
ISBN 1-56043-697-2 $9.99p

ANOINTED OR ANNOYING?
by Ken Gott.
Don't miss out on the powerful move of God that is in the earth today! When you encounter God's Presence in revival, you have a choice—accept it or reject it; become anointed or annoying! Ken Gott, former pastor of Sunderland Christian Centre and now head of Revival Now! International Ministries, calls you to examine your own heart and motives for pursuing God's anointing, and challenges you to walk a life of obedience!
ISBN 0-7684-1003-7 $9.99p

Available at your local Christian bookstore.

Internet: http://www.reapernet.com

Prices subject to change without notice.

B6:20